SECOND EDITION

STEP FORWARD

**STANDARDS-BASED LANGUAGE LEARNING
FOR WORK AND ACADEMIC READINESS**

SERIES DIRECTOR
Jayme Adelson-Goldstein

Lesson Plans

Genevieve Kocienda

198 Madison Avenue
New York, NY 10016 USA

Great Clarendon Street, Oxford, OX2 6DP, United Kingdom

Oxford University Press is a department of the University of Oxford.
It furthers the University's objective of excellence in research, scholarship,
and education by publishing worldwide. Oxford is a registered trade
mark of Oxford University Press in the UK and in certain other countries

ISBN: 978 0 19 474832 2

Printed in China

This book is printed on paper from certified and well-managed sources

ACKNOWLEDGMENTS

Back cover photograph: Oxford University Press building/David Fisher

CONTENTS

The First Step

Lesson Overview	Lesson Notes
MULTILEVEL OBJECTIVES	
On-, Pre-, Higher-level: Review everyday language: alphabet, numbers, greetings, days, months, and the verb *be*	
LANGUAGE FOCUS	
Grammar: The verb *be* (*How are you? I am fine. It's November 21.*) **Vocabulary:** Alphabet, numbers, days, months For vocabulary support, see these **Oxford Picture Dictionary** topics: Meeting and Greeting, pages 2–3; Personal Information, page 4; Numbers, page 16; The Calendar, pages 20–21	
READINESS CONNECTION	
In this lesson, students explore the alphabet, numbers, and the calendar and communicate personal information.	
PACING	
To compress this lesson: Conduct 3 and 5B as whole-class activities. Have students practice 5D with just one partner. **To extend this lesson:** Have students introduce themselves to each other. (See end of lesson.) And/or have students complete **Multilevel Activities 2 Pre-Unit pages 15–16**.	

CORRELATIONS	
CCRS: SL.1.A Participate in collaborative conversations with diverse partners in small and larger groups. L.1.A Demonstrate command of the conventions of standard English grammar and usage when writing and speaking. g. Use frequently occurring nouns and verbs.	**ELPS:** 8. An ELL can determine the meaning of words and phrases in oral presentations and literary and informational text. 9. An ELL can create clear and coherent level-appropriate speech and text. 10. An ELL can demonstrate command of the conventions of standard English to communicate in level-appropriate speech and writing.

Warm-up
10–15 minutes (books closed)

Introduce yourself to students by writing some words on the board that give students some clues about your life, i.e., names, dates, and places that you are comfortable sharing. Tell students the words refer to important people, places, and events in your life and have them guess what they mean to you. When they have finished guessing, tell students why the items on the board are important to you.

Introduction and Presentation I
5 minutes

1. Write your name on the board and spell it out loud. Tell students: *You often have to spell your name when you talk on the telephone, so it's very important to know how to spell it aloud. Who can spell their name for the class?* Call on volunteers to demonstrate.

2. State the objective: *Today we're going to review everyday English: the alphabet, numbers, greetings, days, months, and the verb* be.

1 Review the alphabet

Guided Practice I
10–20 minutes

A 🔊 **1-02** Play the audio. Have students repeat the letters of the alphabet.

B 1. Have students repeat the phrase *How do you spell...?*

2. Model the sample question and answer with a volunteer.

3. Set a time limit (five minutes). Have students practice with a partner. Circulate and monitor.

> **TIP**
>
> Provide extra practice for students who may mix up the names of the letters in English with the ones in their first language. Some ideas are:
>
> Have them say the alphabet backwards.
>
> Write the alphabet on the board. Point to letters randomly and have students say the letter. Increase your speed as students get more comfortable.
>
> Have students work in groups of two to three to perform a dictation activity. One at a time, students spell their name. As they say each letter, the other student(s) write it.

2 Meet, greet, and say goodbye

Communicative Practice and Application
15–25 minutes

A 🔊 **1-03** 1. Introduce the topic: *Now we are going to review how to meet new people.* Direct students to look at the photo. Ask: *Where are they?*

2. Play the conversation. Have students read along silently.

B 1. Model the conversation with two volunteers.

2. Have students work in groups of three and practice the conversation using their own names. Set a time limit (five minutes).

3. Circulate and monitor. Ask volunteers to introduce you to another student.

4. Ask volunteers to present their conversation to the class.

> **MULTILEVEL STRATEGIES**
>
> Use 1B to help you determine the speaking level of your students.
>
> • **Pre-level** Put the first six lines of the conversation in 2A on the board with blanks where names belong. Tell pre-level students to practice only these lines if they find the conversation difficult.
>
> • **Higher-level** Challenge these students to ask their partners more questions. Write these ideas on the board: *Where are you from? Are you a new student at this school?*
>
> Monitor and make a note of which students will need extra help and which students are ready for extra challenges.

3 The verb *be*

Presentation II
5 minutes

Write *I, you, he/she/it, we, they* in a column on the board and *am, is, are* in another column. Review subject-verb agreement. Say: *I _____ a teacher* (clap or hum to indicate the blank) and have students fill in the blank. Repeat for each subject.

Guided Practice II
5 minutes

Have students work individually to complete the sentences. Ask volunteers to share the correct answers.

Answers	
1. I'm	4. are
2. You're	5. I'm
3. We're	6. is

4 Personal information

Guided Practice III
10–15 minutes

1. Review the vocabulary. Write your first and last name and the school's address and phone number on the board. Ask: *What's my first name? My last name? The school's address? Telephone number?*

2. Set a time limit (5 minutes). Direct students to look at the student ID card and to ask and answer the questions with a partner.

Answers
1. Mia
2. Wong
3. 1530 Hill Street Los Angeles, CA 90001
4. 213-555-4768
5. Eastside Adult School

5 Days and months

Presentation III
3 minutes

Introduce the topic. Ask: *What day is today? What month is it?*

Guided Practice IV
20–25 minutes

A 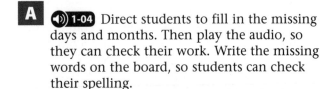 Direct students to fill in the missing days and months. Then play the audio, so they can check their work. Write the missing words on the board, so students can check their spelling.

Answers	
Monday, Wednesday, Friday	February, April, June, August, October, December

B Have students work with a partner to complete the exercise. Ask volunteers to share their answers.

C 1-05 1. Say and have students repeat the ordinal numbers in the chart. Ask: *When do we use ordinal numbers?* [when we want to talk about the order of days, months, different items, etc.]

2. Play the audio. Have students read along silently.

Communicative Practice and Application
10 minutes

D 1. Model the conversation with a volunteer. Then model it again with your own information.

2. Set a time limit (five minutes). Ask students to practice the conversation with several partners.

Evaluation
10–15 minutes

Ask the class to listen to you and write answers to these questions as you read them aloud:
1. *What's your first name?* 2. *What's your last name?* 3. *What day was yesterday?* 4. *What month is it?* 5. *When is your birthday?* Collect and correct their writing.

EXTENSION ACTIVITY
Introduce Yourself
Have students circulate around the room and talk to other students.
1. Tell them to greet other students, state their first and last names, say sentences with *I am*, and tell their birthdays.
2. Have them circulate until each student has introduced him/herself to at least five other people.

1 Learning to Learn

Unit Overview

This unit explores students' preferred learning styles and strategies, making introductions, and using the simple present and question words.

KEY OBJECTIVES	
Lesson 1	Identify personal learning styles
Lesson 2	Identify effective study strategies
Lesson 3	Use the simple present to describe study habits
Lesson 4	Introduce self and others; request clarification
Lesson 5	Identify education and training options
Teamwork & Language Review	Review unit language

UNIT FEATURES	
Academic Vocabulary	*transfer, transition*
Employability Skills	• Reflect on personal learning styles • Compare study habits and personal learning styles • Set goals • Schedule study time into a busy work schedule • Understand teamwork • Work with others • Communicate information • Communicate verbally • Listen actively

Resources	**Class Audio** CD1, Tracks 06–24
	Workbook Unit 1, pages 2–8
	Teacher Resource Center
	    Multilevel Activities 2 Unit 1
	    Multilevel Grammar Exercises 2 Unit 1
	    Unit 1 Test
	Oxford Picture Dictionary Meeting and Greeting, Personal Information, A Classroom, Studying

Lesson Overview	Lesson Notes
MULTILEVEL OBJECTIVES	

On-level: Identify learning styles

Pre-level: Recognize learning styles

Higher-level: Talk and write about learning styles

LANGUAGE FOCUS

Grammar: *Like to*, present continuous (*Min likes to draw. Kyle is using flashcards.*)

Vocabulary: Classroom objects, learning tools; *like, want, need*

For vocabulary support, see these **Oxford Picture Dictionary** topics: A Classroom, pages 6–7; Studying, pages 8–9

STRATEGY FOCUS

Talk about ways to learn English.

READINESS CONNECTION

In this lesson, students reflect on, compare, and communicate information about personal learning styles.

PACING

To compress this lesson: Conduct 2A as a whole-class activity.

To extend this lesson: Have students take a class poll. (See end of lesson.)

And/or have students complete **Workbook 2 page 2** and **Multilevel Activities 2 Unit 1 page 18**.

CORRELATIONS

CCRS: SL.2.A Confirm understanding of a text read aloud or information presented orally or through other media by asking and answering questions about key details and requesting clarification if something is not understood.

L.6.A Use words and phrases acquired through conversations, reading and being read to, and responding to texts, including using frequently occurring conjunctions to signal simple relationships (e.g., *because*).

ELPS: 8. An ELL can determine the meaning of words and phrases in oral presentations and literary and informational text.

Warm-up and Review
10–15 minutes (books closed)

Ask students to name the classroom items that help them learn. Write one or two of their ideas on the board. Hand a piece of chalk to one student and have that student write a word on the board. Ask him/her to pass the chalk to another student. Students who can think of a new word should write it on the board. Students who can't think of a new word should pass the chalk on. Pronounce the words with the class and correct any spelling errors on the board.

Introduction
3 minutes

1. Point out that some of the items mentioned in the warm-up (books, computers, wall posters) are there to help students learn new words.

2. State the objective: *Today we're going to talk about ways to learn new words.*

1 Learn ways to study English

Presentation I
20–25 minutes

A 1. Direct students to look at the phrases. Have them circle the words they know.

2. Direct students to look at the pictures. Ask: *What objects are in the pictures that were not named during the warm-up?* Write any new words on the board.

B **1-06** 1. Have students listen to the audio. Ask them to point to the correct picture in 1A as they listen. Circulate and monitor. If necessary, use the warm-up activity as an example of what it means to brainstorm ideas.

2. Check comprehension by asking *yes/no* questions. Have students hold up one finger for *yes* and two for *no* in order to get a nonverbal response. *Is Dana practicing with a partner?* [yes] *Is Linda using the computer?* [no]

3. Pair students and ask them to take turns pointing to each picture and asking: *What is [Sam] doing?*

C **1-07** 1. Ask students to listen and repeat the words.

2. While students are repeating, circulate and listen for pronunciation difficulties. Provide choral practice as necessary.

(Note: 1D and 1E will confirm students' understanding of the target vocabulary.)

Guided Practice I
15–20 minutes

D 1. Have students complete the sentences using the new vocabulary. Set a time limit (two to three minutes).

2. Encourage students to take turns reading the completed sentences with a partner.

Answers	
1. use the computer	4. brainstorm ideas
2. look up words	5. listen to recordings
3. practice with a partner	6. copy new words

E Read the question aloud. Have pairs take turns asking and answering the question. Circulate and listen for any pronunciation or vocabulary difficulties.

2 Talk about learning tools

Guided Practice II
35–40 minutes

A 1. Ask: *Which classroom items do you like to use the most?* Introduce the new topic: *Now we're going to talk about our learning tools—the things we use to learn.*

2. Group students and assign roles: manager, researcher, administrative assistant, and reporter. Explain that students work with their groups to match the words and pictures.

3. Check comprehension of the exercise: *Who looks up the words in the picture dictionary?* [researcher] *Who writes the numbers in the book?* [administrative assistant] *Who tells the class your answers?* [reporter] *Who helps everyone and manages the group?* [manager]

4. Set a time limit (three minutes) and have students work together to complete the task. While students are working, copy the wordlist onto the board.

5. Call "time" and have the reporters from each group take turns calling out the numbers for the wordlist. Record students' answers on the board. If groups disagree, write each group's choice next to the word.

6. Draw students' attention to the illustration. Prompt students to use vocabulary not labeled in the art. Ask: *Where are the people?* [in a library] *What are they doing?* [Answers will vary.] *What is a person who works in a library called?* [a librarian]

> **MULTILEVEL STRATEGIES**
>
> For 2A, use mixed-level groups.
> - **Pre-level** Assign these students the role of administrative assistant.
> - **Higher-level** Assign these students the role of manager.

B **1-08** 1. Play the audio. Ask students to listen and check their answers.

2. Have students correct the wordlist on the board and then write the correct numbers in their books.

3. Tell the groups from 2A to split into pairs to practice the words. Set a time limit (two minutes).

Answers	
10–tablet	12–the Internet
9–chart	8–marker
6–dictionary	4–notebook
1–flashcards	2–pair
3–group	5–picture
11–headphones	7–whiteboard

C Have students work with a partner to mark the sentences *T* (true) or *F* (false). Set a time limit (five minutes). Discuss answers as a class.

Answers	
1. T	4. T
2. F	5. F
3. T	6. T

Communicative Practice and Application
10–15 minutes

D 1. Model the conversation with a volunteer. Then model it again with your own information.

2. Review the words in the *Need help?* box.

3. Ask: *How do you learn new words?* Write students' ideas on the board in a verb-noun combination that will fit into the model conversation (e.g., *watch TV in English, read my children's books*). Encourage them to use these ideas when they practice the conversation.

4. Set a time limit (five minutes). Ask students to practice the conversation with several partners.

Evaluation
10–15 minutes

TEST YOURSELF

1. Make a four-column chart on the board with the headings *Listening, Pronunciation, Vocabulary*, and *Writing*. Have students give an example strategy for practicing each skill.

2. Have students copy the chart into their notebooks.

3. Set a time limit (five to ten minutes). Have students test themselves by writing the words they recall from the lesson in the chart.

4. Call "time" and have students check their spelling in *The Oxford Picture Dictionary* or another dictionary.

EXTENSION ACTIVITY

Class Poll

Have students take a class poll about favorite learning tools and create a bar graph showing the results. Discuss which tools are the most popular and why.

LESSON 2 WRITING

Lesson Overview	Lesson Notes
MULTILEVEL OBJECTIVES	
On-, Pre-, and Higher-level: Read and write about study strategies and learning-style preferences	
LANGUAGE FOCUS	
Grammar: Simple present (*Tom practices every day. What do you listen to?*) **Vocabulary:** Study-strategy words For vocabulary support, see these **Oxford Picture Dictionary** topics: A Classroom, pages 6–7; Studying, pages 8–9	
STRATEGY FOCUS	
Remember to indent at the beginning of the first line of a paragraph.	
READINESS CONNECTION	
In this lesson, students communicate information about the learning strategies that work best for them.	
PACING	
To compress this lesson: Have students practice the conversation in 2B with only one partner. **To extend this lesson:** Have students create examples of their preferred learning activities. (See end of lesson.) And/or have students complete **Workbook 2 page 3** and **Multilevel Activities 2 Unit 1 page 19**.	
CORRELATIONS	
CCRS: R.1.A Ask and answer questions about key details in a text. SL.1.A Participate in collaborative conversations with diverse partners in small and larger groups. SL.2.A Confirm understanding of a text read aloud or information presented orally or through other media by asking and answering questions about key details and requesting clarification if something is not understood.	**ELPS:** 6. An ELL can analyze and critique the arguments of others orally and in writing. 9. An ELL can create clear and coherent level-appropriate speech and text.

Warm-up and Review
10–15 minutes (books closed)

1. Make a two-column chart on the board with the headings *Ways to Study* and *Learning Tools*.

2. Ask students to give one example for each column.

3. Tell students to remember as many words as they can from Lesson 1 and decide which column they go in.

4. Ask volunteers to come up and write one word (or phrase) on the board in the correct column.

5. Discuss the words in each column and move any items that need to be moved.

6. Ask students about the items on the board using *Do you like to...?* questions.

Introduction
5 minutes

1. Say sentences about your students based on the information from the warm-up: *Maria likes to copy new words. Tien likes to listen to recordings.*

2. State the objective: *Today we're going to read and write about the ways we like to learn.*

1 Prepare to write

Presentation

20–25 minutes

A 1. Direct students to look at the pictures and read and answer the question. [They are studying.] Build students' schema by asking questions about the pictures. Ask: *Who are these people?*

2. Have students work with a partner. Give them one minute to discuss their answers to the questions. Elicit responses from the class.

B 1-09 1. Direct students to look at the pictures again. Ask: *What objects are in the pictures that were not named during the warm-up?* Write any new words on the board.

2. Have students listen to the audio. Ask them to point to the correct picture as they listen. Circulate and monitor.

C 1-09 1. Introduce the model paragraph and its purpose: *You're going to read a paragraph about the ways someone learns a new language. As you read, look for the details of the paragraph: How does Dan learn English?* Play the audio again and have students read along silently.

2. Check comprehension. Ask: *How often does Dan practice English?* [every day] *What four things does he do when he reads a new word?* [He underlines it, looks it up in the dictionary, copies it, and writes an example sentence or word with a similar meaning.] *What will Dan do to improve his English?* [ask more questions in class]

3. Point out the *Writer's Note*. Ask: *Why are all the sentences in one paragraph?* [All the sentences are about the same thing: how Dan studies English.] Ask: *Could this paragraph be split into two? If so, how?* [Yes. One paragraph could be about how Dan learns English at home and the other about how he learns in school.] Ask: *Where would the second indent be?* [before "In class..."]

Guided Practice I

5–10 minutes

D 1. Have students work individually to mark the sentences as *T* (true) or *F* (false). Set a time limit (three to five minutes).

2. Discuss answers as a class. If students finish a *true/false* exercise early, ask them to rewrite the false sentences to make them correct.

Answers	
1. T 2. F 3. F	4. F 5. F 6. F

Guided Practice II

10–15 minutes

E 1-10 1. Ask students to put their pencils down and listen for the answer to this question: *How do Mina and Dan learn?* Play the entire audio once.

2. Play the audio again in segments. After the answer for each question comes up, stop the audio and check in with students. If necessary, replay the segment. Have students listen again and work individually to write *M* (Mina) or *D* (Dan) for each phrase.

Answers	
M–listen to stories D–watch movies M–use the Internet	D–read newspapers D–write new words in a notebook M–play games

F 1-10 Have students compare answers with a partner. Then play the audio again for them to check their work. Discuss answers as a class.

2 Plan

Communicative Practice I

20–25 minutes

A 1. Read the instructions and sentences aloud. Set a time limit (one minute). Have students complete the exercise individually.

2. Write the numbers *1–6* on the board. Ask for a show of hands for each sentence. Write the number of students who checked each sentence next to the corresponding sentence number on the board. Guide a class discussion about which methods are the most popular and why.

B 🔊 **1-11** 1. Play the audio. Have students read along silently.

2. Model the conversation with a volunteer. Then model it again with your own information.

3. Set a time limit (five minutes). Ask students to practice the conversation with several partners.

C Have students think about their answers to the questions and take notes to use in 3A. Have students compare notes with a partner.

3 Write

Communicative Practice II and Application
15–20 minutes

A 1. Copy three sentences from the paragraph template onto the board, but write them as a numbered list. Ask: *Is this a paragraph?* Elicit the differences between the numbered list and the form of the paragraph template on page 7.

2. Rewrite the sentences in paragraph form. Read the sample paragraph aloud.

3. Have students look at the paragraph template as you read it aloud. At each blank, have a volunteer give a sample answer.

4. Set a time limit for writing (five minutes). Have students complete the paragraph template with their own information.

B Ask students to read their paragraphs to a partner. Call on volunteers to share what they learned about their partners.

MULTILEVEL STRATEGIES

In 3A, target the writing to the level of your students.

• **Pre-level** Write a wordlist on the board for these students to use to complete their paragraphs. Then work with these students to write a group paragraph. Read through the template. At each blank, stop and elicit completions. Decide as a group what to write. Have these students copy the group paragraph into their notebooks.

• **Higher-level** Ask these students to include answers to these questions as well: *What activities do you like the most in English class? Why?*

Evaluation
10 minutes

TEST YOURSELF

1. Read the instructions aloud. Assign a time limit (five minutes) and have students work individually.

2. Before collecting student work, invite two or three volunteers to share their sentences. Ask students to raise their hands if they wrote similar answers.

EXTENSION ACTIVITY

Role-play

1. Have students work in groups of four and perform the role-play for each other. Partner A is having problems learning English, and Partner B will give advice. Circulate and monitor as groups work.

2. Put a structure on the board for the pairs to follow:

A: What's the problem?

B: I'm not good at [describe problem].

A: To improve your skills, you can [describe solution].

B: That's great. I'll try that.

3. Have pairs take turns demonstrating their role-plays to the other pair in the group.

Lesson Overview	Lesson Notes
MULTILEVEL OBJECTIVES	
On- and Higher-level: Ask and answer questions about study habits using *want to*, *like to*, and *need to* **Pre-level:** Answer questions about study habits using *want to*, *like to*, and *need to*	
LANGUAGE FOCUS	
Grammar: Simple present (*She needs to study. What does she need to study?*) **Vocabulary:** Studying verbs, *want to*, *like to*, *need to* For vocabulary support, see these **Oxford Picture Dictionary** topics: A Classroom, pages 6–7; Studying, pages 8–9	
READINESS CONNECTION	
In this lesson, students communicate verbally using the simple present to explore their preferred study habits.	
PACING	
To compress this lesson: Assign the matching in 2C as homework. **To extend this lesson:** Have students create a Study Habits Survey. (See end of lesson.) And/or have students complete **Workbook 2 pages 4–5**, **Multilevel Activities 2 Unit 1 page 20**, and **Multilevel Grammar Exercises 2 Unit 1**.	
CORRELATIONS	
CCRS: L.1.A Demonstrate command of the conventions of standard English grammar and usage when writing or speaking. c. Use singular and plural nouns with matching verbs in basic sentences (e.g., *He hops*; *We hop*). g. Use frequently occurring nouns and verbs.	**ELPS:** 7. An ELL can adapt language choices to purpose, task, and audience when speaking and writing. 10. An ELL can demonstrate command of the conventions of standard English to communicate in level-appropriate speech and writing.

Warm-up and Review
10–15 minutes (books closed)

Write two things on the board that you do every day, such as: *I check my email in the morning. I read a book before going to sleep at night.* Ask students what they do every day and write their ideas on the board. Using the words on the board, ask: *Do you like to _____? Do you need to _____? Do you want to _____?* Point out that some activities fit into all three sentences and some into only one. In other words, the words *want*, *like*, and *need* have distinct meanings. Leave the words on the board.

Introduction
5–10 minutes

1. Using the words on the board, say present-tense sentences about yourself and your students. *Kyong likes to clean the house. I don't like to clean the house. I need to clean the house.*

2. State the objective: *Today we're going to learn how to use* need to, like to, *and* want to *to talk about study habits.*

1 Explore the simple present with *want to*, *like to*, and *need to*

Presentation I
20–25 minutes

 1-12 1. Write on the board: *How many people are talking?* [two] *Are they teachers or students?* [students] *What are they studying?* [math] Before students open their books, play the conversation one time and have them answer the questions on the board.

2. Have students open their books. Direct them to look at the picture and read along silently as they listen again.

3. Read the instructions aloud. Ask students to read the conversation silently and mark the sentences as *T* (true) or *F* (false).

4. Read the first sentence aloud. Call on a volunteer for the answer. Ask the volunteer where in the conversation they found the answer. Read the second sentence aloud, calling on a different volunteer for the answer.

Answers
1. T
2. F

B 1. Read the conversation aloud. Shake your head each time you read one of the negative sentences.

2. Read the instructions aloud and have students underline the negative statements.

3. Call on volunteers to say which word makes each sentence negative. [There are two negative statements: *I don't want to study alone* and *I don't like to study after work*. The words *not* and *don't* (*do not*) are used to make negative statements.]

C 1. Demonstrate how to read the grammar charts as complete sentences. Read through the charts sentence by sentence. Then read them again and have students repeat after you.

2. Use the conversation in 1A to illustrate points in the grammar charts. *Cam Tu doesn't like to study after work. Brenda and Cam Tu both need to pass their test.*

Guided Practice I
15–20 minutes

D 1. Read the instructions aloud. Give students time (five minutes) to silently review the charts again and circle the answers.

2. Ask volunteers to write the sentences on the board. Have other students read the sentences aloud.

3. Assess students' comprehension of the charts. Ask: *Is there an -s on the verb after* doesn't? *When do we put an -s on the verb?*

Answers	
1. needs	4. doesn't
2. wants	5. don't
3. want	6. want

2 Ask and answer information questions

Presentation II
10–15 minutes

A **1-13** 1. Write the question words *what*, *where*, *when*, and *how* on the board. Call out examples of places, times, and learning methods: *library, in the morning, with the dictionary*. Ask students to tell you which question word goes with each of your examples.

2. Give students time to read the chart. Play the conversations. Have students repeat the conversations with a partner.

3. Check comprehension of the grammar and content by asking questions and having students answer in complete sentences: *Monica, where do you like to study? Liu, where does Monica like to study?*

Guided Practice II
10–15 minutes

B 1. Have students complete the exercise individually.

2. Ask volunteers to say the answers.

Answers
1. How does, likes to study
2. What does, likes to study
3. Where do, like to study
4. When do, like to study

TIP

For more practice, distribute sets of cards with the words *does* and *do* (one word on each card). Call out questions with blanks in them. *When _____ Martin like to study?* Tell students to hold up the correct card. Call on volunteers to say the complete question.

C Have students work individually to match the questions and answers. Ask volunteers to read the question-and-answer pairs aloud.

Answers
1. c
2. e
3. d
4. a
5. b

3 Ask and answer *yes/no* questions

Presentation III
20–25 minutes

A 1. Assess what students know/remember about forming a *yes/no* question. Write the sentence *He likes to study.* Ask: *Is this a statement or a question?* [statement] *What word do we have to add to make it a question?* [Does] *What word has to change?* [*likes* becomes *like*] Write the question: *Does he like to study?* Then below the question, write two possible answers: *Yes, he does.* and *In the library.* Ask students which one is correct. [*Yes, he does.*]

2. Give students time to read the chart. Play the audio and have students repeat.

3. Check comprehension of the grammar and content by asking questions and having students answer in complete sentences: *Jan, do you like to read? Yes, I like to read.*

Guided Practice III
15–20 minutes

B 1. Read the instructions aloud. Have students complete the sentences individually.

2. Ask volunteers to read the question-and-answer pairs aloud.

Answers
A: Do
B: don't
A: Do, want
B: do

C 1. Have students look at the picture and identify anything that they recognize. Ask: *Where are they?* [a hospital / medical office]

2. Read the question aloud. Play the conversation. Give students time to think of their answer. Have volunteers answer the question.

MULTILEVEL STRATEGIES

In 3C, pair same-level students together.

• **Pre-level** Play the conversation again, stopping after every line and checking students' understanding.

• **On- and Higher-level** Have pairs ask and answer each other's questions about the conversation.

D 1. Read the instructions aloud. Make sure students understand that they will be hearing the questions in the audio. Play the first question and choose the correct answer as a class. Play the rest of the questions. Have students complete the rest of the exercise individually.

2. Play each question again, pausing after each one for students to say the answer.

Answers	
1. a	4. a
2. b	5. b
3. b	6. a

E 🔊 1-15 1. Read the instructions aloud. Play the conversation again. Encourage students to take notes as they listen to help them write their questions.

2. Give students time to write their questions. Set a time limit (five minutes).

3. Have students practice asking and answering their questions with a partner and then share them with the class.

4. As students share their questions with the class, write them on the board and have volunteers answer.

MULTILEVEL STRATEGIES

In 3E, target the writing to the level of your students.

• **Pre-level** Write key words from the conversation on the board as hints for students' questions. [e.g., *Laura/busy, study/together, key words/tablet*]

• **On- and Higher-level** Challenge pairs to take turns writing an answer first and then writing a question for that answer: S1: *No, they don't.* S2: *Do they want to study on a laptop?*

4 Use *want, like,* and *need* to talk about your learning style

Communicative Practice and Application
10–15 minutes

A 1. Ask: *What do you think is the most popular way to (learn new words, practice conversation, learn grammar)?* Have students share their ideas. Write them on the board.

2. Give students time to read the survey and check the answers that are true for them.

B 1. Model the sample conversation with a student. Then have two high-level students model a question and answer for the class.

2. Have pairs take turns asking and answering questions from 4A. Circulate and monitor to make sure students are using the correct question forms.

C 1. Read the instructions aloud. Have students write their sentences. Set a time limit (five minutes).

2. Have pairs take turns reading their sentences to each other and correcting any mistakes, if necessary. Then have students read their partner's sentences to the class.

TIP

Write students' sentences on the board, but leave out a word (e.g., *He likes use flashcards.*). Have students rewrite the sentences correctly in their notebooks, or have volunteers come to the board to correct the sentence (e.g., add the word *to*).

Evaluation
10 minutes

TEST YOURSELF

Ask students to write five questions and answers about their learning styles individually. Collect and correct their writing.

EXTENSION ACTIVITY

Make a Survey

1. Divide students into groups. Ask them to create a "Study Habits Survey" using information questions (e.g., *When do you like to study?*).

2. Each group member writes a question and interviews students from other groups.

3. Students return to their groups. Assign the role of reporter and recorder in each group. Students compile their answers, and the recorders write simple-present sentences: *Ten students like to study at night.*

4. Reporters then share their group's findings with the class.

Lesson Overview	Lesson Notes
MULTILEVEL OBJECTIVES	
On- and Higher-level: Make introductions and clarify information	
Pre-level: Make introductions	
LANGUAGE FOCUS	
Grammar: Questions with *be* (*What's your name?*)	
Vocabulary: Expressions used for introductions	
For vocabulary support, see these **Oxford Picture Dictionary** topics: Meeting and Greeting, pages 2–3; Personal Information, page 4	
STRATEGY FOCUS	
Practice language for making workplace introductions.	
READINESS CONNECTION	
In this lesson, students communicate information about making introductions and asking for clarification.	
PACING	
To compress this lesson: Skip 4B.	
To extend this lesson: Have students compose short question-and-answer conversations. (See end of lesson.)	
And/or have students complete **Workbook 2 page 6** and **Multilevel Activities 2 Unit 1 page 21**.	

CORRELATIONS	
CCRS: SL.1.A Participate in collaborative conversations with diverse partners in small and larger groups.	**ELPS:** 2. An ELL can participate in level-appropriate oral and written exchanges of information, ideas, and analyses, in various social and academic contexts, responding to peer, audience, or reader comments and questions. 9. An ELL can create clear and coherent level-appropriate speech and text.

Warm-up and Review
10–15 minutes (books closed)

Draw on the board two stick figures shaking hands. Draw a speech bubble from each head. Ask students: *What are they saying?* Give students one minute to discuss quietly with a partner. Elicit and write their ideas in the speech bubbles. As students give you ideas, ask for clarification: *Excuse me?* and *How do you spell that?*

TIP

When drawing on the board or overhead, it's OK if you don't draw well; students will just be more creative with their ideas!

Introduction
5 minutes

1. Tell the students: *The people in my picture are shaking hands.* Ask: *When do people shake hands?*

2. State the objective: *Today we're going to learn how to introduce people and how to check what you hear.*

1 Listen to learn: introducing yourself and others

Presentation I and Guided Practice I
20–30 minutes

 1. Direct students to look at the pictures. Ask: *Where are the people in each picture?* [an office building, a classroom, a park or outside in a neighborhood]

2. Read the question aloud. Have pairs ask and answer the question with each other before reviewing the answer as a class.

Answer
People are making introductions.

B 🔊 **1-17** 1. Direct students to look at the pictures again. Ask them to guess what they do and/or what the situation is. [1. They work for the same company. One of them is a new employee. 2. Ms. Morgan is a teacher. The other woman is a new student. 3. Chanda and the boy are new neighbors.]

2. Have students put down their pencils before they listen. Play the audio and ask them to think about which name they will write. Replay the audio and have them write the names in the blanks.

3. Ask students to compare their answers with a partner. Circulate and monitor to ensure students understand the audio.

4. Ask students if their guesses about the illustrations were correct. Confirm understanding of each situation.

Answers
1. Ling
2. Zoila
3. Achir

C 🔊 **1-17** Play the audio again and have students match the names with the questions. Discuss answers as a class.

Answers
1. b
2. c
3. a

2 Practice your pronunciation

Pronunciation Extension
10–15 minutes

 🔊 **1-18** 1. Have students close their books. Write the words *rising* and *falling* on the board. Slowly draw a line on the board starting at the bottom and moving up. Ask students: *Is this line rising or falling?* Hum a note from low to high and ask: *Is my voice rising or falling?*

2. Explain that in English, rising and falling intonation is a very important part of communication. Demonstrate this by bumping into a student and saying with a falling intonation: *Excuse me.* Then, when the student responds, say with a rising intonation: *Excuse me?* Point out that the same phrase can have different meanings because of intonation.

3. Write *Excuse me.* on the board four times, numbered 1–4. Pronounce each one with rising or falling intonation and ask students to show you which one they heard by indicating rising or falling with a hand movement. Mark the intonation above the phrases.

4. Have students open their books. Play the audio. Have students listen to and repeat the example sentences.

B 🔊 **1-19** 1. Ask students to put down their pencils and listen to the audio, indicating rising or falling with their hands. Review the information in the *Need help?* box.

2. Replay the audio and have students work individually to check the appropriate column in their books.

Answers
1. Falling
2. Falling
3. Rising
4. Falling

MULTILEVEL STRATEGIES

For 2B, pair same-level students together.

• **Pre-level** Have students practice the conversation with a partner while you listen and ensure correct intonation.

• **Higher-level** Have students practice the conversation with a partner and add one more exchange.

3 Practice statements with *this, that, these,* and *those*

Presentation II and Guided Practice II
15–20 minutes

A 🔊 **1-20** 1. Play the audio. Ask students to read along silently.

2. Have pairs take turns asking and answering the question. [Ned is introducing Emmy.]

3. Play the audio again and have students repeat the conversation. Replay if necessary.

TIP

After 3A, have students practice listening for *this, that, these,* and *those*. Distribute a pair of index cards to each student, one with *this* on one side and *that* on the other, and one with *these* on one side and *those* on the other. (Each student should have one of each card.) Say a sentence and have students hold up the word they hear. Call on a student to repeat the sentence. Continue with other sentences, moving as quickly as you can from one sentence to the next.

B 🔊 **1-21** 1. Introduce the new grammar. Write sentences on the board. *1. This is my student. 2. That is my student.* Ask one student to stand at the front of the classroom and another to stand at the back of the classroom. Stand next to one of the students and ask the rest of the class to read which sentence is correct. [*This is my student.*] Then gesture (be careful not to point) toward the other student and have the class read the correct sentence. [*That is my student.*] Explain that position is important when using *this* and *that*. For *these* and *those*, repeat the process with two students at the front and the back of the class. Instead of students, you could use books or some other objects.

2. Give students time (one to two minutes) to look at the illustrations and read the information in the chart. Confirm that they understand *singular* and *plural*.

3. Play the audio and have students repeat.

4. Check comprehension of the grammar in the chart. Repeat the process in step 1, but this time, have students say the sentences aloud as you change position and the number of students (or objects).

C 1. Read the instructions aloud and have students work in pairs to describe people in the classroom. Circulate and ensure that students are using the grammar correctly.

MULTILEVEL STRATEGIES

For 3C, pair same-level students together.

• **Pre-level** Provide sentence frames on the board for students to use in their conversations: ___ are my friends, ___ and ___. ___ is my classmate, ____.

• **Higher-level** Direct these students to use their imaginations and use other designations in their descriptions: *Those are my co-workers, Jim and Jon. This is my boss, Mr. Lee.*

4 Make conversation: clarifying

Communicative Practice I
15–20 minutes

A 1. Ask students if they know what the verb *clarify* means. Explain that *to clarify* means to ask for information again to make sure you understand it. Demonstrate by asking a student: *What is your name?* After they answer, ask: *What is your name again?* After the student answers, explain that asking someone to repeat something is one way to clarify information.

2. Read the instructions aloud and the sentences in the *Need help?* box. Model a conversation with two students. Ask: *Which sentences ask for clarification?* [*What's your name again?* and *Is that ___?*]

3. Have groups of two to three students create a conversation and take turns performing each part.

B 1. Set a time limit (ten minutes). Ask groups to share their conversation with another group.

2. Have groups present their conversation to the class.

AT WORK

Workplace introductions

Presentation III and Communicative Practice II
20–25 minutes

A **1-22** 1. Direct students to look at the illustrations. Ask them to describe what they see and what they think the different situations are. Confirm that students understand the meaning of *formal* and *informal*. Ask for examples of when someone is more formal and when they are less informal [more formal: with your boss, meeting someone new at work; less formal: with co-workers, with friends of friends].

2. Play the audio and have students read along silently. Give students time to think of their answer.

B 1. Read the instructions and questions aloud.

2. Have students discuss the questions with a partner. Circulate and help as needed.

3. Have volunteers share their answers. Ask students to show where in the conversation they found the answer.

C 1. Have groups of three take turns practicing each part of the conversations. Circulate and make sure students are using their own names.

2. Have groups say the conversations for the class.

Evaluation
10 minutes

TEST YOURSELF

Have pairs stand up and walk around the room taking turns to introduce each other to five classmates. Circulate and assess students' progress. Take note of any mistakes you hear in intonation, pronunciation, grammar, or vocabulary. When all students have finished the activity, as a class, review the kinds of mistakes you heard (without naming any students who made them).

EXTENSION ACTIVITY

Intonation Practice

Have students compose short question-and-answer conversations.

1. Divide students into groups. Have groups compose short question-and-answer conversations.

2. Tell the groups to exchange papers and mark the intonation on the conversations.

3. Check students' intonation by having them read their conversations aloud.

Lesson Overview	Lesson Notes
MULTILEVEL OBJECTIVES	
On- and Higher-level: Read about and discuss courses, course listings, and degrees **Pre-level:** Read about courses, course listings, and degrees	
LANGUAGE FOCUS	
Grammar: Simple present (*I want to take this class.*) **Vocabulary:** Expressions used for introductions For vocabulary support, see these **Oxford Picture Dictionary** topics: A Classroom, pages 6–7; Studying, pages 8–9	
STRATEGY FOCUS	
Use subheadings to predict what a text is about.	
READINESS CONNECTION	
In this lesson, students communicate information about getting classes and training for a current or new job.	
PACING	
To compress this lesson: Assign 1E and/or 1F for homework. **To extend this lesson:** Have students research course listings and discuss their learning and/or career goals. (See end of lesson.) And/or have students complete **Workbook 2 page 7** and **Multilevel Activities Level 2 Unit 1 page 22**.	

CORRELATIONS	
CCRS: R.1.A Ask and answer questions about key details in a text. R.5.A Know and use various text features (e.g., headings, tables of contents, glossaries, electronic menus, icons) to locate key facts or information in a text.	**ELPS:** 1. An ELL can construct meaning from oral presentations and literary and informational text through level-appropriate listening, reading, and viewing. 3. An ELL can speak and write about level-appropriate complex literary and informational texts and topics.

Warm-up and Review
10–15 minutes (books closed)

Ask students if they have ever taken, or are taking, classes other than their English class. If so, for what purpose? Discuss reasons why adults take classes after they have left school.

Introduction
5 minutes

1. Use students' ideas from the warm-up to talk about the different kinds of training programs and degrees needed for different kinds of jobs.

2. State the objective: *Today we're going to read about and discuss classes that help you get special training for your current job, or for a new job or career.*

1 Build reading strategies

Presentation
10–15 minutes

 A Read the definitions aloud and brainstorm jobs that require different kinds of training or degrees. Use ideas from the introduction to help guide discussion.

Possible Answers
Diploma: receptionist, customer service representative Certificate: plumber, mechanic Degree: engineer, doctor

Guided Practice: Pre-reading
5–10 minutes

 B Read the instructions aloud and confirm that students understand where the subheadings are. Have students answer the question with a partner. Then check answers as a class. If any students answer incorrectly, ask them to support their answer using the subheadings. Establish the correct answers as a class.

Possible Answers
Basic Skills: reading, math Adult Transitions: study skills, how to do research Vocational Studies: construction site safety, building codes

Guided Practice: While Reading
15–20 minutes

 C 1. Ask students to read the information silently and answer the question.

2. Have students work in pairs to compare and discuss their answers and then check answers as a class.

3. Check comprehension. Ask: *Is this program for children?* [no] *What skills can the Basic Skills class help you improve?* [language, reading, writing, and math] *Which class helps you choose college classes?* [Adult Transitions] *Which course will help you change you job?* [Vocational Studies] *How can you get a catalog?* [download or call a counselor]

MULTILEVEL STRATEGIES

Adapt 1C to the level of your students.
- **Pre-level** Read the text aloud to these students as they follow along.
- **On- and Higher-level** Pair students and have them read the web page aloud to each other, taking turns to read each paragraph.

Guided Practice: Rereading
10–15 minutes

 D ◀)) **1-23** 1. Provide an opportunity for students to extract evidence from the web page. Have students reread the web page and underline any words or phrases that are unfamiliar. Have them guess the meaning of the words through the context and then check their answers in a dictionary or online.

2. Pair students and tell them to tell each other which classes they want to learn more about. Have volunteers report their partner's responses to the class.

TIP

Have students go online to find out about other adult education and job training courses in their area. Decide which device(s) students might use and elicit search terms (e.g., *job training* + your city; *RN training* + your city).

Guided Practice: Post-reading
15 minutes

 E 1. Have students work individually to mark the answers *T* (true) or *F* (false) and then note where they found the answers.

2. If time allows or students finish early, have them rewrite false sentences to make them correct.

Answers
1. F
2. F
3. T
4. F
5. T

3. Elicit and discuss any additional questions about the reading. You could introduce new questions for class discussion: *What does equivalency mean? Which course would be the most helpful for you? Is it more important for you to have language skills or math skills?*

F 1. Have students work individually to complete the sentences.

2. Have pairs read each other their sentences before checking answers as a class.

Answers
1. certificate
2. vocational
3. transition
4. transfer
5. career

MULTILEVEL STRATEGIES

For 1F, work with pre-level students.

• **Pre-level** Ask these students *yes/no* and short-answer information questions about the reading while other students are completing 1F. Additionally, have them copy the answers to 1F into their notebooks and underline the words that are new for them and write definitions or examples.

2 Interpret a course listing

Communicative Practice
20–25 minutes

A 1. Direct students to look at the course listing. Model the sample conversation with a student.

2. Have pairs discuss the course listing. Circulate and help as needed.

3. Call on pairs to say their conversation for the class.

MULTILEVEL STRATEGIES

For 2A, pair same-level students together.

• **Pre-level** Provide these students with sentence frames for their conversation:

Which class...

meets three times a week?

takes one week?

is on the weekend?

Which classes...

are at night?

are in the morning?

B 1. Have students work individually to complete the task.

2. Check answers as a class.

Answers
Office Technology (Vocational Studies), College Writing Skills (Adult Transitions), Food Safety and Preparation (Vocational Studies)

C 1. Read the questions aloud. Allow students time to think of their own answers and make notes.

2. Set a time limit (ten minutes). Have pairs discuss the questions. Circulate and help as needed.

3. Have pairs share their responses with another pair. Have volunteers share their partner's answers with the class.

Application
5–10 minutes

BRING IT TO LIFE

Ask students to research courses on the Internet that will help them reach their goals. Have them report their findings to the class.

EXTENSION ACTIVITY

Role-play

1. Have students work in pairs. Tell them they will role-play being a student and a career counselor.

2. Have the career counselor ask: *What job do you want in one year? What job do you want in five years?*

3. Have students take turns with each role.

TEAMWORK & LANGUAGE REVIEW

Lesson Overview	Lesson Notes
MULTILEVEL OBJECTIVES	
On-, Pre-, and Higher-level: Expand upon and review unit grammar and life skills	
LANGUAGE FOCUS	
Grammar: Simple present and present continuous sentences and questions with *be* **Vocabulary:** Educational and job training goals For vocabulary support, see these **Oxford Picture Dictionary** topics: Meeting and Greeting, pages 2–3; Personal Information, page 4; A Classroom, pages 6–7; Studying, pages 8–9	
STRATEGY FOCUS	
Talk about long-term goals.	
READINESS CONNECTION	
In this review, students work in teams to practice describing classroom items, making introductions, and exploring their learning goals.	
PACING	
To extend this review: Have students complete **Workbook 2 page 8**, **Multilevel Activities 2 Unit 1 pages 23–26**, and **Multilevel Grammar Exercises 2 Unit 1**.	
CORRELATIONS	
CCRS: SL.1.A Participate in collaborative conversations with diverse partners in small and larger groups.	**ELPS:** 5. An ELL can conduct research and evaluate and communicate findings to answer questions or solve problems. 6. An ELL can analyze and critique the arguments of others orally and in writing.

Warm-up and Review
10–15 minutes (books closed)

Review 2C from the previous lesson and the *Bring It to Life* activity if students have done it. Ask students if they learned anything useful from their conversation about getting job training. Ask if they might pursue any of the training or classes that they discussed.

Introduction and Presentation
5 minutes

1. Pair students and direct them to look at the picture in their book. Ask them to describe what they see to their partner.

2. Ask volunteer pairs to share their ideas with the class.

Guided Practice
15–20 minutes

 1. Direct students to work in groups of three to four and look at the picture. Ask: *Who are these people? How old are they? What are they doing? What could they be saying?*

2. Set a time limit (five minutes). Circulate and answer any questions.

3. Have students from each group share the group's responses with the class. If you have a large class, you may not want all of the groups to report their responses. Instead, have groups share their responses with each other. Call "time" and tell all groups to work with a new group and to repeat their responses. Repeat this process as desired, making sure each group gets to share their responses at least once.

 1. Have students work in groups of three to four to complete the task.

2. To check answers, have one group say the conversation for the class. Have the rest of the class say if they agree or disagree with the order and why.

Answers	
1–Cathy:	Hi, Victor. I want to introduce my friend Elise.
5–Elise:	That's right.
3–Elise:	Elise.
9–Elise:	Yes, I do. How about you? Where do you study?
7–Elise:	Nice to meet you.
6–Victor:	Hi, Elise. I'm Victor.
4–Victor:	Is that E-L-I-S-E?
2–Victor:	What's your name again?
8–Victor:	Do you like to study in the library?
10–Victor:	I like to study on my tablet in the coffee shop.

3. Explain that groups will now rewrite the conversation with their own ideas. Ask: *Which parts of the conversation should be changed?* [names, spelling, places to study]

4. Set a time limit (ten minutes) for groups to rewrite the conversation and then practice it.

5. Have groups say their new conversation to the class.

Communicative Practice and Application
30–45 minutes

 1. Put students in new groups of four. Tell them they will role-play being in a new class together, introducing each other, and talking about study habits. One pair will practice introducing themselves to the other pair. The other pair will ask questions. Then they switch.

2. Direct students to first think individually about the study habits they will ask and answer questions about. Each group should choose who will begin the introductions and who they will introduce first. The other students ask for clarification of the person's name, and are ready to ask and answer one question about study habits.

3. Circulate and monitor as students carry out the role-play. Provide global feedback once the activity ends.

4. Have volunteer groups perform their role-play for the class.

 1. Group students and assign roles: manager, researcher, administrative assistant, and reporter. Read the instructions and the sentence stems aloud. Check students' understanding of the phrase *long-term goal*.

2. Set a time limit (five minutes) to complete the task.

3. Have volunteers say Lisa's goals to the class. [Lisa's long-term goal is to get work as a childcare worker. First, she wants to get first aid and CPR training. Next, she wants to prepare a resume that lists her childcare experience. Then she wants to check websites and bulletin boards in the local community for jobs.]

E Read the instructions aloud. Students work in their groups from D. Encourage students to make notes of their ideas so they can refer to them in the next exercises. Circulate and monitor.

F Read the instructions aloud. Students work in their groups from D. Explain that students should make a list with each group member's name as a heading. Suggest that students talk about one person's goals at a time and write them on the list. Circulate and monitor.

G Read the instructions aloud and refer students to the model in D. Have students work individually to complete their chart.

H 1. Read the instructions aloud. Model the sample conversation with a volunteer.

2. Give students time to think of (and if necessary, write down) questions they will ask the other students.

3. Set a time limit (ten minutes). Have students interview one or two other students as time allows.

4. Have volunteers share what they learned about their classmates.

MULTILEVEL STRATEGIES

Adapt D–H to the level of your students.

• **Pre-level** Pair these students and work with them directly by supplying sentence frames as needed. Have them interview their partner.

• **Higher-level** After H, have these students give opinions and advice (constructive only!) about the other students' goals and plans.

PROBLEM SOLVING
10–15 minutes

A 1. Ask: *Do you ever feel too tired to study? What things in your life can keep you from studying?* Tell students they will read a story about a woman who is having difficulty studying. Direct students to read Noreen's story silently.

2. Play the audio and have students read along silently again.

B 1. Elicit answers to question 1. Guide students to a class consensus on the answer.

2. As a class, brainstorm answers to question 2. Ask students if they know someone who has this problem and has overcome it, or what they have done themselves to overcome the same.

Evaluation
20–25 minutes

To test students' understanding of the unit language and content, have them take the Unit 1 Test, available on the Teacher Resource Center.

Unit Overview

This unit explores words for feelings, weather, and giving directions, and using the future tense with *will*.

KEY OBJECTIVES	
Lesson 1	Interpret information about feelings and weather
Lesson 2	Identify and describe seasonal events
Lesson 3	Use the future with *will* and *won't* to describe future plans
Lesson 4	Ask for, give, and clarify directions
Lesson 5	Interpret information about small talk; interpret an invitation
Teamwork & Language Review	Review unit language

UNIT FEATURES	
Academic Vocabulary	*energetic, relax*
Employability Skills	• Reflect on a favorite season • Analyze scheduled events • Choose the dates and times of events • Examine routes on a map • Resolve conflicts between scheduled events and childcare • Understand teamwork • Communicate information • Work with others • Communicate verbally

Resources	**Class Audio** CD1, Tracks 25–39
	Workbook Unit 2, pages 9–15
	Teacher Resource Center
	    Multilevel Activities 2 Unit 2
	    Multilevel Grammar Exercises 2 Unit 2
	    Unit 2 Test
	Oxford Picture Dictionary The Calendar, Feelings, Weather, Downtown, City Streets, Directions and Maps

LESSON **1** VOCABULARY

Lesson Overview	Lesson Notes
MULTILEVEL OBJECTIVES	
On-level: Identify feelings and weather **Pre-level:** Recognize words for feelings and weather **Higher-level:** Talk and write about feelings and weather	
LANGUAGE FOCUS	
Grammar: Simple present statements (*It's 32 degrees.*) **Vocabulary:** Words for feelings and weather conditions For vocabulary support, see these **Oxford Picture Dictionary** topics: Feelings, pages 42–43; Weather, page 13	
STRATEGY FOCUS	
Talk about different kinds of weather.	
READINESS CONNECTION	
In this lesson, students communicate information about their feelings, especially related to weather.	
PACING	
To compress this lesson: Conduct 2A as a whole-class activity. **To extend this lesson:** Have students do a research activity. (See end of lesson.) And/or have students complete **Workbook 2 page 9** and **Multilevel Activities 2 Unit 2 page 28**.	
CORRELATIONS	
CCRS: L.6.A Use words and phrases acquired through conversations, reading and being read to, and responding to texts, including using frequently occurring conjunctions to signal simple relationships (e.g., *because*).	**ELPS:** 8. An ELL can determine the meaning of words and phrases in oral presentations and literary and informational text.

Warm-up and Review
10–15 minutes (books closed)

Draw a happy face, a sad face, and a face with a straight mouth on the board. Point to each face and ask: *How does this person feel?* Write the students' ideas on the board. Have students tell you any other words they know for feelings. Draw a sun and a cloud with rain coming from it. Ask: *What kind of day is it? How do you feel on sunny/rainy days?*

Introduction
3 minutes

1. Mime the words on the board and let the class guess the word for each mime.

2. State the objective: *Today we're going to explore words to describe how we feel and words to talk about the weather.*

1 Learn words for feelings

Presentation
20–25 minutes

A 1. Direct students to look at the words as you read them aloud. Have them circle the words they know.

2. Direct students to look at the pictures. Ask: *What feelings that were named during the warm-up are similar to the feelings of the people in the pictures? Which feelings are different?*

B **1-25** 1. Have students listen to the audio. Ask them to point to the correct picture in 1A as they listen. Circulate and monitor.

2. Check comprehension by asking *yes/no* questions. Have students hold up one finger for *yes* and two for *no* in order to get a nonverbal response. *Is Donna bored?* [yes] *Is Jai sleepy?* [no].

3. Pair students and ask them to take turns describing what is happening in each picture. Circulate and monitor.

C **1-26** 1. Ask students to listen and repeat the words.

2. Point out that although *bored, surprised,* and *frustrated* all end in *-ed*, the last syllable is pronounced differently in *frustrated*. Ask students to count the syllables in each word as you say them. The *-ed* ending is pronounced as an additional syllable after the /t/ sound. While students are repeating, circulate and listen for pronunciation difficulties. Provide choral practice as necessary.

Guided Practice I
15–20 minutes

D 1. Have students complete the sentences using the new vocabulary. Set a time limit (two to three minutes).

2. Encourage students to take turns reading the completed sentences in pairs.

Answers	
1. energetic	4. upset
2. surprised	5. bored
3. frustrated	6. sleepy

MULTILEVEL STRATEGIES

For 1D, pair same-level students together.

• **Pre-level** While the others are writing, assist pre-level students with the exercise.

• **Higher-level** When these students finish, have them write about situations where they feel cheerful, bored, etc., without writing the feeling itself. For example: *I'm waiting for the bus.* After reviewing the correct answers for 1D, ask these students to say their sentences. Other students can guess the feeling that goes with the situation.

E 1. Read the instructions aloud and model the sample conversation with a volunteer.

2. Set a time limit (three minutes). Have students take turns asking and answering questions with a partner. Circulate and listen for any pronunciation or vocabulary difficulties.

2 Talk about the weather

Guided Practice II
35–40 minutes

A 1. Ask: *How's the weather today? How was it last month?* Introduce the new topic: *Now we're going to learn some weather words.*

2. Group students and assign roles: manager, researcher, administrative assistant, and reporter. Explain that students will work with their groups to match the words and pictures and write the missing temperatures.

3. Check comprehension of the exercise, asking: *Who looks up the words in the picture dictionary?* [researcher] *Who writes the numbers and temperatures in the book?* [administrative assistant] *Who tells the class your answers?* [reporter] *Who helps everyone and manages the group?* [manager]

4. Set a time limit (three minutes) and have students work together to complete the task. While students are working, copy the wordlist onto the board.

5. Call "time" and have the reporters from each group take turns calling out the numbers for the wordlist and the temperatures. Record students' answers on the board. If groups disagree about temperatures, write each groups' choices next to the word.

6. Draw students' attention to the illustrations. Prompt them to use vocabulary not labeled in the art. Ask: *What objects do you see in the first picture?* [trees, road, clouds, etc.] *What is the man wearing in the second picture?* [a yellow coat, hat, gloves, jeans, etc.] *What parts of a car can you name?* [wheels, headlights, windshield, etc.] *What is the man wearing/carrying in the fourth picture?* [blue shirt, striped tie, suit jacket, briefcase, etc.]

Answers	
80°F/27°C	8–warm
32°F/0°C	9–humid
50°F/10°C	5–icy
84°F/29°C	2–lightning
6–cool	3–snowstorm
7–foggy	1–thunderstorm
4–freezing	

MULTILEVEL STRATEGIES

For 2A, use mixed-level groups.

• **Pre-level** Assign these students the role of administrative assistant.

• **Higher-level** Assign these students the role of manager.

B (audio) 1-27 1. Play the audio. Ask students to listen and check their answers.

2. Have students correct their answers based on the wordlist on the board and then write the correct numbers in their books.

3. Tell the groups from 2A to split into pairs to practice the words. Set a time limit (two minutes).

C 1. Ask students to work individually to complete the sentences. Set a time limit (three minutes).

2. Have students read the conversations aloud with a partner.

3. Have volunteers write the answers on the board.

Answers
1. thunderstorm, lightning
2. freezing, icy, snowstorm
3. foggy, cool
4. warm, humid

Communicative Practice and Application
10–15 minutes

D 1. Read the instructions aloud. Check students' understanding of *mood*. Ask: *When are you in a good mood? When are you in a bad mood?*

Provide sentence frames: *I'm in a good mood when ____. Rainy days put me in a ____ mood.*

2. Read the questions aloud and model a conversation with a student.

3. Review the sentences in the *Need help?* box.

4. Set a time limit (five minutes). Ask students to practice the conversation with several partners.

5. Have students share some of the responses they heard with the class: *Jan said rainy days make her sad.*

MULTILEVEL STRATEGIES

Target the *Test Yourself* to the level of your students.

• **Pre-level** Have these students work with their books open.

• **Higher-level** Have these students write sentences about how different kinds of weather make them feel.

Evaluation
10–15 minutes

TEST YOURSELF

1. Make a chart with two columns and two rows on the board. Write the headings *Feelings* and *Weather* across the top and *good* and *bad* down the left side. Have students give you an example for each section.

2. Have students copy the chart into their notebooks.

3. Set a time limit (five to ten minutes). Have students test themselves by writing the words they recall from the lesson in the chart.

4. Call "time" and have students check their spelling in *The Oxford Picture Dictionary* or another dictionary.

EXTENSION ACTIVITY

Conduct Research

If you have access to the Internet, write on the board a list of five to ten cities from around the country. Assign one to each student. Have each student look up the weather in his/her city. Then have students ask each other *How's the weather in___?* until they have heard the weather for all of the cities listed.

Lesson Overview	Lesson Notes
MULTILEVEL OBJECTIVES	
On-, Pre-, and Higher-level: Read and write about seasonal events	
LANGUAGE FOCUS	
Grammar: Simple present (*Summer is a wonderful season.*) **Vocabulary:** Words related to the seasons For vocabulary support, see these **Oxford Picture Dictionary** topics: The Calendar, pages 20–21; Feelings, pages 42–43; Weather, page 13	
STRATEGY FOCUS	
Talk about different kinds of weather.	
READINESS CONNECTION	
In this lesson, students write to communicate information about feelings and the weather.	
PACING	
To compress this lesson: Complete 1E as a class and omit 1F. **To extend this lesson:** Have students plan a seasonal activity. (See end of lesson.) And/or have students complete **Workbook 2 page 10** and **Multilevel Activities 2 Unit 2 page 29**.	

CORRELATIONS	
CCRS: R.1.A Ask and answer questions about key details in a text. SL.1.A Participate in collaborative conversations with diverse partners in small and larger groups. W.8.A With guidance and support, recall information from experiences or gather information from provided sources to answer a question.	**ELPS:** 6. An ELL can analyze and critique the arguments of others orally and in writing. 9. An ELL can create clear and coherent level-appropriate speech and text.

Warm-up and Review
10–15 minutes (books closed)

Ask: *How's the weather today? How was the weather in (December)?* Write the weather-related words students produce on the board. Discuss what kinds of weather and which seasons they like the best. Ask for a show of hands: *How many people like cold weather? Rain? Snow? Hot weather? Is summer/spring your favorite season?*

Introduction
5 minutes

1. Using the information on the board, tell students which is your favorite season and why.

2. State the objective: *Today we're going to read and write about our favorite seasons.*

1 Prepare to write

Presentation
20–25 minutes

A 1. Direct students to look at the picture and read the questions. Build students' schema by asking questions about the pictures. Ask: *Where is this? What products are people selling? What is the weather like? Do you ever go to a place like this?*

2. Have students work in pairs. Give them one minute to discuss their responses to the questions. Elicit responses from the class.

B **1-28** 1. Direct students to look at the picture again. Ask: *What things can you see in the picture?* Write any new words on the board.

2. Have students listen to the audio. Ask them to point to the items/actions in the picture as they listen. Circulate and monitor.

C **1-28** 1. Introduce the model paragraph and its purpose: *You're going to read a paragraph about the writer's favorite season. As you read, look for the weather and feeling words: How does Ana feel in summer? What's the weather like?* Play the audio again and have students read along silently. Answer any questions about unfamiliar vocabulary.

2. Check comprehension. Ask: *What activities does Ana do in summer?* [hiking or cycling] *What events happen?* [music festivals and the country fair] *What does Ana do at the farmers' marker?* [sells fruit and vegetables]

MULTILEVEL STRATEGIES

After the comprehension check in 1C, call on volunteers and tailor your questions to the level of your students.

• **Pre-level** Ask *yes/no* questions. *Is the weather humid?* [no]

• **On-level** Ask information questions. *What does Ana want to do after the farmers' market?* [She relaxes while enjoying some lemonade or ice cream.]

• **Higher-level** Ask these students to compare themselves to Ana. Ask: *What is the same about you and Ana? What is different?*

---

3. Point out the *Writer's Note.* Ask: *What is the topic sentence in Ana's paragraph?* [*Summer is a wonderful season in Eugene, Oregon.*] Ask: *Where is the topic sentence usually located?* [Usually, it's the first sentence.] Ask: *How do the other sentences in the paragraph relate to the topic sentence?* [They support or give more information about the topic sentence.] Ask students to say which details support the topic sentence.

Guided Practice I
5–10 minutes

D 1. Look at sentence 1 together. Ask: *How do we know this is false?* Ask students to point to or highlight the place in the text where they can find the answer.

2. Have students work individually to mark the sentences as *T* (true) or *F* (false). Set a time limit (three to five minutes).

3. Discuss answers as a class. If students finish the *true/false* exercise early, ask them to rewrite the false sentences to make them correct.

Answers	
1. F	4. F
2. F	5. T
3. T	6. F

TIP

Activate students' knowledge of the seasons before playing the audio for 1E. In addition to asking what seasons they connect with given events, check for student understanding of the words *spring, summer, winter,* and *fall.*

Guided Practice II
10–15 minutes

E **1-29** 1. Direct students to look at the flyer. Ask students to think about what seasons they connect with each event. Explain that they will listen to an announcer talking about different community events during the year, and that they should pay special attention to the dates mentioned and write them in the blanks. Play the entire audio once.

2. Play the audio again in segments. After the answer for each question comes up, stop the audio and check in with students. If necessary, replay the segment. Have students listen again and work individually to write the dates.

F 🔊 **1-29** Have students compare answers with a partner. Then play the audio again for them to check their work. Discuss answers as a class.

Answers
St. Patrick's Day Parade: March 17th
Garden Show: April 16–19
Country Music Festival: July 24th–26th
Seafood Festival September: 13 &14
Pumpkin Patch: October 25–30
Snow and Ice Festival: December 3–21

2 Plan

Communicative Practice I
20–25 minutes

A 1. Write the chart on the board. Fill it out with your own answers as an example for students. Have students complete the exercise individually.

B 🔊 **1-30** 1. Play the audio. Have students read along silently.

2. Draw students' attention to the information in the *Need help?* box. Ask volunteers to say sentences using the sentence frame.

3. Based on the chart on the board, model asking and answering questions with a volunteer. *Why do you like fall? I like fall because there's a harvest festival in October.*

4. Set a time limit (five minutes). Ask students to ask and answer questions with a partner. Circulate and monitor.

3 Write

Communicative Practice II and Application
15–20 minutes

A 1. Copy three sentences from the example paragraph onto the board, but write them as a numbered list. Ask: *Is this a paragraph? Which sentence is the topic sentence?* Elicit the differences between the numbered list and the form of the paragraph template on page 21.

2. Have students look at the paragraph template as you read it aloud. At each blank, have a volunteer give a sample answer.

3. Set a time limit for writing (five minutes). Have students complete the paragraph template with their own information.

B Ask students to read their paragraphs to a partner. Call on volunteers to share what they learned about their partners.

MULTILEVEL STRATEGIES
In 3B, target the writing to the level of your students.
• **Pre-level** Write a wordlist on the board for these students to use to complete their paragraphs. Then work with these students to write a group paragraph. Read through the template. At each blank, stop and elicit completions. Decide as a group what to write. Have these students copy the group paragraph into their notebooks.
• **Higher-level** Ask these students to write a few sentences about their least favorite season.

Evaluation
10 minutes

TEST YOURSELF

1. Read the instructions aloud. Assign a time limit (five minutes) and have students work individually.

2. Before collecting student work, invite two or three volunteers to share their sentences. Ask students to raise their hands if they wrote similar answers.

EXTENSION ACTIVITY
Plan an Event
Bring in copies of the weekend events section of the local newspaper/magazine or have students research events on the Internet. Have them choose one event and plan a class trip (either imaginary or real). Have students tell the class why they chose the event, why they think it's a good thing to do for the season, and the other details such as time, price, and transportation possibilities.

Lesson Overview

	Lesson Notes

MULTILEVEL OBJECTIVES

On-level: Ask and answer questions with *will* to talk about future events

Pre-level: Answer questions with *will* to talk about future events

Higher-level: Write a paragraph about the future using *will*

LANGUAGE FOCUS

Grammar: The future with *will* (*I will visit in August. When will they meet?*); prepositions of time

Vocabulary: Months and ordinal numbers

For vocabulary support, see this **Oxford Picture Dictionary** topic: The Calendar, pages 20–21

STRATEGY FOCUS

Use appropriate time expressions for different points in the future.

READINESS CONNECTION

In this lesson, students practice communicating information about future events.

PACING

To compress this lesson: Skip the partner interaction in 2B.

To extend this lesson: Have students practice *Present or future?* (See end of lesson.)

And/or have students complete **Workbook 2 pages 11–12, Multilevel Activities 2 Unit 2 page 30,** and **Multilevel Grammar Exercises 2 Unit 2.**

CORRELATIONS

CCRS: L.1.A Demonstrate command of the conventions of standard English grammar and usage when writing or speaking. e. Use verbs to convey a sense of past, present, and future (e.g., *Yesterday I walked home; Today I walk home; Tomorrow I will walk home.*) j. Use frequently occurring prepositions (e.g., *during, beyond, toward*).

ELPS: 7. An ELL can adapt language choices to purpose, task, and audience when speaking and writing. 10. An ELL can demonstrate command of the conventions of standard English to communicate in level-appropriate speech and writing.

Warm-up and Review
10–15 minutes (books closed)

1. Write the names of the next few months on the board. For example, if it is now October, write *November, December,* and *January.* Tell students about something you will do in one of those months and about one event that will occur. Ask: *What will you do in November? What will you do in December?* They may talk about community events, holidays, or personal events.

2. Elicit and write their short answers under the correct month.

Introduction
5–10 minutes

1. Using the information on the board, say some sentences using *will.* Examples: *We'll celebrate Thanksgiving in November. Maria will have her baby in December.*

2. State the objective: *Today we're going to explore how to use* will *to talk about things that will happen in the future.*

1 Focus on the future with *will*

Presentation I
20–25 minutes

 1-31 1. Direct students to look at the illustration in the center. Ask: *What is this?* [a text message] *What are Lara and Ana messaging about?* [a visit]

2. Play the audio. Have students read along silently as they listen.

3. Read the questions aloud. Ask students to read the conversation again and answer the questions individually.

4. Read the first question aloud. Call on a volunteer for the answer. Ask the volunteer where in the conversation they found the answer. Read the second sentence aloud, calling on a different volunteer for the answer.

Answers
1. in August
2. by plane

B 1. Have students work individually to identify each verb in the conversation.

2. Call on volunteers to say which words show that the women are talking about the future.

C 1. Demonstrate how to read the grammar charts as complete sentences. Read through the charts sentence by sentence. Then read them aloud again and have students repeat after you.

2. Use the message conversation in 1A to illustrate points in the grammar charts, e.g., *Will you have free time in August?*

3. Read the information in the contraction boxes aloud. On the board, write sentences with no contractions: *I will not visit in August. They will take the train to New York City. He will not study tomorrow. I will go to school next Monday.* Have students rewrite the sentences in their notebooks with contractions. Have volunteers come to the board to rewrite the words with contractions for students to check their answers.

Guided Practice I
15–20 minutes

 1. Read the instructions aloud. Give students time to silently review the charts again and complete the sentences. Play the audio again, if necessary.

2. Ask volunteers to write the sentences on the board. Have other students read the sentences aloud.

3. Assess student understanding of the charts. Ask: *What is the verb? Is there an -s on the verb? Do we change the verb for* he *or* she?

Answers
1. will
2. will
3. won't
4. won't
5. will

2 Explore asking and answering questions with *will*

Presentation II
10–15 minutes

 1-32 1. Review the question words *what, where, when,* and *how (long)*. Write them on the board. Call out examples of events, days/months, and transportation methods: *farmers' market, spring festival, Tuesday, July, train.* Ask students to tell you which question word goes with each of your examples.

2. Give students time to read the chart. Point out that the information questions have a longer, more specific answer than the *yes/no* questions. Ask: *What is the first word in a* yes/no *question?* [will] 3. Play the conversations. Have students repeat the conversations with a partner.

3. Ask: *When do we not use a contraction?* [in a short, affirmative answer]

4. Check comprehension of the grammar and content by asking questions and having students answer in complete sentences: *Sam, when will you do your homework? Lee, will you walk home today?*

Guided Practice II
10–15 minutes

B 1. Look at "Peter's yearly planner" as a class. Ask: *What will Peter do in January?*

2. Have students put their pencils down and review the exercise orally with a partner before they write. Circulate and monitor.

3. Have students write the answers individually.

4. Ask volunteers to write their complete conversations on the board. Review and correct them together.

Answers
1. When will, go / He'll go in January.
2. What will, do / He'll visit Mexico.
3. Will, go / No, he won't. He'll go by plane.
4. Will, take / Yes, he will.

MULTILEVEL STRATEGIES

For 2B, pair same-level students together.

• **Pre- and On-level** Have these students read the conversations aloud together when they finish writing.

• **Higher-level** Have these students cover the exercise and ask and answer questions using only the "yearly planner" as a guide.

3 Practice: prepositions of time with *will*

Presentation III and Guided Practice III
15–20 minutes

 1. Ask students to give examples of prepositions. Write them on the board. Ask: *Which prepositions do we use for time?* Circle them if they are already on the board, and if not, write them [*at, in, on*]. Write on the board the words *time, month, year, day,* and *date.* Ask students to give an example of each one. Explain that they will practice using prepositions of time with the correct kinds of time.

2. Read the instructions aloud and have students complete the task individually.

3. Have students check their answers with a partner. Then discuss answers as a class.

Answers		
at + time	*in* + month/ year	*on* + day/date
11 a.m. 3 p.m. 9:15 p.m. 8:30 a.m.	December 2021 April 2019	Monday Friday, January 22nd Thursday, August 3rd Saturday

B 1. Read the instructions aloud and model the task. On the board, fill out one of your own events for the week and the year. Have students fill out the information for themselves individually.

2. Model the sample conversation with a student, using the information you wrote on the board. Direct students' attention to the *Need help?* box. Read the information aloud. Explain that they should use each sentence in the box as a model. They create their own sentences to illustrate the time expressions. [For example, *Right now it's Tuesday, May third, 2018 at 3:30 p.m. This time tomorrow it will be Wednesday at 3:30 p.m.,* etc.]

3. Have students work in pairs to ask and answer questions about each other's events. Circulate and monitor.

4. Have volunteers report one of their partner's responses to the class.

4 Practice talking about the future

Communicative Practice and Application
10–15 minutes

A 1. Read the instructions aloud. Then read the complete questions in the chart. [*Where will you be at 11 a.m. tomorrow?*]

2. Students fill out their chart individually. Circulate and monitor.

B 1. Read the instructions aloud. Model the conversation with a volunteer.

2. Students take turns asking and answering questions from 4A with a partner.

3. Students share their partner's responses with the class.

MULTILEVEL STRATEGIES

For 4B, pair same-level students together.

• **Pre-level** Provide sentence frames for students to answer questions: *At 11:00 a.m. tomorrow, I'll ___.*

• **On- and Higher-level** Challenge pairs to ask and answer two or three more questions about future plans.

Evaluation
10 minutes

TEST YOURSELF

Before students begin, have them ask their partners: *How do you spell your name?* Write example sentences, one about you and one about a volunteer, using the structures in 4A.

MULTILEVEL STRATEGIES

Adapt the *Test Yourself* to the level of your students.

• **Pre-level** Give these students sentence frames to fill out. Examples: *At this time tomorrow ___. Next week ___.*

• **Higher-level** Have these students write a paragraph titled "My Next Five Years."

EXTENSION ACTIVITY

Present or Future?

Give students more practice deciding if a sentence is in the present or future.

1. Write *Present* and *Future* on the board. Say sentences and ask students to tell you whether they are present or future.

2. Ask volunteers to write the sentences in the two columns.

Lesson Overview	Lesson Notes
MULTILEVEL OBJECTIVES	
On- and Higher-level: Ask for and give directions **Pre-level:** Follow directions	
LANGUAGE FOCUS	
Grammar: Imperatives (*Go straight.*) **Vocabulary:** Expressions for giving directions For vocabulary support, see these **Oxford Picture Dictionary** topics: Downtown, pages 126–127; City Streets, pages 128–129; Directions and Maps, page 159	
STRATEGY FOCUS	
Interrupt politely.	
READINESS CONNECTION	
In this lesson, students communicate verbally to give and receive directions.	
PACING	
To compress this lesson: Skip Exercise 4B. **To extend this lesson:** Have students write directions to a place. (See end of lesson.) And/or have students complete **Workbook 2 page 13** and **Multilevel Activities 2 Unit 2 page 31**.	

CORRELATIONS	
CCRS: SL.1.A Participate in collaborative conversations with diverse partners in small and larger groups. SL.6.A Speak audibly and express thoughts, feelings, and ideas clearly. Produce complete sentences when appropriate to task and situation.	**ELPS:** 2. An ELL can participate in level-appropriate oral and written exchanges of information, ideas, and analyses, in various social and academic contexts, responding to peer, audience, or reader comments and questions. 9. An ELL can create clear and coherent level-appropriate speech and text.

Warm-up and Review
10–15 minutes (books closed)

Write the word *library* on the board. Tell students how often you go to the library. Ask them to think of places in the community that they often go. Have a group of five or six volunteers line up at the board and have them take turns writing names of places. After they finish, allow any student with a new idea to write the word on the board.

Introduction
5 minutes

1. Point to the places on the board and ask students how to get there. This will give you an idea of which direction words they already know.

2. State the objective: *Today we're going to learn how to give directions to places in the community.*

1 Listen to learn: give and get directions

Presentation I
10–15 minutes

 1. Direct students to look at the pictures. Ask: *What do you see?* [bridge, steps, library]

2. Ask questions using the vocabulary in the pictures and the places written on the board during the warm-up: *When you drive to the mall, do you go <u>under</u> the freeway or <u>over</u> it?*

3. Have students match the directions to the pictures. Discuss answers as a class.

Answers	
3–Go past the library.	4–Go around the traffic circle.
2–Go up the steps.	1–Go over the bridge.

Guided Practice I
20–25 minutes

 1-33 1. Direct students to look at the chart and the headings. Ask: *What is the difference between a destination and directions?* [A destination is the place you want to go and directions are how you get there.] Explain that they will listen to four conversations of people asking for and giving directions. The first time they listen, they will listen for the destination and then write it in the chart.

2. Play the audio and have students complete the task.

3. Have students compare their answers in pairs and then as a class.

Answers
1. library
2. bus station
3. shopping mall
4. hospital

MULTILEVEL STRATEGIES

Target instruction for 1B to the level of your students.

• **Pre-level** Explain to these students that the destination will be in the first sentence of each conversation.

• **Higher-level** Challenge these students to fill in the directions column of the chart for the first conversation.

 1-33 Play the audio again and have students write the directions for each conversation. Have students compare answers with a partner and then with the class.

Answers
1. Go up the steps and you'll see it on the right.
2. Go over the bridge and then turn left.
3. Drive around this traffic circle and take the first left.
4. Go past the police station and the hospital is on your right.

TIP

Before you play the audio, explain to pre-level students that in each conversation, the person will give directions, and then the other person will repeat them back, so they will hear each set of directions twice.

2 Practice your pronunciation

Pronunciation Extension
15–20 minutes

1-34 1. Direct students' attention to the underlined words before they listen.

2. Play the audio. After students listen, illustrate the concept of stressing contrasting words by writing this alternative version of conversation one on the board: *A: Do I take the next street on the left? B: No, take the next street on the right.* Say the sentence (stressing *right*) and ask students to identify the word you stressed.

1-34 Play the audio again. As students repeat the conversations, monitor and provide feedback on pronunciation.

1-35 Play the audio and have students complete the exercise individually. Replay the audio and have them check their work. Discuss answers as a class.

Answers
1. second, right
2. past, school
3. under, bridge
4. around, supermarket

D 1. Have students practice the conversations in 2C with a partner. Circulate and monitor.

> **MULTILEVEL STRATEGIES**
>
> For 2D, pair same-level students together.
>
> • **Pre-level** Have students practice the conversation in pairs while you listen and ensure correct intonation.
>
> • **Higher-level** Have students practice the conversation in pairs and add one more exchange.

3 Practice using conjunctions *and* and *but*

Presentation II and Guided Practice II
15–20 minutes

A Read the instructions aloud. Have students complete the task individually.

B 1. Write sentences on the board: *1. I have a brother and a sister. 2. I have a brother, but I don't have a sister.* Have students work in pairs to discuss the sentences they marked in the reading and the sentences on the board. Tell them to work with a partner to come up with a rule for when to use *and* and when to use *but.* Don't check answers yet.

C 🔊 1-36 1. Read the sentences in the grammar chart aloud. Play the audio and have students repeat.

2. Have pairs who worked together in B confirm that their rules are correct. Have students discuss the rules as a class and come to a consensus on the best explanation.

D 1. Read the instructions aloud and give students time to study the map.

2. Have pairs talk about the map and complete the sentences. Circulate and ensure that students are using the grammar correctly.

Answers
1. but, park
2. but, bank
3. and, High Street, Oak Street
4. and, pharmacy, bookstore

> **MULTILEVEL STRATEGIES**
>
> Target instruction for 3D to the level of your students.
>
> • **Pre-level** Work with these students and help them fill in the blanks. Direct them to use their finger to follow the route as you read the sentence aloud.
>
> • **Higher-level** Direct these students to cover the locations at the beginning of each set of directions. Then have them take turns finding the destination as their partner reads the starting point and the directions aloud.

4 Make conversation: asking for and giving directions

Communicative Practice I
15–20 minutes

A 1. Ask students to remember the last time they asked for or gave directions. Ask: *What is a polite phrase you can use to stop and ask someone something?* [Say "Excuse me."] Then review clarifying from Unit 1. Ask: *What is one way to clarify information?* [Repeat the information that you heard.]

2. Write the sample conversation on the board. Point to each blank and ask what kind of information can be used to fill it [e.g., direction, location, verb]. Then ask the class for an example. Model the conversation with a volunteer.

3. Have students work in pairs to create a conversation and take turns performing the parts.

B 1. Set a time limit (ten minutes). Ask pairs to share their conversation with another pair. Circulate and monitor.

2. Have pairs present their conversation to the class.

> **TIP**
>
> Whenever you observe students creating conversations, you can take notes of any common mistakes you hear. Without identifying who made the mistakes, discuss them as a class when the activity is finished.

AT WORK

Interrupting politely

Presentation III and Communicative Practice II
25–35 minutes

A 1. Direct students to look at the illustrations. Ask them to describe what they see and what they think the different situations are. Confirm that students understand the meanings of *interrupt* and *polite*.

2. Play the audio and have students read along silently. Give students time to study the conversations.

3. Direct students' attention to the *Need help?* box. Read the sentences aloud and have them say which ones are used in the conversations.

B Have students practice the conversations in A with a partner. Challenge them to substitute the other sentences from the *Need help?* box into the conversation. Circulate and help as needed.

C 1. Read the questions aloud. Have pairs discuss answers to the questions.

2. Have pairs share their ideas with the class.

Evaluation
10–15 minutes

TEST YOURSELF

Read the instructions aloud. Model the conversation with a student. Set a time limit (five minutes). Have students work in pairs to act out the situation. Circulate and assess students' progress.

> **MULTILEVEL STRATEGIES**
>
> For the *Test Yourself*, pair same-level students together.
>
> • **Pre-level** Read simple directions to these students and have them trace the route on the map on page 26, or prepare a list of short directions for students to read while their partners follow along.

> **EXTENSION ACTIVITY**
>
> **Give Directions**
>
> Have students use the Internet to find driving directions to different places.
>
> 1. Have students work in pairs and use an Internet map site to find driving directions to different locations. If you don't have access to the Internet, have groups of students write directions to a place they know.
>
> 2. Ask students to read the directions to each other. Have the groups share their directions.

Lesson Overview	Lesson Notes
MULTILEVEL OBJECTIVES	
On- and Higher-level: Read about and discuss making small talk and invitations **Pre-level:** Read about making small talk and invitations	
LANGUAGE FOCUS	
Grammar: Future with *will* (*Who will bring the food?*) **Vocabulary:** *In the mood, feel like, look at, make eye contact* For vocabulary support, see this **Oxford Picture Dictionary** topic: Feelings, pages 42–43	
STRATEGY FOCUS	
Use examples to illustrate ideas.	
READINESS CONNECTION	
In this lesson, students communicate information about making small talk in various social situations.	
PACING	
To compress this lesson: Assign 1E and/or 1F as homework **To extend this lesson:** Talk about invitations (See end of lesson.) And/or have students complete **Workbook 2 page 14** and **Multilevel Activities 2 Unit 2 page 32**.	

CORRELATIONS	
CCRS: R.1.A Ask and answer questions about key details in a text. R.7.A Use the illustrations and details in a text to describe its key ideas (e.g., maps, charts, photographs, political cartoons, etc.).	**ELPS:** 1. An ELL can construct meaning from oral presentations and literary and informational text through level-appropriate listening, reading, and viewing. 3. An ELL can speak and write about level-appropriate complex literary and informational texts and topics.

Warm-up and Review
10–15 minutes (books closed)

Tell your students about places you often go, such as the bank or a park. Write the words on the board. Ask volunteers to tell you where they go. As they give you the names of places, write them on the board. Ask: *Do you speak English there? Whom do you speak to?*

Introduction
5 minutes

1. Point to places on the board and tell students whom you talk to in those places. *When I go to the bank, I talk to the teller, and sometimes I also talk to the people who are waiting in line.*

2. State the objective: *Today we're going to learn how to make small talk. Small talk is a conversation we have with someone we don't know very well.*

1 Build reading strategies

Presentation
10–15 minutes

 1. Have students read along silently as you read the sentences aloud. Help students with definitions as needed.

be in the mood for: Tell students about yourself to illustrate the definition: *I usually eat a salad for lunch, but today I'm not in the mood for salad. I'm in the mood for a sandwich. I want to eat a sandwich today.* Check comprehension.

make eye contact: Demonstrate eye contact and ask: *Is it polite to make eye contact with the teacher? With people you don't know?* Note that answers may vary depending on students' cultural backgrounds.

stranger: Clarify the definition by giving examples of people who are not strangers: *My mother is not a stranger. My friend is not a stranger.*

2. Have students complete the activity. Check answers as a class.

Answers
3–strangers
2–make eye contact
1–be in the mood for

Guided Practice: Pre-reading
5–10 minutes

 Read the instructions aloud and confirm that students understand what *small talk* means. Have students answer the question with a partner. Then check answers as a class. If any students answer incorrectly, ask them to support their answer using the photo and title in 1C. Establish the correct answer as a class.

Guided Practice: While Reading
15–20 minutes

1. Ask students to read the article silently and think about their answer to the question. Answer any questions about unfamiliar vocabulary.

2. Have students work in pairs to compare and discuss their answers, and then check answers as a class.

3. Check comprehension. Ask: *What are good topics for small talk? Is small talk easy for everyone? How do many people begin making small talk?*

MULTILEVEL STRATEGIES

Adapt 1C to the level of your students.
- **Pre-level** Read the text aloud to these students as they follow along.
- **On- and Higher-level** Have students work in pairs and read the article aloud to each other, taking turns to read each paragraph.

Guided Practice: Rereading
10–15 minutes

 🔊 1-38 1. Play the audio and have students listen and read along silently.

2. Provide an opportunity for students to extract evidence from the article. Have students reread the article and underline any words or phrases that give examples of small talk topics and language.

3. Have students discuss their answers to the question with a partner. Circulate and monitor. Have volunteers report their partner's responses to the class.

TIP

Have students raise their hands if they think small talk is difficult. As a class, brainstorm topics and opening lines, with the idea of making small talk easier to start. Write ideas on the board. Have students copy the ideas into their notebooks.

Guided Practice: Post-reading
15 minutes

 1. Have students work individually to complete the items and identify the sentences where they found the answers.

Answers
1. b
2. b
3. a
4. a

2. Elicit and discuss any additional questions about the reading and the topic. You could introduce new questions for class discussion: *What are other possible topics for small talk? What topics are NOT good for making small talk?*

F 1. Have students work individually to complete the sentences.

2. Have students read their sentences to a partner before checking answers as a class.

Answers
1. strangers
2. nervous
3. in the mood
4. compliment

MULTILEVEL STRATEGIES

For 1F, work with pre-level students.

• **Pre-level** Ask these students *yes/no* and short-answer information questions about the reading while other students are completing 1F. Have these students copy the answers to 1F into their notebooks and underline the words that are new for them.

2 Read an invitation

Communicative Practice
10–15 minutes

A 1. Direct students to look at the invitation. Read the questions aloud.

2. Have students answer the questions individually before comparing answers with a partner.

3. Check answers as a class.

Answers
1. the technology department
2. employees in the technology department
3. noon / 12 p.m.
4. 2nd floor conference room

B 1. Read the questions aloud. Allow students time to think of their own answers and make notes.

2. Set a time limit (five minutes). Have students discuss the questions with a partner. Circulate and help as needed.

3. Have pairs share their responses with another pair. Have volunteers share their partner's answers with the class.

MULTILEVEL STRATEGIES

Target instruction for 2B for the level of your students.

• **Pre-level** Provide these students with sentence frames for their conversation:

I like/don't like parties with _____.

I like/don't like parties with _____ because _____.

When I talk to people at parties, I feel _____.

When I talk to a co-worker at a party, I say _____.

Application
5–10 minutes

BRING IT TO LIFE

To help students plan for this exercise, discuss where they might have the opportunity to start a conversation with someone in English outside of school. *Do you wait for the bus? Work with people who don't speak your language? Have friendly neighbors?* If your school has students of different language backgrounds, suggest they start a conversation at break time with a student who speaks a different language.

TIP

Make this *Bring It to Life* more concrete and practice *will* by having students make an action-plan chart for their group. *Sonya will talk to a woman at the bus stop. Nasrim will talk to her neighbor.* Post the charts.

EXTENSION ACTIVITY

Talk about Invitations

Bring in party invitations and see if students can identify the type of event from the words and illustrations.

1. Post and number the invitations and write questions for students to answer. Ask: *Which one is for a baby shower? Which one is for a birthday party? Which one is a wedding invitation?*

2. Discuss *RSVP* and any words on the invitations that students don't know.

Lesson Overview

Lesson Notes

MULTILEVEL OBJECTIVES

On-, Pre-, and Higher-level: Expand upon and review unit grammar and life skills

LANGUAGE FOCUS

Grammar: Future with *will* (*Next weekend, Jim and Mario will...*)

Vocabulary: *Farmers' market*

For vocabulary support, see these **Oxford Picture Dictionary** topics: The Calendar, pages 20–21; Feelings, pages 42–43; Weather, page 13; Downtown, pages 126–127; Directions and Maps, page 159

STRATEGY FOCUS

Talk about feelings in different situations.

READINESS CONNECTION

In this review, students work in teams to communicate information about feelings, the weather, future plans, and giving and using directions.

PACING

To extend this review: Have students complete **Workbook 2 page 15**, **Multilevel Activities 2 Unit 2 pages 33–36**, and **Multilevel Grammar Exercises 2 Unit 2**.

CORRELATIONS

CCRS: R.1.A Ask and answer questions about key details in a text.

R.7.A Use the illustrations and details in a text to describe its key ideas (e.g., maps, charts, photographs, political cartoons, etc.).

W.3.A Write narratives in which they recount two or more appropriately sequenced events, include some details regarding what happened, use temporal words to signal event order, and provide some sense of closure.

SL.1.A Participate in collaborative conversations with diverse partners in small and larger groups.

ELPS: 5. An ELL can conduct research and evaluate and communicate findings to answer questions or solve problems. 6. An ELL can analyze and critique the arguments of others orally and in writing.

Warm-up and Review
10–15 minutes (books closed)

1. Review the *Bring It to Life* assignment from Lesson 5.

2. Have students who made small talk with someone share their experiences.

3. If the groups made action-plan charts, have students who completed the assignment check off their names.

4. Encourage students who haven't completed the assignment yet to try it.

Introduction and Presentation
5 minutes

1. Tell students some of your plans and ask about theirs: *This summer I'll go to the mountains. What will you do?*

2. State the objective: *Today we'll review sentences and questions with* will *and ask for and give directions.*

Guided Practice
15–20 minutes

A 1. Direct students to work in groups of three to four and look at the picture. Ask: *Who are these people? How old are they? What are they doing? What could they be saying?*

2. Set a time limit (five minutes) to complete the exercise. Circulate and answer any questions.

3. Have students from each group share the group's responses with the class. If you have a large class, you may not want all of the groups to report their responses. Instead, have groups share their responses with each other. Call "time" and tell all groups to work with a new group and to repeat their responses. Repeat this process as desired, making sure each group gets to share their responses at least once.

B 1. Read the instructions and the sample story beginning aloud. Have students complete the task individually.

2. Have students read their stories to a partner. Have volunteers share them with the class.

> **TIP**
>
> After students read their stories, you can collect them and correct any mistakes for students to review later. Students naturally can be sensitive to being corrected in front of others and it can affect their confidence.

Communicative Practice
30–45 minutes

C Draw a map on the board of the neighborhood near the school (or class meeting place). Have students call out places that can be included on the map.

D 1. Put students in new groups of three to four. Check students' understanding of the word *destination*.

2. Have students work in their teams to write directions from the school to another place on the map. Set a time limit (five minutes).

3. Have each team take a turn giving their directions, but make sure they don't say what their final destination is. Have the rest of the class listen to the directions, following along on the map, and guess the destination.

E 1. Read the instructions and the questions aloud. Check students' understanding of any new vocabulary in the questions.

2. Have students work in their teams from D. Ask them to copy the questionnaire into their notebooks. Set a time limit (ten minutes). Explain that each student in the group should fill out the questionnaire.

F Read the instructions and the sample summary aloud. Students work in their teams from D to complete the task.

G Have the reporter from each team present their summary to the class.

> **MULTILEVEL STRATEGIES**
>
> Adapt D–G to the level of your students.
> - **Pre-level** Work with these students directly by supplying sentence frames as needed. Have them interview other students in pairs.
> - **Higher-level** After G, have these students give advice about the situations that make people nervous.

PROBLEM SOLVING AT HOME
10–15 minutes

A 1. Ask students to read the paragraph silently. Then play the audio and have them read along silently.

2. Check comprehension. Write *Friday* on the board and ask: *What is happening on Friday at Gina's work? What is Gina nervous about? Which family members are mentioned? What does Sofia like to do on Friday nights?* Write the answers in an abbreviated format so that students can see the conflict. [office party; She's nervous about small talk.; children and mother, Sofia; Sofia watches favorite TV program.]

B 1. Read the questions aloud. Have students work with a team to answer the questions. Circulate and monitor.

2. Come to a class consensus of what problem Gina has. Then have teams share their solutions. Write each one on the board.

3. As a class, discuss the pros and cons of each solution. Have students choose the top three of each.

Evaluation
20–25 minutes

To test students' understanding of the unit language and content, have them take the Unit 2 Test, available on the Teacher Resource Center.

3 Moving Out

Unit Overview

This unit focuses on common household problems, using ads to find a place to live, understanding rental agreements, and using the comparative to describe features of places to live.

KEY OBJECTIVES	
Lesson 1	Identify household problems and repairpeople; recognize household maintenance
Lesson 2	Identify different housing features; interpret classified ads
Lesson 3	Use the comparative to compare different types of housing
Lesson 4	Respond to housing ads
Lesson 5	Evaluate information about different ways to find housing; interpret rental agreements
Teamwork & Language Review	Review unit language

UNIT FEATURES	
Academic Vocabulary	*available, regulations*
Employability Skills	• Compare and contrast homes • Interpret rental information in housing ads • Draw conclusions about types of housing • Summarize housing information • Interpret a rental agreement • Determine whether to rent or buy a new home • Understand teamwork • Communicate information • Work with others • Communicate verbally

Resources	**Class Audio** CD1, Tracks 40–55
	Workbook Unit 3, pages 16–22
	Teacher Resource Center
	    Multilevel Activities 2 Unit 3
	    Multilevel Grammar Exercises 2 Unit 3
	    Unit 3 Test
	Oxford Picture Dictionary The Home, Finding a Home, Apartments, Different Places to Live, Household Problems and Repairs

Lesson Overview	Lesson Notes
MULTILEVEL OBJECTIVES	
On-level: Identify household problems and repairpeople **Pre-level:** Recognize household problems and repairpeople **Higher-level:** Talk and write about household problems and repairpeople	
LANGUAGE FOCUS	
Grammar: *There is, there are* (*There's no electricity. There are mice in the garage.*); present continuous (*The pipe is dripping.*) **Vocabulary:** Words for household problems and repairpeople, *get rid of* For vocabulary support, see these **Oxford Picture Dictionary** topics: The Home, pages 46–47; Household Problems and Repairs, pages 62–63	
STRATEGY FOCUS	
Talk about common household problems and repairs.	
READINESS CONNECTION	
In this lesson, students communicate information about common household problems.	
PACING	
To compress this lesson: Conduct 2A as a whole-class activity. **To extend this lesson:** Have students extend a conversation. (See end of lesson.) And/or have students complete **Workbook 2 page 16** and **Multilevel Activities 2 Unit 3 page 38**.	
CORRELATIONS	
CCRS: L.6.A Use words and phrases acquired through conversations, reading and being read to, and responding to texts, including using frequently occurring conjunctions to signal simple relationships (e.g., *because*). SL.1.A Participate in collaborative conversations with diverse partners in small and larger groups.	**ELPS:** 8. An ELL can determine the meaning of words and phrases in oral presentations and literary and informational text.

Warm-up and Review
10–15 minutes (books closed)

1. Ask students to name some rooms in a house.

2. Pass out four pieces of paper, each labeled with a different room: *Living Room, Bedroom, Bathroom, Kitchen*. Tell students to write the name of one item that belongs in that room and then pass the paper to another student who will add another item. Set a time limit (ten minutes).

3. While students are writing, draw four columns on the board with columns labeled *Living Room,*

Bedroom, Bathroom, and *Kitchen*. Call "time" and have volunteers copy the completed lists under the correct heading onto the board.

TIP

For a livelier warm-up, have teams line up at the board. The first person in line writes a word and then runs to the back of the line. Teammates can shout out ideas.

Introduction
3 minutes

1. Indicate items on the board that sometimes cause problems. Ask: *Do you ever have a problem with your sink? Your lights?*

2. State the objective: *Today we're going to learn how to talk about household problems.*

1 Learn about common household problems

Presentation
20–25 minutes

A Direct students to look at the words as you read them aloud. Have them circle the words they know.

B 🔊 **1-40** 1. Direct students to look at the pictures and name the parts of the house. Ask: *What items in the pictures are not on the list on the board?* Write any new words to the lists on the board.

2. Have students listen to the audio. Ask them to point to the correct picture as they listen. Circulate and monitor.

3. Check comprehension by asking *yes/no* questions. Have students hold up one finger for *yes* and two for *no* in order to get a nonverbal response. Ask: *Is the leaking pipe in the kitchen?* [yes] *Are there mice in the bathroom?* [no]

4. Pair students and ask them to take turns describing what is happening in each picture. Circulate and monitor.

C 🔊 **1-41** 1. Ask students to listen and repeat the words. Point out that *broken* has two syllables, but *cracked* has only one.

2. While students are repeating, circulate and listen for pronunciation difficulties. Provide choral practice as necessary.

Guided Practice I
15–20 minutes

D 1. Have students work individually to complete the sentences using the new vocabulary. Set a time limit (two minutes).

2. Encourage students to take turns reading the completed sentences with a partner.

Answers	
1. no electricity	4. leaking pipe
2. cracked window	5. broken door
3. dripping faucet	6. mice

MULTILEVEL STRATEGIES

For 1D, pair same-level students together.

• **Pre-level** While other students are writing, assist pre-level students with the exercise.

• **Higher-level** When these students finish, have them write about any situations they may have in their own home. After correcting 1D, ask these students to say their sentences.

E 1. Read the instructions aloud and model the sample conversation with a volunteer.

2. Set a time limit (three minutes). Have students take turns asking and answering the questions with a partner. Circulate and listen for any pronunciation or vocabulary difficulties.

2 Talk about household repairs

Guided Practice II
35–40 minutes

A 1. Ask: *When a pipe is leaking, whom do I call to fix it?* Introduce the new topic: *Now let's talk about household repairs.*

2. Group students and assign roles: manager, researcher, administrative assistant, and reporter. Explain that students work with their groups to match the words and pictures.

3. Check comprehension of the exercise: *Who looks up the words in the picture dictionary?* [researcher] *Who writes the numbers in the book?* [administrative assistant] *Who tells the class your answers?* [reporter] *Who helps everyone and manages the group?* [manager]

4. Set a time limit (three minutes) and have students work together to complete the task. While students are working, copy the wordlist onto the board.

5. Call "time" and have the reporters from each group take turns calling out the numbers for the wordlist. Record students' answers on the board. If groups disagree, write each group's choice next to the word.

6. Draw students' attention to the illustration. Prompt students to use vocabulary not labeled in the art. Ask: *What objects do you see in kitchen?* [oven, sink, toolkit, cap, etc.] *What parts of a house can you see?* [a door, floor, wall, closet, etc.] *What parts of a truck can you name?* [wheels, headlights, windshield, etc.]

Answers	
5–carpenter	6–lock
9–cockroach	7–locksmith
3–electrician	2–plumber
8–exterminator	1–repairperson
4–fuse box	

MULTILEVEL STRATEGIES

Have students work in mixed-level groups for 2A.

• **Pre-level** Assign these students the role of administrative assistant.

• **Higher-level** Assign these students the role of manager.

B ◀)) 1-42 1. Play the audio. Ask students to listen and check their answers.

2. Have students correct the wordlist on the board and then write the correct numbers in their books.

3. Tell the groups from 2A to split into pairs to practice the words. Set a time limit (two minutes).

C 1. Before students write, check for comprehension. Have them put their pencils down. Ask: *Who is repairing the door in the bedroom?* [the carpenter] *Who is checking the fuse box?* [the electrician]

2. Note the verb *get rid of* and explain that it can mean "throw away." *When my clothes are too old, I get rid of them.*

3. Have students work individually to complete the paragraph and check their work with a partner. Set a time limit (three minutes).

4. Discuss answers as a class.

Answers	
1. electrician	4. locksmith
2. plumber	5. repairperson
3. carpenter	6. exterminator

Communicative Practice and Application
10–15 minutes

D 1. Model asking and answering the questions with a volunteer.

2. Set a time limit (five minutes). Direct students to ask and answer the questions with several partners.

TIP

For more practice after 1D, write this conversation on the board: *A: There's a(n) / There are _____ [housing problem(s)]. B: You need to call a(n) _____ [repairperson].* Have students practice with a partner.

Evaluation
10–15 minutes

TEST YOURSELF

1. Make a two-column chart on the board with the headings *Problem* and *Repairperson*. Have students give you an example for each column.

2. Have students copy the chart into their notebooks.

3. Set a time limit (five to ten minutes). Have students test themselves by writing the words they recall from the lesson in the chart.

4. Call "time" and have students check their spelling in *The Oxford Picture Dictionary* or another dictionary.

MULTILEVEL STRATEGIES

Target the *Test Yourself* to the level of your students.

• **Pre-level** Have these students work with their books open.

• **Higher-level** Ask these students to write sentences. *There's a leaking faucet in the kitchen. / I need to call a plumber.*

EXTENSION ACTIVITY

Extend the Conversation

Have students write out their conversations for the activity in the *Tip* after 2D. To challenge students, have them extend the conversation.

Lesson Overview	Lesson Notes
MULTILEVEL OBJECTIVES	
On-, Pre-, and Higher-level: Read and write about housing	
LANGUAGE FOCUS	
Grammar: Simple present (*My dream home has five bedrooms.*) **Vocabulary:** Adjectives for homes and neighborhoods, *security deposit* For vocabulary support, see these **Oxford Picture Dictionary** topics: The Home, pages 46–47; Finding a Home, pages 48–49; Apartments, pages 50–51; Different Places to Live, page 52	
STRATEGY FOCUS	
Use *finally* to introduce the last point in a list.	
READINESS CONNECTION	
In this lesson, students compare and contrast homes and interpret rental information in housing ads.	
PACING	
To compress this lesson: Omit 1F. **To extend this lesson:** Have students do a "drawing dictation." (See end of lesson.) And/or have students complete **Workbook 2 page 17** and **Multilevel Activities 2 Unit 3 page 39**.	

CORRELATIONS	
CCRS: SL.1.A Participate in collaborative conversations with diverse partners in small and larger groups. SL.2.A Confirm understanding of a text read aloud or information presented orally or through other media by asking and answering questions about key details and requesting clarification if something is not understood. W.2.A Write informative/explanatory texts in which they name a topic, supply some facts about the topic, and provide some sense of closure.	**ELPS:** 6. An ELL can analyze and critique the arguments of others orally and in writing. 9. An ELL can create clear and coherent level-appropriate speech and text.

Warm-up and Review
10–15 minutes (books closed)

Tell students about your home—if it's large or small, how many bedrooms you have, if you are near stores and your children's schools, and so on. Write adjectives on the board as you describe your home: *old/new, large/small, near/far*. Ask *yes/no* questions: *Is my home old/new?*

Introduction
5 minutes

1. Use the opposites on the board to compare a place you used to live with the home you live in now: *My old home was smaller than my new home. It was too noisy.*

2. State the objective: *Today we're going to read and write about our homes or the homes we want.*

1 Prepare to write

Presentation
20–25 minutes

A 1. Have students close their books. Ask: *Have you ever looked at ads for apartments or homes?* Ask where they saw the ads.

2. Write the following abbreviations on the board: *lg, 2BR, kit., stud., 1BA, nr, mo., sec. dep., 2nd fl., mgr.,* and *eves.* Ask students to guess what the abbreviations stand for, but don't tell them yet if they are correct.

3. Direct students to open their books and read the ad silently. Build students' schema by asking questions about the ad. Ask: *Which abbreviations are the same as the ones on the board?* Challenge students to call out the meaning of each abbreviation without looking at the word box. Then have them confirm answers by matching each abbreviation to a word in the box. Ask students to guess the meaning of the abbreviations not in the book (*kit., stud., 2nd fl.*). Confirm their answers [kit. = kitchen, stud. = studio apartment, 2nd fl. = second floor].

4. Have students work in pairs. Give them time (one to two minutes) to discuss their completed sentences. Elicit responses from the class.

Answers
1. large, bathroom
2. month, security deposit
3. manager, evenings

B 🔊1-43 1. Direct students to look at the pictures. Ask: *What things can you see in the pictures?* Write any new words on the board.

2. Have students listen to the audio. Ask them to point to any items in the picture as they listen. Circulate and monitor.

C 🔊1-43 1. On the board, write: *dream home.* Ask students what they think it means.

2. Introduce the model paragraph and its purpose: *You're going to read a paragraph about the writer's dream home. As you read, look for the differences between the home she wants and where she lives now. What doesn't she like about her apartment?* [It has only one bedroom; it's too dark; windows are too small.] *What does she want in her dream apartment?* [She wants two bedrooms; a larger, sunnier apartment; and a safer street closer to the school and park.]

Play the audio again and have students read along silently. Answer any questions about unfamiliar vocabulary.

3. Point out the *Writer's Note.* Ask: *What is a word that means the same as* finally? [last(ly)] Explain that many times, but not always, a writer will make the last point in a paragraph the most important point.

Guided Practice I
5–10minutes

D Have students work individually to circle the correct words. Set a time limit (three minutes). Discuss answers as a class.

Answers
1. apartment
2. two
3. noisy
4. near

MULTILEVEL STRATEGIES

After the comprehension check in 1D, call on volunteers and tailor your questions to the level of your students.

• **Pre-level** Ask *yes/no* questions. *Does Teresa like the apartment she has now?* [no]

• **On-level** Ask other information questions. *What does Teresa say about her street?* [It's dangerous.]

• **Higher-level** Ask these students to compare their dream house to Teresa's. *What is the same about you and Teresa? What is different?*

Guided Practice II
10–15 minutes

E 🔊1-44 1. Read the instructions aloud. Have students read the items that they will listen for in the audio. Play the entire audio once.

2. If necessary, play the audio again in segments. After the answer for each question comes up, stop the audio and check in with students. If necessary, replay the segment. Have students listen again and work individually to circle the correct answers.

Answers
1. 3
2. 2
3. school
4. $900

F 1-44 Have students compare answers to 1E with a partner. Then play the audio again for them to check their work. Discuss answers as a class.

2 Plan

Communicative Practice I

15–20 minutes

A 1. Write the questionnaire on the board. Fill it out with your own answers as an example for students. Have students complete the exercise individually.

B 1. Read the sample conversation with a volunteer. Then based on your questionnaire on the board, model the role-play with a volunteer.

2. Set a time limit (five minutes). Ask students to practice the role-play with a partner. Circulate and monitor.

3 Write

Communicative Practice II and Application

15–20 minutes

A 1. Have students look at the paragraph template as you read it aloud. At each blank, have a volunteer give a sample answer.

2. Set a time limit for writing (five minutes). Have students complete the paragraph template with their own information.

MULTILEVEL STRATEGIES

Target the writing in 3A to the level of your students.

- **Pre-level** Write a wordlist on the board for these students to use to complete their paragraphs. Then work with these students to write a group paragraph. Read through the template. At each blank, stop and elicit a word to complete it. Decide as a group what to write. Have these students copy the group paragraph into their notebooks.
- **Higher-level** Ask these students to include explanations of what they want in their dream home. *I need three bedrooms because I have a son and a daughter.*

B Ask students to read their paragraphs to a partner. Call on volunteers to share what they learned about their partners.

Evaluation

10 minutes

TEST YOURSELF

1. Read the instructions aloud. Assign a time limit (five minutes) and have students work individually.

2. Before collecting student work, invite two or three volunteers to share their sentences. Ask students to raise their hands if they wrote similar responses.

EXTENSION ACTIVITY

Plan an Event

Do a "drawing dictation." Dictate a description of your dream home and have students draw it. Have students compare drawings and describe what they drew to their partners.

LESSON 3 GRAMMAR

Lesson Overview	Lesson Notes
MULTILEVEL OBJECTIVES	
On-level: Express opinions orally and in writing using comparative adjectives	
Pre-level: Express opinions using comparative adjectives	
Higher-level: Express opinions orally and write a paragraph using comparative adjectives	
LANGUAGE FOCUS	
Grammar: Comparative adjectives (*An apartment is cheaper than a house.*)	
Vocabulary: Adjectives to describe homes and neighborhoods	
For vocabulary support, see these **Oxford Picture Dictionary** topics: The Home, pages 46–47; Finding a Home, pages 48–49; Apartments, pages 50–51; Different Places to Live, page 52	
READINESS CONNECTION	
In this lesson, students use comparative adjectives to describe features of places to live.	
PACING	
To compress this lesson: Skip the partner interaction in 3A and 3B.	
To extend this lesson: Have students make a poster. (See end of lesson.)	
And/or have students complete **Workbook 2 pages 18–19**, **Multilevel Activities 2 Unit 3 page 40**, and **Multilevel Grammar Exercises 2 Unit 3**.	
CORRELATIONS	
CCRS: L.1.A Demonstrate command of conventions of standard English grammar and usage when writing or speaking. f. Use frequently occurring adjectives. i. Use determiners (e.g., articles, demonstratives). SL.1.A Participate in collaborative conversations with diverse partners in small and larger groups.	**ELPS:** 7. An ELL can adapt language choices to purpose, task, and audience when speaking and writing. 10. An ELL can demonstrate command of the conventions of standard English to communicate in level-appropriate speech and writing.

Warm-up and Review
10–15 minutes (books closed)

Write familiar items on the board, or bring in pictures for comparison: *apples, strawberries, a sunny day, a rainy day, a regular car, a fancy car, a hamburger, a salad.* Ask: *Do you like apples? Do you like strawberries? Which do you like more?* Restate students' ideas using the word *better*: *Kyong thinks strawberries are better than apples.* Write on the board the sentence frame: _____ *is/are better than* _____.

Introduction
5–10 minutes

1. Point to the board. Say: *Apples are good, but I think strawberries are better than apples. When I talk about two things, I am comparing them.*

2. State the objective: *Today we're going to learn to give our opinions using comparisons.*

1 Explore the comparative

Presentation I
20–25 minutes

 1-45 1. Direct students to look at the floor plans and the notes. Ask: *Which apartment is bigger?*

2. Have students read the paragraph silently as they listen to the audio.

3. Ask: *Which apartment is better?* Elicit their ideas. Don't correct their grammar at this point.

B 1. Briefly review adjectives. Ask students to give a definition of the word *adjective* and examples of adjectives they already know.

2. Ask students to underline the adjectives, working individually.

3. Call on volunteers to say what they notice that is different between the adjectives ending in *-er* and the ones preceded by *more*. Don't correct or confirm answers yet.

Answers
smaller, cheaper, bigger; more convenient, more comfortable, more expensive

C 1. Read and ask students to repeat each example in the chart.

2. Use the story in 1A to illustrate points in the grammar chart: *Apartment A is sunnier than Apartment B. It's also smaller.*

3. Give students time to silently review the chart.

4. Assess students' understanding of the chart. Write *tall, young, interesting,* and *funny* on the board. Ask: *What are the comparative forms of these words?* Use *wet* and *sad* to check the doubling rule.

Guided Practice I
15–20 minutes

D 1. Read the instructions aloud. Model the sample conversation with a volunteer.

2. Give students time to silently review the charts again and think of what they want to say about the apartments.

3. Have students work in pairs to make comparisons of the apartments in 1A. Circulate and monitor.

4. Ask students to say one of their comparisons to the class.

E 1. Read the instructions aloud. Have students complete the task with a partner.

2. Ask students to share their sentences with another pair and check for any errors. Then have volunteers share one of their sentences with the class.

2 Practice: ask and answer questions with *which*

Presentation II and Guided Practice II
20–25 minutes

A **1-46** 1. Remind students that *which* is used to ask questions comparing two or more things.

2. Play the audio and have students repeat.

3. Use the pictures from the warm-up to check comprehension. Have volunteers ask you comparative questions. *Which is more expensive, the hamburger or the salad?*

B Have students complete the questions and answers individually. Ask volunteers to read the questions and answers aloud.

Answers
1. cheaper
2. safer
3. more dangerous
4. more expensive

MULTILEVEL STRATEGIES
Adapt 2B to the level of your students.
• **Pre-level** Encourage these students to fill in only the questions. Give them time to copy the answers from the board after volunteers have written them.
• **On- and Higher-level** Have these students read the questions and answers to each other while the pre-level students are copying.

1. Read the instructions aloud. Model the sample conversation with a volunteer.

2. Set a time limit (five minutes) for students to write their questions.

3. Have students ask three students their questions. Circulate and monitor.

MULTILEVEL STRATEGIES

Adapt 2C to the level of your students.

• **Pre-level** Provide key words for students to use in their sentences (e.g., *more expensive/Joe's Coffee Shop/The Coffee Place; quieter/the park/ the library*).

• **On- and Higher-level** Have these students expand on their answers to the questions (*I think Ben's Restaurant is cheaper because the lunch special is only $5.99.*).

3 Practice: adverbs of degree with comparatives

Presentation III
5–10 minutes

 1. On the board, write *much, a lot, a little*, and *a bit*. Explain that degree is how much or little there is of something. Ask: *Which words have similar meaning?* [*much* and *a lot; a little* and *a bit*]

2. Have students open their books and study the chart.

3. Direct students to look at the graph next to the chart. Read the instructions aloud and have students complete the task individually. Circulate and monitor.

4. Have students compare their sentences with a partner, before checking answers as a class.

Guided Practice III
20–25 minutes

B 1. Read the instructions and the example aloud. Explain that there isn't one correct answer. Have students complete the task individually.

2. Have students compare sentences with a partner. Circulate and monitor.

3. Have volunteers report one of their partner's responses to the class.

Possible Answers
1. much quieter
2. a lot easier
3. a little more expensive
4. a bit safer
5. much more convenient

C 1. Read the instructions aloud. Ask several volunteers to use the adjectives in the box to describe one of the pictures. *The first house is large and expensive. The second house is new.*

2. Model the sample conversation with a volunteer.

3. Remind students to use adverbs of degree in their conversation. Have students ask and answer questions with a partner. Circulate and monitor.

D 1. Read the instructions and the example aloud. Have students complete the task individually.

2. Have volunteers read one or two of their sentences aloud.

TIP

When students say their sentences, challenge them to say their sentences from memory, rather than just reading from their notebooks.

4 Practice: questions and answers with the comparative

Communicative Practice and Application
10–15 minutes

A Read the instructions and the questions aloud. Before students write, ask the questions to higher-level students to provide a model for answering the "why" part of the question. Set a time limit (five minutes) for students to write their own answers in their notebooks.

B 1. Read the instructions aloud. Model the conversation with a volunteer.

2. Have students take turns asking and answering questions from 4A with a partner.

C Discuss the class's answers. Ask for a show of hands: *Who said a new house was better?* Elicit reasons from both sides.

> **TIP**
>
> For additional review of adjectives, give every student a piece of paper or a card with an adjective on it. Tell them to look for the person with the opposite adjective. To make this easier, put the opposites on different colored paper. As a follow-up, ask student pairs to tell you the comparative forms of their adjectives, or have them write sentences with their adjectives.

Evaluation
10–15 minutes

TEST YOURSELF

Have students complete their work individually. Collect and correct their writing.

> **MULTILEVEL STRATEGIES**
>
> Adapt the *Test Yourself* to the level of your students.
>
> • **Pre-level** Have these students fill in a sentence frames. *My partner thinks a(n) _____ house is better. It's _____.* Allow them to work with their books open.
>
> • **Higher-level** Ask these students to write a paragraph about their own and their partners' opinions.

> **EXTENSION ACTIVITY**
>
> **Make a Poster**
>
> Bring in magazines and have groups of students cut out pictures, glue them on poster paper, and write comparative sentences about them. Ask each group to present its poster to the class.

Lesson Overview	Lesson Notes
MULTILEVEL OBJECTIVES	
Pre- and On-level: Interpret housing ads, ask questions about an apartment, and listen for the answers	
Higher-level: Ask and answer questions about an apartment	
LANGUAGE FOCUS	
Grammar: Simple-present questions (*How much is the rent? Does it have a stove?*)	
Vocabulary: *Available, included, utilities*	
For vocabulary support, see these **Oxford Picture Dictionary** topics: The Home, pages 46–47; Finding a Home, pages 48–49; Apartments, pages 50–51; Different Places to Live, page 52	
STRATEGY FOCUS	
Ask about rules and regulations.	
READINESS CONNECTION	
In this lesson, students verbally communicate and listen actively for information about housing ads.	
PACING	
To compress this lesson: Skip Exercise 2C and/or 4B.	
To extend this lesson: Have students do a role-play. (See end of lesson.)	
And/or have students complete **Workbook 2 page 20** and **Multilevel Activities 2 Unit 3 page 41**.	

CORRELATIONS	
CCRS: SL.1.A Participate in collaborative conversations with diverse partners in small and larger groups. SL.2.A Confirm understanding of a text read aloud or information presented orally or through other media by asking and answering questions about key details and requesting clarification if something is not understood. SL.4.A Describe people, places, things, and events with relevant details, expressing ideas and feelings clearly.	**ELPS:** 2. An ELL can participate in level-appropriate oral and written exchanges of information, ideas, and analyses, in various social and academic contexts, responding to peer, audience, or reader comments and questions. 9. An ELL can create clear and coherent level-appropriate speech and text.

Warm-up and Review
10–15 minutes (books closed)

Review apartment ad abbreviations. Write an ad on the board that contains abbreviations: *Beautiful 3BR 2BA hse., nr. shopping, $1400/mo. $1000 sec. dep. New cpt., big yd.* Have students discuss with their classmates what the abbreviations mean. Put a number above each abbreviation and write the numbers again in a list (1–9). Ask volunteers to come up and write the full words.

Introduction
5 minutes

1. Write questions about the ad on the board: *How many bedrooms does the house have? Is this house expensive or cheap?*

2. State the objective: *When you look for an apartment or a house, you need to ask questions. Today we'll learn how to ask and answer questions about apartments.*

1 Listen to learn: asking about an apartment

Presentation I
15–20 minutes

 1. Have students read the housing ad and circle any words or abbreviations they don't understand. Discuss the words and abbreviations as a class.

2. Have students ask and answer the questions with a partner. One person asks all of the questions and the other answers them. Then have students switch roles and repeat.

Answers	
1. 1	4. Yes
2. Yes	5. Yes
3. $800	

 1-47 **1.** Explain that students will listen to three conversations with a lot of details. Emphasize that the first time through, they should just listen for the general topic of the conversations and not worry about the details. Play the audio.

2. Come to a class consensus about the answer to the question.

Answers
apartments for rent

Guided Practice I
5–10 minutes

 1-47 **1.** Direct students to look at the notes. Ask: *What are the notes about?* [different apartments] Explain that they will listen to the three conversations again and fill in the notes as they listen.

2. Play the audio and have students complete the task individually.

3. Students compare their answers with a partner, before checking answers as a class.

Answers
1. 114 Maple Street
Rent $1,000
Deposit: $1,000
Utilities included: No
Available: January 1
2. 15 Center Street
Rent: $950
Deposit: $600
Utilities included: No
Available: December 15
3. 198 Second Avenue
Rent: $1,100
Deposit: $550
Utilities included: Yes
Available: January 1

MULTILEVEL STRATEGIES

Adapt 1C to the level of your students.

• **Pre-level** Stop the audio after each piece of information is given and play it again if necessary.

• **Higher-level** Challenge these students to write other details that they hear (e.g., when Sharon will see the apartment; if she thinks the security deposit is cheap).

2 Practice your pronunciation

Pronunciation Extension
10–15 minutes

 1-48 **1.** Focus students' attention on the headings and questions before they listen. Mime the words *falling* and *rising*.

2. Play the audio. Ask students which questions have a rising intonation and which have a falling intonation.

3. Replace the questions with nonsense syllables (e.g., *la la la*) so that students can focus on the intonation. Tell them to listen to the last word and tell you if the intonation is rising or falling.

4. Explain the importance of rising and falling intonation: *If people don't hear your question intonation, they may not answer your question!*

5. Play the audio again and have students repeat.

B 🔊 **1-49** Have students complete the chart individually. Play the audio so they can check their answers. Discuss answers as a class.

Answers
1. Falling
2. Rising
3. Falling
4. Rising

C Have students practice the questions in 2B with a partner. Circulate and monitor.

MULTILEVEL STRATEGIES

Adapt 2C to the level of your students.

• **Pre-level** Have students practice the questions while you listen and ensure correct intonation.

• **Higher-level** Have students practice the questions in pairs and include an answer to turn it into a conversation.

3 Practice asking about apartment regulations

Presentation II and Guided Practice II
20–25 minutes

A 🔊 **1-50** 1. Write the word *regulations* on the board. Ask students what it means and/or to give some examples. [For example, rules made by owners of a place or the people in charge of a school or apartment building; Rent must be paid on the first of the month.]

2. Read the instructions aloud. Play the audio and have students read along silently.

3. Ask a volunteer for the answer. [*Are pets allowed?*]

B 🔊 **1-51** 1. Read the instructions aloud. Play the audio and have students complete the task individually. Play the audio again, if necessary.

2. Check answers as a class.

Answers
1. b
2. b
3. b
4. b

C 1. Read the instructions and the questions aloud. Give students time to read the conversation again and think about the answers.

2. Have students work in pairs to share their answers and confirm that their grammar rules are correct. Have students tell the class the rules and come to a consensus on the best explanation.

D 🔊 **1-52** 1. Give students time to study the chart.

2. Play the audio and have students repeat.

E 1. Read the instructions aloud. Draw students' attention to the apartment regulations in the picture.

2. Model the sample conversation with a volunteer.

3. Have students take turns asking and answering questions about the regulations with a partner. Circulate and monitor.

4 Make conversation: asking about an apartment

Communicative Practice I
15–20 minutes

A 1. Ask students if they have ever called to ask about an apartment. Brainstorm questions to ask when calling about an apartment.

2. Write the sample conversation on the board. Point to each blank and ask what kind of information can be used in each blank (e.g., *a number, a regulation*) and then ask the class for an example. Model the sample conversation with a volunteer.

3. Have students work in pairs to create a conversation and take turns performing the parts.

TIP

If necessary, write possible answers for each blank on the board for students to use in their conversations.

B 1. Set a time limit (ten minutes). Ask pairs to share their conversation with another pair. Circulate and monitor.

2. Have pairs present their conversation to the class.

AT WORK

Asking about regulations

Presentation III and Communicative Practice II
25–35 minutes

A 🔊 1-53 1. Discuss workplace regulations. Ask students to share any regulations that they know of in their workplace. Ask which regulations would be the same or different in a factory and in an office.

2. Play the audio and have students read along silently. Give students time to study the conversation. Discuss any unfamiliar vocabulary.

3. Direct students' attention to the *Need help?* box. Read the sentence stems aloud and have students say examples sentences using each stem.

B Have students work in pairs to practice the conversation in A. Challenge them to substitute the other phrases from the *Need help?* box in the conversation. Circulate and help as needed.

C 1. Ask: *When you have a question about regulations at work, what department do you go to?* [human resources] Further explain that the human resource department in a company makes sure that both employees and management follow regulations. They also take care of payroll, hiring, firing, and workplace safety.

2. Read the questions aloud. Have pairs discuss the questions and then share their ideas with the class.

Evaluation
10–15 minutes

TEST YOURSELF

Read the instructions aloud. Model the conversation with a student. Set a time limit (five minutes). Have students work in pairs to act out the situation. Circulate and assess students' progress.

MULTILEVEL STRATEGIES

For the *Test Yourself*, pair same-level students together.
• **Pre-level** Provide a list of regulations for these students to ask about.

EXTENSION ACTIVITY

Role-play

Have students create their own apartment ad, but not show it to their classmates. Have students create a framework of notes as in 1C. Have students sit back to back with a partner and role-play a phone conversation asking for information about an apartment. They take turns being the apartment manager and the renter. "Renters" ask for the information and take notes. Students check that they have written down the correct information after each role-play.

Lesson Overview	Lesson Notes
MULTILEVEL OBJECTIVES	
On- and Higher-level: Read about and discuss finding an apartment and different places to live **Pre-level:** Read about finding an apartment and different places to live	
LANGUAGE FOCUS	
Grammar: Simple present, comparative adjectives (*New Jersey is more crowded than Wyoming.*) **Vocabulary:** *Own, rent, rental agreement, roommate, share, utilities* For vocabulary support, see these **Oxford Picture Dictionary** topics: Finding a Home, pages 48–49; Apartments, pages 50–51; Different Places to Live, page 52	
STRATEGY FOCUS	
Identify the purpose of the text.	
READINESS CONNECTION	
In this lesson, students communicate information about understanding rental agreements.	
PACING	
To compress this lesson: Assign 1E and/or 1F as homework. **To extend this lesson:** Have students talk about regulations (See end of lesson.) And/or have students complete **Workbook 2 page 21** and **Multilevel Activities 2 Unit 3 page 42**.	
CORRELATIONS	
CCRS: R.1.A Ask and answer questions about key details in a text.	**ELPS:** 1. An ELL can construct meaning from oral presentations and literary and informational text through level-appropriate listening, reading, and viewing. 3. An ELL can speak and write about level-appropriate complex literary and informational texts and topics.

Warm-up and Review
10–15 minutes (books closed)

As a class, brainstorm any words associated with finding/renting an apartment. Leave the words on the board for students to refer to during the lesson.

Introduction
5 minutes

1. Ask students if they have ever read and signed a rental agreement. Ask: *What kind of information is in a rental agreement?*

2. State the objective: *Today we're going to learn about finding and renting an apartment.*

1 Build reading strategies

Presentation
10–20 minutes

 1. Read the instructions aloud. Have students complete the task individually. Check answers as a class.

Answers	
1. own	3. utilities
2. rent	4. share

Guided Practice: Pre-reading
5–10 minutes

 1. Read the instructions aloud. Have students circle their answers.

2. Ask students to talk about each possible source. Possible questions to ask: *Which newspaper do you use? Where in the newspaper will you find ads? What Internet sites are helpful? Where is the local community center? How will it help you? Which supermarket do you go to and where are the ads? How can your friends help?*

Guided Practice: While Reading
15–20 minutes

 1. Read the *Reader's Note* aloud. Explain that identifying why the writer is writing and who they are writing for makes it easier to understand any kind of text.

2. Ask students to read the article silently and think about their answer to the questions. Answer any questions about unfamiliar vocabulary.

3. Have students work in pairs to compare and discuss their answers and then check answers as a class.

4. Check comprehension. Ask: *Which is cheaper, buying a house or renting? What do you call money that you borrow from a bank to buy a house? What should you bring with you when you look at an apartment? What should you discuss if you are going to share an apartment?*

> **MULTILEVEL STRATEGIES**
>
> Adapt 1C to the level of your students.
>
> • **Pre-level** Read the text aloud to these students as they follow along.
>
> • **On- and Higher-level** Pair students and have them read the article aloud to each other, taking turns to read each paragraph.

Guided Practice: Rereading
10–15 minutes

 ◀)) 1-54 1. Play the audio and have students listen and read along silently.

2. Give students time to extract evidence from the article. Have students reread the article and write what they think are the three most important pieces of information.

3. Have students work in pairs to compare their three points and see if they agree. Circulate and monitor. Have volunteers report their partner's responses to the class.

Guided Practice: Post-reading
15 minutes

 1. Have students work individually to choose the correct answers and then identify the sentences where they found each answer.

Answers
1. b
2. c
3. a
4. c

2. Elicit and discuss any additional questions about the reading and the topic. You could introduce new questions for class discussion: *Do you think looking for an apartment in your neighborhood is easy or difficult? Why?*

F 1. Have students work individually to complete the sentences.

2. Have students read their sentences to a partner, before checking answers as a class.

Answers
1. landlord
2. agreement
3. roommate
4. utilities

> **MULTILEVEL STRATEGIES**
>
> For 1F, work with pre-level students.
>
> • **Pre-level** Ask these students *yes/no* and short-answer information questions about the reading while other students are completing 1F. Have these students copy the answers to 1F into their notebooks and underline words that are new for them.

2 Read a rental agreement

Communicative Practice
10–15 minutes

 1. Direct students to look at the rental agreement. Read the questions aloud.

2. Have students answer the questions individually before comparing answers with a partner.

3. Check answers as a class.

Answers
1. 1573 New Street, Jackson, Mississippi 39202 2. Mr. Ken Mason 3. $850 4. heating

 1. Read the question aloud. Allow students time to think of their own answer and make notes.

2. Set a time limit (ten minutes). Have students compare their answers with a partner. Circulate and help as needed.

3. Have pairs share their responses with another pair. Have volunteers share their partner's answers with the class.

Answer
utilities (gas and electricity)

Application
5–10 minutes

BRING IT TO LIFE

To help students plan for this exercise, discuss where they might find the information about apartment regulations, such as their own apartment building website or the names/ websites of specific apartment buildings in the area.

Make this *Bring It to Life* more concrete and practice *allowed to* by having students make a poster of the regulations they found. Display their posters in the classroom.

EXTENSION ACTIVITY

Role-play

Have students work in groups. Groups imagine they own an apartment building together. Ask them to make a list of information and regulations about apartments in their building. Groups share their information with the class. Everyone discusses which regulations are reasonable or not.

Lesson Overview	Lesson Notes
MULTILEVEL OBJECTIVES	
On-, Pre-, and Higher-level: Expand upon and review unit grammar and life skills	
LANGUAGE FOCUS	
Grammar: Comparative adjectives (*I want a smaller home.*) **Vocabulary:** Comparative adjectives, housing-ad abbreviations For vocabulary support, see these **Oxford Picture Dictionary** topics: The Home, pages 46–47; Apartments, pages 50–51; Different Places to Live, page 52; Household Problems and Repairs, pages 62–63	
STRATEGY FOCUS:	
Talk about places to live and how to solve repair problems.	
READINESS CONNECTION	
In this review, students work in teams to explore household problems, places to live, and opinions about them.	
PACING	
To extend this review: Have students complete **Workbook 2 page 22**, **Multilevel Activities 2 Unit 3 pages 43–46**, and **Multilevel Grammar Exercises 2 Unit 3**.	

CORRELATIONS	
CCRS: SL.1.A Participate in collaborative conversations with diverse partners in small and larger groups. SL.4.A Describe people, places, things, and events with relevant details, expressing ideas and feelings clearly. R.1.A Ask and answer questions about key details in a text. W.2.A Write informative/explanatory texts in which they name a topic, supply some facts about the topic, and provide some sense of closure.	**ELPS:** 5. An ELL can conduct research and evaluate and communicate findings to answer questions or solve problems. 6. An ELL can analyze and critique the arguments of others orally and in writing.

Warm-up and Review
10–15 minutes (books closed)

1. Review the *Bring It to Life* assignment from Lesson 5.

2. Have students talk about what regulations are important for them to have in an apartment and, if they have done the Extension Activity in Lesson 5, which group's apartment building would best match their needs.

Introduction and Presentation
5 minutes

1. Tell students about the advantages and problems of where you live.

2. State the objective: *Today we'll review adjectives and comparatives and talk about the good points and possible problems in different kinds of places to live.*

Guided Practice
15–20 minutes

A 1. Direct students to work in groups of three to four and look at the pictures. Ask: *Have you lived in any of these places? Do you know anyone who lives in these places?* Check students' understanding of each kind of place. Ask volunteers to give definitions and examples of each place in the area.

2. Set a time limit (five minutes) to complete the exercise. Circulate and answer any questions.

3. Have students from each group share the group's responses with the class. If you have a large class, you may not want all of the groups to report their responses. Instead, have groups share their responses with each other. Call "time" and tell all groups to work with a new group and to repeat their responses. Repeat this process as desired, making sure each group gets to share their responses at least once.

Communicative Practice
30–45 minutes

B Put students in new groups of four and assign roles: manager, researcher, administrative assistant, and reporter. Have researchers share information from their groups in A. Set a time limit (five minutes) to complete the task.

C 1. Check students' understanding of the word *opinion*. Read the sample summary aloud. Have volunteers say the comparative forms in the sample.

2. Set a time limit (ten minutes) to complete the task.

3. Have volunteer reporters present their team's summary to the class.

D 1. Read the instructions aloud. As a class, brainstorm different kinds of repairpeople and write them on the board for students to refer to. Check students' understanding of any vocabulary new to them in the list of problems. Explain the word *handy* (to be good with tools and fixing things).

2. Set a time limit (five minutes) to complete the task.

3. Have teams compare their answers with another team.

E Read the instructions aloud. Have one student from each group report their summary to the class. Have a class vote on who seems to be the most handy.

F 1. Read the instructions and the sample note aloud. Set a time limit (ten minutes) for groups to write their note.

2. Have a volunteer from each group share their note with the class.

MULTILEVEL STRATEGIES

Adapt F to the level of your students.

• **Pre-level** Pair these students and work with them directly by supplying sentence frames as needed.

• **Higher-level** Have these students include three problems in their note that they want fixed.

PROBLEM SOLVING
10–15 minutes

A 🔊 **1-55** 1. Ask students to read the paragraphs silently. Then play the audio and have them read along silently.

2. Check comprehension. Write the headings *City* and *Riverville* on the board. Ask: *What are the good points for Dan and Lia in the city? What are the bad points? What are the good and bad points of them living in Riverville?* Write the answers in an abbreviated format so that students can see the conflict [City: expensive, close to work; Riverville: cheaper, no job for Lia, long car commute for Dan].

B 1. Read the questions aloud. Have students work with a team to answer the questions. Circulate and monitor.

2. Come to a class consensus of what Dan and Lia's problem is. Then have teams share their solutions. Write each one on the board.

3. As a class, discuss the pros and cons of each solution. Choose the top three of each.

Evaluation
20–25 minutes

To test students' understanding of the unit language and content, have them take the Unit 3 Test, available on the Teacher Resource Center.

Unit Overview

This unit explores the skills and processes involved in searching and interviewing for a job, career planning, and using the simple past to describe job experience.

KEY OBJECTIVES	
Lesson 1	Identify common jobs; identify job application vocabulary
Lesson 2	Evaluate job interview performance; interpret job ads
Lesson 3	Use the simple past to describe past events related to work and study
Lesson 4	Respond to interview questions
Lesson 5	Identify job training opportunities
Teamwork & Language Review	Review unit language

UNIT FEATURES	
Academic Vocabulary	*assistant, evaluate*
Employability Skills	• Reflect on and draw conclusions about jobs • Analyze job interview behavior • Speculate about required job skills and education for jobs • Determine lengths of education and on-the-job training • Determine opportunities for career development • Understand teamwork • Communicate information • Work with others • Communicate verbally

Resources	**Class Audio** CD1, Tracks 56–72
	Workbook Unit 4, pages 23–29
	Teacher Resource Center
	    Multilevel Activities 2 Unit 4
	    Multilevel Grammar Exercises 2 Unit 4
	    Unit 4 Test
	Oxford Picture Dictionary The Workplace, Jobs and Occupations, Job Skills, Career Planning, Job Search, Interview Skills, Schools and Subjects

LESSON 1 VOCABULARY

Lesson Overview	Lesson Notes
MULTILEVEL OBJECTIVES	
On-level: Identify jobs and job-application vocabulary **Pre-level:** Recognize jobs and sections of a job application **Higher-level:** Talk and write about jobs and job applications	
LANGUAGE FOCUS	
Grammar: Simple-present statements (*He delivers mail.*) **Vocabulary:** Words for job applications and occupations For vocabulary support, see these **Oxford Picture Dictionary** topics: Jobs and Occupations, pages 170–173; Job Skills, page 176; Job Search, pages 168–169	
STRATEGY FOCUS	
Talk about different kinds of jobs.	
READINESS CONNECTION	
In this lesson, students communicate information about jobs and job applications.	
PACING	
To compress this lesson: Conduct 2C as a whole-class activity. **To extend this lesson:** Have students take a class poll. (See end of lesson.) And/or have students complete **Workbook 2 page 23** and **Multilevel Activities 2 Unit 4 page 48**.	

CORRELATIONS	
CCRS: L.6.A Use words and phrases acquired through conversations, reading and being read to, and responding to texts, including using frequently occurring conjunctions to signal simple relationships (e.g., *because*). SL.1.A Participate in collaborative conversations with diverse partners in small and larger groups.	**ELPS:** 8. An ELL can determine the meaning of words and phrases in oral presentations and literary and informational text.

Warm-up and Review
10–15 minutes (books closed)

Write the alphabet on the board in rows and say: *Today we're going to begin a unit on jobs. Let's see how many job names you remember.* Elicit job names to go with as many of the letters as possible. Write and leave the words on the board.

Introduction
3 minutes

1. Using examples from the board, talk about job duties. *A doctor prescribes medicine.*

2. State the objective: *Today we're going to talk about jobs and job applications.*

1 Learn about job applications

Presentation
20–25 minutes

A Direct students to look at the job application and read the words. Ask: *Did you ever fill out a job application? What job did you apply for?* Have students give examples for each part of the job application.

B 🔊 **1-56** 1. Direct students to look at Katia's job application again. Tell students to read the application and tell you what they know about Katia.

2. Have students listen to the audio. Ask them to point to the correct section of the application as they listen. Circulate and monitor.

3. Check comprehension. Ask: *What information goes in the personal information section? The employment history section? The references section?*

4. Have pairs discuss which parts of the application will help Katia the most. Have students share their answers with the class.

C 🔊 **1-57** 1. Ask students to listen and repeat the words.

2. While students are repeating, circulate and listen for pronunciation difficulties. Provide choral practice as necessary.

3. Discuss job skills in more depth: *What are Katia's job skills?* Referring to the jobs from the warm-up, ask: *What are some job skills of a secretary? A plumber?*

4. Discuss references: *Who makes a good reference? Your mother? Your teacher?*

Guided Practice I
15–20 minutes

D 1. Have students complete the sentences using the new vocabulary. Set a time limit (two minutes).

2. Encourage students to take turns reading the completed sentences with a partner.

Answers	
1. references	4. personal information
2. job skills	5. employment history
3. education	6. interests

TIP

To prepare for 1E, write labels of the sections of the application to display on the board. Then write different kinds of information on strips of paper: *Mary Hall, Donny's Restaurant, use a cash register.* Distribute the strips of paper to students and have them put the information in the right category on the board. Correct together.

E 1. Read the instructions aloud and model the sample conversation with a volunteer.

2. Set a time limit (three minutes). Have students take turns asking and answering questions with a partner. Circulate and listen for any pronunciation or vocabulary difficulties.

MULTILEVEL STRATEGIES

For 1E, pair same-level students together.
- **Pre-level** Assist these students with the exercise.
- **Higher-level** When these students finish, have them brainstorm ideas for what can be written in the skills section of the application. Have volunteers write their ideas on the board.

2 Talk about jobs

Guided Practice II
35–40 minutes

A 1. Ask: *Did you ever apply for a job? Where did you go?* Introduce the new topic: *Now let's talk about jobs and job duties.*

2. Group students and assign roles: manager, researcher, administrative assistant, and reporter. Explain that students work with their groups to match the words and pictures.

3. Check comprehension of the exercise: *Who looks up the words in the picture dictionary?* [researcher] *Who writes the numbers in the book?* [administrative assistant] *Who tells the class your answers?* [reporter] *Who helps everyone and manages the group?* [manager]

4. Set a time limit (three minutes) and have students work together to complete the task. While students are working, copy the wordlist onto the board.

5. Call "time" and have the reporters from each group take turns calling out the numbers for the wordlist. Record students' answers on the board. If groups disagree, write each group's choice next to the word.

6. Draw students' attention to the illustrations. Prompt students to use vocabulary not labeled in the art. Ask: *What is the chef using?* [pots and pans, plate, spoon, etc.] *What is the sales clerk selling?* [laptops, cellphones] *What is the veterinarian doing?* [checking the dog's heart with a stethoscope] *Describe what the movers are wearing* [a white cap, brown shirt, and white pants; red cap, blue shirt, black pants].

MULTILEVEL STRATEGIES

Have students work in mixed-level groups for 2A.

• **Pre-level** Assign these students the role of administrative assistant.

• **Higher-level** Assign these students the role of manager.

Answers

3–accountant	4–mail carrier
7–chef	5–mover
9–computer programmer	8–sales clerk
2–job applicant	6–veterinarian
1–job counselor	

B 🔊 **1-58** 1. Play the audio. Ask students to listen and check their answers.

2. Have students correct the wordlist on the board and then write the correct numbers in their books.

3. Tell the groups from 2A to split into pairs to practice the words. Set a time limit (two minutes).

Communicative Practice and Application
10–15 minutes

C 1. Read the instructions and the phrases in the box. Answer any questions about vocabulary. Model the conversation with a volunteer.

2. Set a time limit (five minutes). Ask students to use the phrases and practice the conversation with several partners.

MULTILEVEL STRATEGIES

For 2C, seat same-level students together.

• **Pre-level** Have students work in pairs or small groups. Assist those groups.

• **Higher-level** After students complete the exercise, ask them to compose additional sentences about other jobs. They can say their sentences without using job names for the rest of the class to guess the job title.

TIP

For more vocabulary practice, pass out pictures of people in different occupations or use the picture cards on page 54 of Multilevel Activities 2 Unit 4. Have less-verbal students use the cards for flashcard vocabulary practice. Have more-verbal students ask questions: *What does this person do? Would you like this job?*

D 1. Read the questions aloud. Have students discuss the questions in groups of three to four. Circulate and monitor.

2. Have one volunteer from each group share their group's responses with the class.

Evaluation
10–15 minutes

TEST YOURSELF

1. Make a three-column chart on the board with the headings *Education, Employment history,* and *Job skills.* Have volunteers give you an example for each column.

2. Have students copy the chart into their notebooks.

3. Set a time limit (five to ten minutes). Have students fill out the chart with their own information.

4. Call "time" and have students check their spelling in *The Oxford Picture Dictionary* or another dictionary.

EXTENSION ACTIVITY

Class Poll

Have students decide which job in 2A requires the most education, makes the most money, is the most physically difficult, and is the most in demand at the moment. You or students can check average salaries and educational requirements on the Department of Labor website to find out how accurate their responses are.

Lesson Overview	Lesson Notes
MULTILEVEL OBJECTIVES	
On-, Pre-, and Higher-level: Read and write about job interviews	
LANGUAGE FOCUS	
Grammar: Simple present (*He wears nice clothes. He doesn't smile very much.*) **Vocabulary:** Words for feelings, job-ad words, and abbreviations For vocabulary support, see these **Oxford Picture Dictionary** topics: The Workplace, pages 182–183; Jobs and Occupations, pages 170–173; Job Skills, pages 168–169; Interview Skills, page 179	
STRATEGY FOCUS	
Use time words to show sequence.	
READINESS CONNECTION	
In this lesson, students communicate information about preparing for job interviews.	
PACING	
To compress this lesson: Assign 1D for homework and/or skip 2B. **To extend this lesson:** Have students explore job ads. (See end of lesson.) And/or have students complete **Workbook 2 page 24** and **Multilevel Activities 2 Unit 4 page 49**.	

CORRELATIONS	
CCRS: R.1.A Ask and answer questions about key details in a text. SL.1.A Participate in collaborative conversations with diverse partners in small and larger groups. SL.2.A Confirm understanding of a text read aloud or information presented orally or through other media by asking and answering questions about key details and requesting clarification if something is not understood. W.2.A Write informative/explanatory texts in which they name a topic, supply some facts about the topic, and provide some sense of closure.	**ELPS:** 6. An ELL can analyze and critique the arguments of others orally and in writing. 9. An ELL can create clear and coherent level-appropriate speech and text.

Warm-up and Review
10–15 minutes (books closed)

1. Elicit the names of the sections of a job application from Lesson 1, and write them on the board.

2. Ask students what questions they would be asked from each section during a job interview. For example, under Personal Information: *What's your name?* Under Employment History: *What was your last job?*

3. Write their ideas on the board, helping them form the questions correctly.

Introduction
5 minutes

1. Tell students about a job interview experience you have had—what you said and did and how you felt.

2. State the objective: *Today we're going to read and write about job interviews.*

1 Prepare to write

Presentation
20–25 minutes

A 1. Build students' schema by reading the questions aloud and having students look at the pictures in 1B and think of answers individually.

2. Have students work in pairs. Give them one minute to discuss their responses to the questions. Elicit responses from the class.

B 🔊 1-59 1. Direct students to look at the pictures. Ask: *What kind of job do you think the man is looking for?*

2. Have students listen to the audio. Ask them to point to the correct picture as they listen. Circulate and monitor.

C 🔊 1-59 1. Introduce the model text and its purpose: *You're going to read a text about someone looking for a job. As you read, look for which parts of the text match the pictures in B. This can help you understand the text better.* Play the audio again and have students read along silently.

2. Point out the *Writer's Note*. Ask: *What does* sequence *mean?* [the order that things happen] Ask students to find the sequence words in the text.

3. Check comprehension. Ask: *How often does Adam go to interviews?* [every week] *Where does he find information about the company?* [on the Internet] *What is hard for him to do during an interview?* [smile and make eye contact] *What does he do at the end of the interview?* [He shakes hands with the interviewer.]

Guided Practice I
10–15 minutes

D 1. Have students work individually to mark the mistakes. Set a time limit (two minutes).

2. As a class, discuss answers and talk about each of the things Adam does. Ask: *Why is it important to write questions in advance? Why is it bad not to make eye contact?*

Answers
Checks beside 2, 3, and 5

MULTILEVEL STRATEGIES

For 1D, seat same-level groups together.
• **Pre-level** Help these students identify Adam's mistakes.
• **Higher-level** Have these students write five other mistakes that people may make at interviews and share their ideas with the class.

E 1. Read the questions aloud. Have groups of three to four students discuss the questions. Circulate and monitor.

2. Have one volunteer from each group share their group's responses with the class.

Guided Practice II
15–20 minutes

F 1. Introduce the topic: *Before you apply for a job, you need to get some information about it. We're going to talk about job ads.*

2. Direct students to look at the ad and match the abbreviations with the words. Check answers as a class.

Answers
3–references
2–experience
4–immediately
1–part-time

G 🔊 1-60 1. Read the instructions. Review the meaning of the headings in the chart. Ask students to give examples of experience and skills, and to say how they know if someone is nervous or confident. Play the entire audio once.

2. Play the audio again in segments. After the answer for each question comes up, stop the audio and check in with students. If necessary, replay the segment. Have students listen again and work individually to fill in the chart.

3. Have students compare answers with a partner. Then play the audio again for them to check their work. Discuss answers as a class.

Answers			
	Experience	**Job skills**	**Confident or nervous?**
Rick	yes	can talk to customers, can use the computer and answer emails	confident
Alexa	no	can use the computer and answer emails	nervous

H Read the questions and lead a class discussion. To guide the discussion, write a *pro/con* chart on the board and write students' answers.

2 Plan

Communicative Practice I
10–15 minutes

Read the instructions aloud. Have students work in pairs. Circulate and monitor.

3 Write

Communicative Practice II and Application
15–20 minutes

A 1. Read the instructions aloud. Draw students' attention to the *Need help?* box. Discuss times when an adjective applies to how they feel around interviews. Ask students to call out other adjectives that might describe how they feel before, during, or after a job interview. Write them on the board.

2. Have students look at the template as you read it aloud. At each blank, have a volunteer give a sample answer.

3. Set a time limit for writing (five minutes). Have students complete the template with their own information.

B 1. Ask students to read their paragraphs to a partner. Call on volunteers to share one thing they liked about their partner's paragraphs.

2. Have a class discussion about how to improve performance at job interviews.

MULTILEVEL STRATEGIES

Target the writing in 3A to the level of your students.

• **Pre-level** Write a wordlist on the board for these students to use to complete their paragraphs. Then work with these students to write a group paragraph. Read through the template. At each blank, stop and elicit completions. Decide as a group what to write. Have these students copy the group paragraph into their notebooks.

• **Higher-level** Ask these students to write about how they will improve their performance at their next interview.

Evaluation
10 minutes

TEST YOURSELF

1. Read the instructions aloud. Set a time limit (five minutes) and have students work individually.

2. Before collecting student work, invite two or three volunteers to share their sentences. Ask students to raise their hands if they wrote similar answers.

EXTENSION ACTIVITY

Reading Job Ads

Bring in job ads from a newspaper or print some out from the Internet. Divide students into groups of three or four, and give each group a section with 10–15 job ads on it. Write questions on the board: *Are references required? Is the job part-time or full-time? Is experience required?* Tell students to choose three of the ads and report about those jobs to the class.

Lesson Overview	Lesson Notes
MULTILEVEL OBJECTIVES	

On- and Higher-level: Use the simple past to talk about and ask and answer questions about work experience

Pre-level: Use the simple past to talk about work experience

LANGUAGE FOCUS

Grammar: Simple past (*Katia worked at Sam's Supermarket.*)

Vocabulary: Regular verbs

For vocabulary support, see these **Oxford Picture Dictionary** topics: The Workplace, pages 182–183; Jobs and Occupations, pages 170–173; Job Skills, page 176; Interview Skills, page 179

STRATEGY FOCUS

Learn spelling rules for regular verbs in the past tense.

READINESS CONNECTION

In this lesson, students use the past tense to communicate verbally about job experience.

PACING

To compress this lesson: Assign 3C and/or 4A as homework.

To extend this lesson: Have students do a dictation activity. (See end of lesson.)

And/or have students complete **Workbook 2 pages 25–26, Multilevel Activities 2 Unit 4 page 50,** and **Multilevel Grammar Exercises 2 Unit 4.**

CORRELATIONS

CCRS: L.1.A Demonstrate command of the conventions of standard English grammar and usage when writing or speaking. e. Use verbs to convey a sense of past, present, and future (e.g., *Yesterday I walked home; Today I walk home; Tomorrow I will walk home.*) j. Use frequently occurring prepositions (e.g., *during, beyond, toward*).

SL.1.A Participate in collaborative conversations with diverse partners in small and larger groups.

SL.2.A Confirm understanding of a text read aloud or information presented orally or through other media by asking and answering questions about key details and requesting clarification if something is not understood.

ELPS: 7. An ELL can adapt language choices to purpose, task, and audience when speaking and writing. 10. An ELL can demonstrate command of the conventions of standard English to communicate in level-appropriate speech and writing.

Warm-up and Review
10–15 minutes (books closed)

Ask students about what they do on the weekends. Write the verbs they use in a column on the board.

Introduction
5–10 minutes

1. Refer to the words on the board. Say: *This is what you usually do on the weekends, but if we talk about what you did last weekend, we need to change the verb.* Write the past-tense form of the verb and say sentences about your students. *Paula worked last weekend. Esther cleaned the house.*

2. State the objective: *Today we're going to use the past tense to talk about job experience.*

1 Explore the simple past

Presentation I
20–25 minutes

A ◀))1-61 1. Direct students to look at the picture of Katia. Ask: *What's her job? Is she happy? What is she wearing?* Play the audio and have students read along silently. Have a volunteer answer the question.

2. Discuss these questions as a class: *Does Katia work at the pizza restaurant now? Is Katia a student now? Where does Katia want to work?*

Answer
Yes, she worked and studied at the same time.

B 1. Read the paragraph in 1A aloud slowly. Have students raise their hand every time they hear a verb.

2. Read the instructions and have students underline the verbs.

3. Ask students to say what these verbs all have in common. If necessary, give them a hint that it is about the form of the verbs, not the meanings.

Answers
worked, attended, studied, graduated, applied; They all end in *-ed*.

C 1. Demonstrate how to read the grammar charts as complete sentences. Read through the charts sentence by sentence. Then read them again and have students repeat after you.

2. Use the paragraph in 1A to illustrate points in the grammar charts. *She graduated in 2015. Last week, she applied for a job at State Bank.*

Guided Practice I
15–20 minutes

D 1. Read the instructions aloud. Give students time to silently review the charts again and fill in the blanks.

2. Ask volunteers to write the sentences on the board. Have other students read the sentences aloud.

3. Assess students' comprehension of the charts. Write other verbs on the board that illustrate the spelling rules in the grammar chart and have students change them to the past tense: *talk, ask, bake, share, carry, cry.* Ask: *What happens to the verb in the negative form?* [It doesn't change form / add *-ed*.]

Answers	
1. worked	4. didn't study
2. attended	5. didn't graduate
3. studied	6. didn't apply

E Read the instructions aloud. Have pairs make sentences. Have volunteers write their sentences on the board. Guide a short class discussion about the sentences.

2 Practice: the simple past

Presentation II
15–20 minutes

A 1. Read the instructions and give students time to read Katia's to-do list. Answer any questions about vocabulary.

2. Have a volunteer answer the question.

B ◀))1-62 1. Read the instructions aloud. Play the audio and have students circle *True* or *False* individually.

2. Have students compare their answers with a partner. Play the audio again and check answers as a class.

Answers	
1. F	4. T
2. F	5. F
3. T	6. T

MULTILEVEL STRATEGIES
Group same-level students together to complete 2B.
• **Pre-level** Play the audio again and stop it after each sentence for students to choose their answer.
• **On- and Higher-level** After they listen to the audio, have students use the list in 2A and make questions to orally quiz each other about Katia's to-do list.

Guided Practice II
15–20 minutes

 C Read the instructions aloud. Have students work individually to fill in the blanks.

Answers	
1. walked	5. asked
2. didn't pick	6. replied
3. didn't return	7. cooked
4. called	8. baked

MULTILEVEL STRATEGIES

Group same-level students together to complete 2C.

• **Pre-level** Work with these students to form the past tense of each verb in the box before they fill in the blanks.

• **Higher-level** Challenge these students to cover the wordlist and fill in the blanks.

D Read the instructions and model the sample conversation with a volunteer. If necessary, allow students time (two or three minutes) to think of sentences to say and make notes before they have a conversation. Circulate and monitor.

3 Practice: information questions in the simple past

Presentation III
15–20 minutes

 A 1. Assess what students know/remember about information questions. On the board, write: *Mr. Lee did. The restaurant is over there. I feel happy. For one hour. At 3:30.* Ask students to say which question word they would use to start a question for each of the answers on the board.

2. Give students time to read the chart. Play the conversations and have students repeat them.

3. Check comprehension of the grammar and content by asking questions and having students answer in complete sentences. (*Jan, what time did you come to school today? Sam, who did you have dinner with last night?*, etc.)

Guided Practice III
10–15 minutes

 B 1. Read the instructions. Have students complete the sentences individually.

2. Have students compare their sentences with a partner.

3. Challenge pairs to write an answer for each question. Then have volunteers say their conversation to the class.

Answers
1. did he start work
2. did they visit
3. did she graduate
4. did you live

C 1. Read the instructions and the sample question and answer aloud. Explain that more than one question is possible for each answer.

2. Direct students' attention to the *Grammar Note* box and read the information aloud. Check comprehension by asking students questions and having them answer with true information. (For example, *How long did you watch TV yesterday? I watched TV for one hour.*)

3. Have students write the questions individually and then compare answers with a partner. Have pairs say their conversations to the class to check answers.

Possible Answers
1. What did she watch on TV last night?
2. When did you visit your aunt and uncle?
3. How long did you stay in the library?
4. When did they study Spanish?
5. How long did he work in a hospital?

MULTILEVEL STRATEGIES

Target instruction for 3C to the level of your students.

• **Pre-level** Work with these students and guide them in writing the questions. (For example, *In number 2, what question word should you use? What verb will you use? How do we make it past tense in a question?*)

• **On- and Higher-level Have** students write all possible questions for each answer.

4 Talk about past events in your life

Communicative Practice and Application
10–15 minutes

A 1. Read the instructions and the sample question aloud.

2. Set a time limit (five minutes) for students to write the questions. Circulate and monitor.

3. Call "time" and check students' questions as a class. Have volunteers come to the board and write their questions.

B 1. Read the instructions and sample sentence aloud. Explain that students can take notes of their partner's answers to help them write their sentences later.

2. Have pairs take turns asking and answering the questions and then write their sentences individually.

3. Have pairs exchange sentences to check answers. Then have volunteers say their sentences about their partner aloud to the class.

> **TIP**
>
> Write students' sentences on the board, but include one mistake (e.g., *Maria walk home at 3:00 yesterday*.). Have students rewrite the sentences correctly in their notebooks, or have volunteers come to the board to correct the sentence (e.g., *walked*).

Evaluation
10 minutes

TEST YOURSELF

Ask students to write their three sentences about past events. Collect and correct their writing.

> **EXTENSION ACTIVITY**
>
> **Listen and Change**
>
> Dictate some statements and questions in the present tense and have students change them to past tense.

Lesson Overview

Lesson Notes

MULTILEVEL OBJECTIVES

On- and Higher-level: Ask and answer job interview questions

Pre-level: Provide short answers to job interview questions

LANGUAGE FOCUS

Grammar: Simple past tense (*I worked at a restaurant.*)

Vocabulary: Expressions used for introductions

For vocabulary support, see these **Oxford Picture Dictionary** topics: The Workplace, pages 182–183; Job Skills, page 176; Interview Skills, page 179

STRATEGY FOCUS

Form and use adverbs of manner.

READINESS CONNECTION

In this lesson, students communicate verbally in teams to explore how to answer job interviews.

PACING

To compress this lesson: Skip 4B.

To extend this lesson: Have students do a matching activity. (See end of lesson.)

And/or have students complete **Workbook 2 page 27** and **Multilevel Activities 2 Unit 4 page 51**.

CORRELATIONS

CCRS: L.1.A Demonstrate command of the conventions of standard English grammar and usage when writing or speaking. e. Use verbs to convey a sense of past, present, and future (e.g., *Yesterday I walked home; Today I walk home; Tomorrow I will walk home.*) f. Use frequently occurring adjectives. j. Use frequently occurring prepositions (e.g., *during, beyond, toward*).

RF.2.A Demonstrate understanding of spoken words, syllables, and sounds (phonemes).

RF.4.A Read with sufficient accuracy and fluency to support comprehension.

SL.1.A Participate in collaborative conversations with diverse partners in small and larger groups.

SL.2.A Confirm understanding of a text read aloud or information presented orally or through other media by asking and answering questions about key details and requesting clarification if something is not understood.

ELPS: 2. An ELL can participate in level-appropriate oral and written exchanges of information, ideas, and analyses, in various social and academic contexts, responding to peer, audience, or reader comments and questions. 9. An ELL can create clear and coherent level-appropriate speech and text.

Warm-up and Review
10–15 minutes (books closed)

Tell the class about a few things you can do and write them on the board: *work well with people, cook, do math.* Ask students about what they can do. Write their ideas on the board using a simple verb. Leave these words on the board.

Introduction
5 minutes

1. Say: *One thing you have to do at a job interview is talk about your skills. Many of your skills are on the board. Alfredo can cook. Myong can fix things.*

2. State the objective: *Today we're going to learn how to answer job interview questions.*

1 Listen to learn: job interviews

Presentation I and Guided Practice I
20–30 minutes

A 1. Direct students to look at the pictures in 1B. Ask: *Where are the people in each picture?* [a car dealership, outside in front of a house, in an office]

2. Read the questions aloud. Answers will vary. Have pairs ask and answer the question with each other before reviewing the answers as a class.

B 🔊 **1-64** 1. Read the instructions aloud and direct students to look at the pictures again. Explain that they will listen to three different job interviews.

2. Have students put down their pencils before they listen. Play the audio and ask them to listen for key words in each conversation that match actions or items in each picture. Replay the audio and have them write the number of the matching conversation in each blank.

3. Ask students to compare their answers with a partner. Circulate and monitor to ensure students understand the audio.

Answers
2–salesperson
3–mail carrier
1–accountant

C 🔊 **1-64** 1. Read the instructions and the questions aloud. Suggest to students that they take brief notes of the information they hear to help them answer the questions.

2. Play the audio again. Have students write their answers individually before comparing answers with a partner. Check answers as a class.

TIP

You can play the audio twice. The first time, tell students to listen for the answer to the first question, and then the second time for the second question.

Answers
1. She worked as an assistant manager at a supermarket. Good at math
2. He worked in a car rental company and was a mechanic. Good with cars
3. He worked in the mail room at a factory. Is careful and is never late to work, likes to walk and talk to people, and loves dogs

2 Practice your pronunciation

Pronunciation Extension
10–15 minutes

A 🔊 **1-65** 1. Read the instructions aloud. Play the audio. Have students hold up one finger for one syllable and two fingers for two syllables for each word.

2. Pronounce the words and clap or tap a table or desk with each syllable. Have students repeat the words and clap or tap their desks.

3. Read the *Need help?* box. Write the words *work*, *add*, *watch*, and *assist* on the board. Ask students which words will have an extra syllable in the past tense. Add the *-ed* endings and pronounce the words.

Answers
1. 1, 1
2. 2, 2
3. 1, 2
4. 1, 2

B 🔊 **1-66** 1. Read the instructions aloud. Tell students to hold up one or two fingers to indicate the number of syllables they hear for each word. Say the words in the exercise, but intersperse other words to challenge students: *cooked*, *asked*, *arrived*, *studied*.

2. When most students can correctly identify the number of syllables, play the audio and have them circle the answers in their books. Correct the exercise on the board.

3. Replay the audio and have students work individually to circle *1* or *2* in their books for each word.

Answers	
1. 1	4. 1
2. 2	5. 1
3. 2	6. 2

C (1-66) Play the audio again and have students repeat the words. Then call on volunteers to pronounce them.

D Have students repeat the sentences after you. Then have them repeat to a partner. Monitor and provide feedback on pronunciation.

3 Practice job interview questions

Presentation II and Guided Practice II
20–25 minutes

> **TIP**
>
> Before you play the audio for the first time, on the board write the following words: *education, experience, skills,* and *references.* Have students write each topic word on a separate piece of paper. Tell students that they will hear information about each of these topics in the job interview. As you play the audio the first time, tell them to hold up the topic being discussed as they hear it.

A (1-67) Play the audio. Ask students to read along silently.

B (1-68) 1. Read the instructions. Have students read the answer choices silently to themselves.

2. Play the audio and have students circle the correct answer. Replay if necessary.

Answers
1. a
2. a
3. b
4. b

C 1. Introduce the new grammar in 1D. Write sentences on the board. *1. I talk slowly. 2. I talk quickly.* Say the first sentence slowly again and ask: *How do I talk?* [slowly] Repeat with *I talk quickly.*

2. Read the instructions and the questions aloud. Give students time (one to two minutes) to look at the conversation in 3A, underline the questions, and answer the question. Have pairs compare their answers before checking answers as a class.

Answers
1. What did you study? How long did you work there?
2. carefully, fluently

D (1-69) 1. Play the audio and have students repeat.

2. Check comprehension of the grammar in the chart and in the *Grammar Note.* Ask: *What does an adjective describe? What does an adverb describe?* Point out to students that the word *adverb* has the word *verb* in it, and that can help them remember what an adverb does.

3. Write the sentences from the chart on the board, leaving the adverb or adjective blank. Have students come to the board and write the correct word in the blank.

E 1. Read the instructions aloud and model the sample conversation with a volunteer. Set a time limit (three minutes) for students to write their questions.

2. Have pairs take turns asking and answering each other's questions. Circulate and monitor.

> **MULTILEVEL STRATEGIES**
>
> Target instruction for 3E to the level of your students.
>
> • **Pre-level** Provide key words for students to use in their sentences: *eat/quickly, good/driver, study/carefully, slow/walker.*
>
> • **Higher-level** Direct these students to write two or three additional questions using adjectives or adverbs not included in the chart.

4 Make conversation: talking about your job skills

Communicative Practice I
15–20 minutes

A 1. Read the instructions and the examples of job skills in the *Need help?* box. As a class, brainstorm other job skills and write them on the board (e.g., *well organized, quick learner, use a computer*).

2. Have pairs create a conversation and take turns performing parts.

B 1. Set a time limit (ten minutes). Ask pairs to share their conversation with another pair and write the verbs that the other pair used.

2. Have pairs present their conversation to the class.

> **TIP**
>
> As pairs present their conversations to the class, challenge students to write the simple past verbs that they hear. Have a contest to see who can write them all correctly.

AT WORK

Evaluate a job interview

Presentation III and Communicative Practice II
15–20 minutes

A **1-70** 1. Direct students to look at the illustration. Ask them to describe what it shows. Read the checklist aloud. Answer any questions about vocabulary.

2. Play the audio and have students check the things that the job applicant did correctly.

3. Have pairs compare answers. Play the audio again for the class to check their answers.

Answers
Check all.

B 1. Read the instructions and questions aloud.

2. Have students discuss the questions with a partner. Circulate and help as needed.

3. Have volunteers share their answers.

> **MULTILEVEL STRATEGIES**
>
> Target instruction for B to the level of your students.
>
> • **Pre-level** Provide sentence frames for students to answer the questions: *I think I performed ___. I was ___. I asked the interviewer ___. The interviewer asked me ___. I can improve ___.*
>
> • **Higher-level** Direct these students to write an interview guide poster that includes important tips on having a good interview. Display the poster in class.

Evaluation
10–15 minutes

TEST YOURSELF

Have pairs perform the role-play. Circulate and assess students' progress. Take note of any mistakes you hear in intonation, pronunciation, grammar, or vocabulary. When all students have finished the activity, as a class, review the kinds of mistakes you heard (without naming any students who made them).

> **EXTENSION ACTIVITY**
>
> **Match**
>
> Write these sentences on the board or on slips of paper: *Yes, I worked at a restaurant. My boss will be a reference. Do you have experience? I studied accounting in my country. Do you have references? I worked there for two years. Tell me about your education. How long did you work there?* Have students match the questions to the answers.

Lesson Overview	Lesson Notes
MULTILEVEL OBJECTIVES	
On- and Higher-level: Read about and discuss career goals and job training requirements **Pre-level:** Read about career goals and job training requirements	
LANGUAGE FOCUS	
Grammar: Simple present (*My goal is to be a chef.*) **Vocabulary:** *Associate's degree, bachelor's degree, career, diploma, GED certificate, salary* For vocabulary support, see these **Oxford Picture Dictionary** topics: Jobs and Occupations, pages 170–173; Job Skills, page 176; Career Planning, pages 174–175; Schools and Subjects, pages 200–201	
STRATEGY FOCUS	
Understand how to use the navigation bar at the top of a website.	
READINESS CONNECTION	
In this lesson, students communicate information about changing jobs, career planning, and related education.	
PACING	
To compress this lesson: Assign 1A and/or 2F for homework. **To extend this lesson:** Have students play a guessing game. (See end of lesson.) And/or have students complete **Workbook 2 page 28** and **Multilevel Activities 2 Unit 4 page 52**.	
CORRELATIONS	
CCRS: R.1.A Ask and answer questions about key details in the text. SL.1.A Participate in collaborative conversations with diverse partners in small and larger groups.	**ELPS:** 1. An ELL can construct meaning from oral presentations and literary and informational text through level-appropriate listening, reading, and viewing. 3. An ELL can speak and write about level-appropriate complex literary and informational texts and topics.

Warm-up and Review
10–15 minutes (books closed)

Remind students that you have been talking about jobs during this unit and ask them to name jobs they might be interested in having. Write the jobs on the board.

Introduction
5 minutes

1. Ask *yes/no* questions about the educational requirements of the jobs on the board: *Do you need a university degree for this job? Do you need a high school diploma?*

2. State the objective: *Today we'll read about changing jobs and education.*

1 Build reading strategies

Presentation I
10–15 minutes

 Read the instructions aloud. Have students complete the task individually and then share their answers and sentences with the class.

Guided Practice: Pre-reading
5–10 minutes

 1. Read the instructions and the sample sentence aloud. Have students answer the question with a partner and then share their partner's responses with the class.

2. As a class, brainstorm reasons people change careers that were not already mentioned.

Guided Practice: While Reading
15–20 minutes

 1. Read the instructions and the information in the *Reader's Note*. Have students read the article silently.

2. Ask volunteers who they think the website is for.

MULTILEVEL STRATEGIES
Adapt 1C to the level of your students.
• **Pre-level** Read the text aloud to these students as they follow along.
• **On- and Higher-level** Pair students and have them read the web page aloud to each other, taking turns reading each paragraph.

Guided Practice: Rereading
10–15 minutes

 1-71 1. Play the audio. Give students time (three to five minutes) to extract evidence from the web page. Have students reread the web page and underline any words or phrases that are unfamiliar to them. Have them look up definitions in a dictionary and write them in their notebooks.

2. Play the audio again and have students read along silently. Have a volunteer answer the question and show where they got the information.

TIP
Have students go online to find out about career changes and job training courses in their area. Decide which device(s) students might use and elicit search terms (e.g., *career change* + *your city*).

Guided Practice: Post-reading
15 minutes

 1. Have students work individually to choose the correct answers and then identify in the reading where they found each answer. Check answers as a class.

2. Check comprehension further. Ask: *How many reasons does the article give for workers leaving their job?* [four] *What other information can you find on the website?* [information for finding a job; information for how to train for a new job] *What example does the article give of a job/career change?* [a school teacher applying for a job as a sales trainer] *What does* revise *mean?* [to change] *What do you have to change when you apply for a different job?* [your resume]

Answers
1. a
2. c
3. a
4. c

MULTILEVEL STRATEGIES
For 1E, work with pre-level students.
• **Pre-level** Ask these students *yes/no* and short-answer information questions about the reading while other students are completing 1E.
• **Higher-level** Have these students take turns asking and answering comprehension questions about the reading.

 1. Have students work individually to complete the sentences.

2. Have pairs read each other their sentences before checking answers as a class.

Answers
1. employer
2. salary
3. trainer
4. average

2 Read a job training chart

Communicative Practice
10–15 minutes

A 1. Direct students to look at the chart. Model a sample question and answer with a volunteer.

2. Have pairs discuss the chart, asking and answering questions about it. Circulate and help as needed.

B 1. Read the questions aloud. Allow students time to think of their own answers and make notes.

2. Set a time limit (five minutes). Have pairs discuss the questions. Circulate and help as needed.

3. Have pairs share their responses with another pair. Have volunteers share their partner's answers with the class.

Application
5–10 minutes

BRING IT TO LIFE

Ask students to talk to two family members or friends about their career plans. Provide possible questions: *Do you like your job now? What skills do you use in your job? Do you want to change jobs? Why or why not? What skills or training do you need for a new job?* Have them report their findings to the class.

EXTENSION ACTIVITY

Guessing Game

Play a guessing game.

1. Write job titles on cards and tape one card to each student's back. 2. The students give clues to help each other guess the word on their backs. *You work at a hotel. You register guests.* 3. When students correctly guess the jobs, they can take the cards off their backs and put them on the wall. 4. When everybody's card is up, have them describe what their jobs were. *I worked at a hotel. I registered guests.*

TEAMWORK & LANGUAGE REVIEW

Lesson Overview	Lesson Notes
MULTILEVEL OBJECTIVES	
On-, Pre-, and Higher-level: Expand upon and review unit grammar and life skills	
LANGUAGE FOCUS	
Grammar: Simple past (*She studied computers in college. Did Sam sleep late?*) **Vocabulary:** *Job fair* For vocabulary support, see these **Oxford Picture Dictionary** topics: Jobs and Occupations, pages 170–173; Job Skills, page 176; Job Search, pages 168–169; Interview Skills, page 179	
STRATEGY FOCUS	
Talk about learned job skills.	
READINESS CONNECTION	
In this review, students work in teams to explore ways to present their skills, training, and experience at a job fair.	
PACING	
To extend this review: Have students complete **Workbook 2 page 29**, **Multilevel Activities 2 Unit 4 pages 53–56**, and **Multilevel Grammar Exercises 2 Unit 4**.	

CORRELATIONS	
CCRS: R.1.A Ask and answer questions about key details in the text. R.7.A Use the illustrations and details in a text to describe its key ideas (e.g., maps, charts, photographs, political cartoons, etc.). L.1.A Demonstrate command of the conventions of standard English grammar and usage when writing or speaking. e. Use verbs to convey a sense of past, present, and future (e.g., *Yesterday I walked home; Today I walk home; Tomorrow I will walk home.*) j. use frequently occurring prepositions (e.g., *during, beyond, toward*). L.6.A Use words and phrases acquired through conversations, reading and being read to, and responding to texts, including using frequently occurring conjunctions to signal simple relationships (e.g., *because*). SL.1.A Participate in collaborative conversations with diverse partners in small and larger groups. W.2.A Write informative/explanatory texts in which they name a topic, supply some facts about the topic, and provide some sense of closure.	**ELPS:** 5. An ELL can conduct research and evaluate and communicate findings to answer questions or solve problems. 6. An ELL can analyze and critique the arguments of others orally and in writing.

Warm-up and Review
10–15 minutes (books closed)

1. Review the *Bring It to Life* assignment from Lesson 5.

2. Have students who did the exercise share what they learned. Encourage students who didn't do the exercise to ask their classmates questions about their interviews.

Introduction and Presentation
5 minutes

1. Pair students and direct them to look at the picture in their book. Ask them to describe what they see to their partner.

2. Ask volunteer pairs to share their ideas with the class.

Guided Practice
15–20 minutes

 1. Direct students to work in groups of three to four and look at the picture. Ask: *Who are these people? What are they doing? What could they be saying?*

2. Set a time limit (five minutes) for groups to answer the questions. Circulate and monitor.

3. Have students from each group share the group's responses with the class. If you have a large class, you may not want all of the groups to report their responses. Instead, have groups share their responses with each other. Call "time" and tell all groups to work with a new group and to repeat their responses. Repeat this process as desired, making sure each group gets to share their responses at least once.

B 1. Have students complete the task individually.

2. Have pairs compare answers and then practice the conversation.

Answers
1. did, work
2. worked
3. answered, helped
4. didn't, stay
5. wanted

C Read the instructions. Have pairs work together to complete the task. Circulate and help as needed.

MULTILEVEL STRATEGIES

For C, pair same-level students together.

• **Pre- and On-level** Pair these students. Write a conversation on the board with blanks for students to fill in.

A: Hello. My name is ____. I want a job as a _____.

B: Great! Tell me about your _____.

A: I can _____ and I am good at _____.

B: Do you have any special _____?

A: Yes. I have training in _____.

B: Where did you _____ before?

A: I worked at _____ for _____.

• **Higher-level** Have these students include an additional question and answer about education.

Communicative Practice
30–45 minutes

D 1. Put students in new groups of two to three. Tell them they will role-play their conversations from C. Read the sample conversation with a volunteer.

2. Set a time limit (ten minutes) for teams to complete the task.

3. Have students take turns saying each part of the conversation. Circulate and monitor as students carry out the role-play. Provide global feedback after the activity ends.

4. Have volunteer groups perform their role-play for the class.

E 1. Read the instructions aloud. Set a time limit (five minutes) for students to complete the task individually.

Answers
1. b
2. c
3. d
4. a

F Put students in new groups of four and assign roles: manager, researcher, administrative assistant, and reporter. Verify students' understanding of their roles. Set a time limit (five minutes) for teams to complete the task.

G 1. Read the instructions aloud. Have students copy the chart into their notebooks to use as they interview their teammates.

2. Set a time limit (five to ten minutes). Have students interview their teammates and fill in their charts.

TIP

For class interviews, it may help to have students stand in two circles, one inside the other. Students on the outside circle face the students in the inside circle. The students facing each other take turns asking and answering questions. When you call "time," each student moves one place to the right and now faces a new person to interview. Continue until all students have interviewed each other or the time limit has been reached.

For smaller classes, students can stand in two lines facing each other and move one place to the right.

H Read the sample paragraph aloud. Have teams work together to create a summary, with administrative assistants recording a final version. If time allows, have volunteer reporters share their team's summary with the class.

MULTILEVEL STRATEGIES

Adapt D–H to the level of your students.

• **Pre-level** Pair these students and work with them directly by supplying sentence frames as needed. Have pairs interview other students.

• **Higher-level** After H, have these students give career advice to other students based on their skills.

PROBLEM SOLVING AT WORK
10–15 minutes

A 🔊 1-72 1. Ask: *Do you use all of your skills in your job now? What skills would you like to be able to use in the job you have now or in a future job?* Tell students they will read a story about a man who is not happy with some aspects of his job. Direct students to read Jin's story silently.

2. Play the audio and have students silently read along again. Have a volunteer give an answer to the question.

B 1. Elicit answers to question 1. Guide students to a class consensus on the answer.

2. As a class, brainstorm answers to question 2. Ask students if they know someone who has this problem and has overcome it, or what they have done themselves to overcome the same problem.

Evaluation
20–25 minutes

To test students' understanding of the unit language and content, have them take the Unit 4 Test, available on the Teacher Resource Center.

5 On the Job

Unit Overview

This unit explores pay stubs, the workplace, and requesting a schedule change, and using the modals *might*, *should*, and *could*.

KEY OBJECTIVES	
Lesson 1	Identify parts of a pay stub; identify workplace equipment
Lesson 2	Identify appropriate workplace and school behavior
Lesson 3	Use *might* to describe possibilities at work and in everyday life
Lesson 4	Clarify directions on the job; request a schedule change
Lesson 5	Identify factors affecting job retention and advancement
Teamwork & Language Review	Review unit language

UNIT FEATURES	
Academic Vocabulary	*attitude, cooperate, equipment, evaluation, promotion, regulations*
Employability Skills	• Interpret figures on a pay stub • Compare and contrast appropriate workplace and school behavior • Analyze job performance skills • Find solutions to difficulties at a new job • Understand teamwork • Communicate information • Cooperate with others • Communicate verbally
Resources	**Class Audio** CD2, Tracks 02–16 **Workbook** Unit 5, pages 30–36 **Teacher Resource Center** Multilevel Activities 2 Unit 5 Multilevel Grammar Exercises 2 Unit 5 Unit 5 Test **Oxford Picture Dictionary** Prepositions, The Workplace, Job Skills, Office Skills, Job Search, Job Safety, Office Work

Lesson Overview	Lesson Notes

MULTILEVEL OBJECTIVES

On-level: Identify workplace vocabulary

Pre-level: Recognize workplace vocabulary

Higher-level: Talk and write about the workplace

LANGUAGE FOCUS

Grammar: Simple present of *be* and prepositions (*The time clock is on the wall.*)

Vocabulary: Pay stub terms and workplace equipment

For vocabulary support, see these **Oxford Picture Dictionary** topics: Prepositions, page 25; The Workplace, pages 182–183

STRATEGY FOCUS

Read a pay stub and talk about workplace equipment.

READINESS CONNECTION

In this lesson, students interpret figures on a pay stub and explore workplace vocabulary.

PACING

To compress this lesson: Conduct 2D as a whole-class activity.

To extend this lesson: Have students discuss pay stubs. (See end of lesson.)

And/or have students complete **Workbook 2 page 30** and **Multilevel Activities 2 Unit 5 page 58**.

CORRELATIONS

CCRS: R.7.A Use the illustrations and details in a text to describe its key ideas (e.g., maps, charts, photographs, political cartoons, etc.).

L.6.A Use words and phrases acquired through conversations, reading and being read to, and responding to texts, including using frequently occurring conjunctions to signal simple relationships (e.g., *because*).

SL.1.A Participate in collaborative conversations with diverse partners in small and larger groups.

ELPS: 8. An ELL can determine the meaning of words and phrases in oral presentations and literary and informational text.

Warm-up and Review
10–15 minutes (books closed)

1. Lead a brief class discussion about your students' jobs: *Do you work at home? In a factory? In an office? Do you get paid every week? Every month?*

2. Draw a blank check on the board, with blank lines for every item that needs to be filled in (date, amount, etc.). Number each line. Ask students what information goes on each numbered line and fill in the check with sample information.

Introduction
3 minutes

1. Add a rectangle representing a pay stub to the check on the board. Say: *When you get paid, your paycheck has a pay stub.* Find out what students already know about a pay stub by asking: *What information do you see on a pay stub?*

2. State the objective: *Today we're going to explore workplace vocabulary, including words on a pay stub and names of workplace machines.*

1 Learn about reading a pay stub

Presentation
20–25 minutes

A 1. Ask: *Do you look at your pay stub? Do you understand all the parts of it?* Direct students to look at the pay stub. Ask: *What is the name of the company?* [Mills Brothers Company] *What is the name of the employee?* [Pablo Ramirez]

2. Read the words aloud. Ask students to circle the words they know.

B 🔊 **2-02** 1. Have students listen to the audio. Ask them to point to the correct section of the pay stub in 1A as they listen. Circulate and monitor.

2. Ask: *How often does Pablo gets paid?* [once a week] Ask where students can find the answer. Check comprehension by making *true/false* statements about the pay stub. *Pablo's net pay was $427.* [false] *Pablo's state tax deduction was $20.10.* [true] Have students hold up one finger for *true* and two for *false* in order to get a nonverbal response.

MULTILEVEL STRATEGIES

After the group comprehension check in 1B, call on volunteers and tailor your questions to the level of your students.

- **Pre-level** Ask *yes/no* questions. *Did Pablo pay state tax?* [yes]
- **On-level** Ask information questions about the Earnings/Deductions part of the stub. *How much was his gross pay?* [$427]
- **Higher-level** Ask critical-thinking questions. *Where does tax money go? What's the difference between state and federal taxes?*

C 🔊 **2-03** 1. Ask students to listen and repeat the words.

2. While students are repeating, circulate and listen for pronunciation difficulties. Provide choral practice as necessary.

TIP

Take some time to review the meaning of the words and terms on the pay stub: *deduction, gross, net, social security, state, federal, Medicare, total, hourly rate.* Have students work in pairs or small groups and look up the words and terms in dictionaries or online. This can be assigned for homework as well. Have volunteers make a poster using the paystub in the book as a guide and label each of the parts. Have them include definitions of each part. Display it in the classroom.

Guided Practice I
15–20 minutes

D 1. Have students work individually to complete the sentences using the new vocabulary. Set a time limit (two minutes).

2. Encourage students to take turns reading the completed sentences with a partner.

Answers	
1. deductions	5. gross pay
2. Social Security	6. pay period
3. hourly rate	7. Medicare
4. federal tax	8. net pay

E Read the instructions aloud. Set a time limit (three minutes). Have students take turns asking and answering the questions with a partner. Circulate and listen for any pronunciation or vocabulary difficulties.

Answers
1. 01/10/18—1/16/18
2. 4

MULTILEVEL STRATEGIES

For 1E, pair same-level students together.

- **Pre-level** Assist these students with the exercise.
- **Higher-level** When these students finish, have them use the statements in 1D and make questions to ask and answer in pairs.

2 Talk about workplace equipment

Guided Practice II
35–40 minutes

A 1. Ask: *Do you use machines at work?* Introduce the new topic: *Now let's look at different equipment that is used in the workplace.*

2. Group students and assign roles: manager, researcher, administrative assistant, and reporter. Explain that students work with their groups to match the words and pictures.

3. Check comprehension of the exercise: *Who looks up the words in the picture dictionary?* [researcher] *Who writes the numbers in the book?* [administrative assistant] *Who tells the class your answers?* [reporter] *Who helps everyone and manages the group?* [manager]

4. Set a time limit (three minutes) and have students work together to complete the task. While students are working, copy the wordlist onto the board.

5. Call "time" and have the reporters from each group take turns calling out the numbers for the wordlist. Record students' answers on the board. If groups disagree, write each group's choice next to the word.

6. Draw students' attention to the illustrations. Prompt students to use vocabulary not labeled in the art. Ask: *What other items can you name?* [exit sign, recycling bin, warning sign, etc.] *What are the men wearing on their heads?* [hard hats] *Why are the men wearing bright vests?* [so they can be seen easily for safety] *What is the woman doing?* [making a photocopy]

Answers	
4–printer	5–photocopier
7–water cooler	9–hand cart
8–forklift	1–time clock
3–keyboard	6–file cabinet
2–monitor	

MULTILEVEL STRATEGIES

Have students work in mixed-level groups for 2A.

• **Pre-level** Assign these students the role of administrative assistant.

• **Higher-level** Assign these students the role of manager.

B **2-04** 1. Play the audio. Ask students to listen and check their answers.

2. As a class, correct the wordlist on the board and then have students write the correct numbers in their books as needed.

3. Tell the groups from 2A to split into pairs to practice the words. Set a time limit (two minutes).

Communicative Practice and Application
10–15 minutes

C 1. Read the instructions and the phrases in the box aloud. Answer any questions about vocabulary. Model the conversation with a volunteer.

2. Set a time limit (five minutes). Ask students to practice the conversation with several partners.

Answers
1. time clock–check in to work
2. monitor–read email
3. keyboard–type email
4. printer–print documents
5. photocopier–make copies
6. file cabinet–store files
7. water cooler–get a drink of water
8. forklift–lift heavy objects
9. hand cart–move boxes

MULTILEVEL STRATEGIES

For 2C, seat same-level students together.

• **Pre-level** Have students work in pairs or small groups. Assist those groups.

• **Higher-level** After students complete the exercise, ask them to compose additional sentences about other office equipment. They can say their sentences (without naming the equipment) for the rest of the class to guess the piece of equipment.

TIP

For more vocabulary practice, pass out pictures of different occupations or use the picture cards on page 64 of Multilevel Activities Level 2 Unit 5. Have less-verbal students use the cards for flashcard vocabulary practice. Have more-verbal students ask questions: *What does this do? How/When do you use it?*

D 1. Read the questions aloud. Have groups of three to four students discuss the questions. Circulate and monitor.

2. Have a volunteer from each group share their group's responses with the class.

Evaluation
10–15 minutes

TEST YOURSELF

1. Make a three-column chart on the board with the headings *Deductions, Earnings,* and *Equipment.* Have students give you an example for each column.

2. Have students copy the chart into their notebooks.

3. Set a time limit (five to ten minutes). Have students fill out the chart with words from the lesson.

4. Call "time" and have students check their spelling in *The Oxford Picture Dictionary* or another dictionary.

MULTILEVEL STRATEGIES

Target the *Test Yourself* to the level of your students.

• **Pre-level** Have these students work with their books open.

• **Higher-level** Have these students complete the chart and then write at least one sentence for each column in the chart.

EXTENSION ACTIVITY

Discuss Pay Stubs

Bring in real or model pay stubs for students to discuss and compare. You can find copies of pay stubs on the Internet by typing *pay stub* into an image search engine. Most real-life pay stubs are more complicated than the one in the book, but students can identify the items from the vocabulary list.

Lesson Overview | Lesson Notes

MULTILEVEL OBJECTIVES

On-, Pre-, and Higher-level: Read and write about appropriate behavior at work and school

LANGUAGE FOCUS

Grammar: *Can/can't* (*We can't wear sandals.*); *Have to* (*We have to be on time.*)

Vocabulary: *Appropriate, behavior, hairnet, hard hat, regulations, safety glasses*

For vocabulary support, see this **Oxford Picture Dictionary** topic: Job Safety, page 197

STRATEGY FOCUS

Use informal greetings in an email to a friend, such as *Hi* or *Hey*. Then continue with a friendly question.

READINESS CONNECTION

In this lesson, students communicate information about what people wear and how they behave at work.

PACING

To compress this lesson: Skip 2B.

To extend this lesson: Have students play a guessing game. (See end of lesson.)

And/or have students complete **Workbook 2 page 31** and **Multilevel Activities 2 Unit 5 page 59**.

CORRELATIONS

CCRS: R.7.A Use the illustrations and details in a text to describe its key ideas (e.g., maps, charts, photographs, political cartoons, etc.).

SL.1.A Participate in collaborative conversations with diverse partners in small and larger groups.

SL.2.A Confirm understanding of a text read aloud or information presented orally or through other media by asking and answering questions about key details and requesting clarification if something is not understood.

W.2.A Write informative/explanatory texts in which they name a topic, supply some facts about the topic, and provide some sense of closure.

ELPS: 6. An ELL can analyze and critique the arguments of others orally and in writing. 9. An ELL can create clear and coherent level-appropriate speech and text.

Warm-up and Review
10–15 minutes (books closed)

Draw a four-column chart on the board with the headings *Factory, Office, Hospital,* and *Restaurant.* Ask the class to brainstorm words for the clothing people wear in these places. Assign a time limit (two minutes). Call "time" and ask for volunteers to write their ideas in the correct columns. Leave this on the board.

Introduction
5 minutes

1. Make statements using the words on the board: *Nurses wear uniforms.*

2. State the objective: *Today we're going to read and write about what people wear and how they behave at work.*

1 Prepare to write

Presentation
20–25 minutes

 1. Direct students' attention to the pictures in 1B and read the questions aloud. Ask: *What is Lucy wearing?* [a white jacket and a hairnet]

2. Have students work in pairs. Give them one minute to discuss their responses to the questions. Build students' schema by reading the questions aloud again and discussing their responses as a class.

Answers
1. She is a sandwich chef.
2. Answers will vary. Possible answers include: *working with people* and *preparing food*.

 2-05 1. Play the audio.

2. Check comprehension. Ask: *What does Lucy wear at work?* [a hairnet, plastic gloves, and a white coat] Indicate the chart on the board (from the warm-up). Ask: *In which column should we put* hairnet, plastic gloves, *and* white jacket? [Restaurant] Ask volunteers to say if they have worn these items and where they worked.

TIP

Bring in pictures of common workplace machines or use the picture cards on page 64 of Multilevel Activities Level 2 Unit 5 to help students review vocabulary. Have less-verbal students use the pictures as flashcards. Have more-verbal students ask each other questions about the pictures. *Do you know how to use a(n) _____? Do you have a(n) _____ at your job? Do you have to wear _____? Does a(n) _____ have to wear a(n) _____?*

 2-05 1. Introduce the text and its purpose: *You're going to read an email about someone's new job. As you read, look at which parts of the text match the pictures in B. This can help you understand the text better.* Play the audio again and have students read along silently.

2. Point out the *Writer's Note.* Ask: *How do you usually begin an email to a friend or family member?* Ask: *What other friendly questions can you include in an email to someone you know well?* [*How's the weather there? Are you enjoying your new house/car/pet?*]

Guided Practice I
5 minutes

 1. Have students work individually to choose the correct answers. Set a time limit (two minutes).

2. Review the answers as a class.

Answers
1. b
2. b
3. a

MULTILEVEL STRATEGIES

For 1D, seat same-level students together.

• **Pre-level** While the other students are completing 1D, have pre-level students look at the pictures in 1B and list the things they see. As you review the answers to 1D, write them on the board so that pre-level students can copy them into their books.

• **On- and Higher-level** Write additional questions on the board for these students. *Where does Lucy work? What are the important rules at Lucy's job? What do you think her tools are? Why is she happy with her new job?*

Guided Practice II
10–15 minutes

 2-06 Read the instructions and the list of work behaviors aloud. Play the audio and have students complete the task individually. Don't check answers yet.

 2-06 1. Have pairs compare their answers for E. Play the audio again and check answers as a class.

2. Ask: *Which of these things do you have to do for your job? Which ones are you good at? Are there ones that you want to be better at?*

Answers
Checks beside "Be on time for work," "Check in with your time card in the morning," "Check off the delivery times on a list," "Wear appropriate clothing," and "Ask for help."

2 Plan

Communicative Practice I
5 minutes

A Read the instructions and the words in the *Need help?* box aloud. Have students complete the exercise individually. Circulate and monitor.

> **MULTILEVEL STRATEGIES**
>
> Adapt 2A to the level of your students.
> - **Pre-level** Work with these students to assist them with vocabulary.
> - **Higher-level** Ask these students to write a sentence or two explaining why each rule exists.

B Read the instructions and the sample sentences aloud. Have pairs share their lists with each other and talk about the reasons for the rules. Circulate and monitor.

3 Write

Communicative Practice II and Application
15–20 minutes

A 1. Read the instructions aloud. Have students look at the paragraph template as you read it aloud. At each blank, have a volunteer give a sample answer.

2. Set a time limit for writing (five minutes). Have students complete the template with their own information.

B 1. Ask students to read their email to a partner. Call on volunteers to share one thing they liked about their partner's email and also any rules that are similar to their own job.

2. Lead a class discussion about which rules are easy to follow and which ones are harder to follow.

> **MULTILEVEL STRATEGIES**
>
> For 3A, target the writing to the level of your students.
> - **Pre-level** Write a wordlist on the board for these students to use to complete their emails. Then work with these students to write a group email. Read through the template. At each blank, stop and elicit completions. Decide as a group what to write. Have these students copy the group email into their notebooks.
> - **Higher-level** Ask these students to write an email without using the template as a guide.

Evaluation
10 minutes

TEST YOURSELF

1. Read the instructions aloud. Assign a time limit (five minutes) and have students work individually.

2. Before collecting student work, invite two or three volunteers to share their sentences. Ask students to raise their hands if they wrote similar answers.

> **EXTENSION ACTIVITY**
>
> **Guessing Game**
>
> Create a guessing game. Brainstorm a list of sports and games with which most students are familiar. Tell groups to choose a sport/game and write its rules, using *can't* and *have to*. Ask a reporter from each group to read the group's rules aloud without naming the game. Have the class guess the game.

Lesson Overview

Lesson Notes

MULTILEVEL OBJECTIVES

On- and Higher-level: Use *might* and *should* to talk and write about plans

Pre-level: Demonstrate understanding of *might* and *should* by answering questions about plans

LANGUAGE FOCUS

Grammar: *Might* (*He might get hurt.*); *should* (*She should be on time.*)

Vocabulary: *Appropriate, get hurt, make a request*

For vocabulary support, see these **Oxford Picture Dictionary** topics: Job Skills, page 176; Office Skills, page 177

STRATEGY FOCUS

Understand that we use *might* to say that something is possible, and that we do not use *to* after *might*.

READINESS CONNECTION

In this lesson, students compare and contrast appropriate workplace and school behavior and explore how to use *might* and *should*.

PACING

To compress this lesson: Assign 3C as homework.

To extend this lesson: Have students write sentences with modals. (See end of lesson.)

And/or have students complete **Workbook 2 pages 32–33, Multilevel Activities 2 Unit 5 page 60**, and **Multilevel Grammar Exercises 2 Unit 5**.

CORRELATIONS

CCRS: L.1.A Demonstrate command of the conventions of standard English grammar and usage when writing or speaking.

SL.1.A Participate in collaborative conversations with diverse partners in small and larger groups.

SL.2.A Confirm understanding of a text read aloud or information presented orally or through other media by asking and answering questions about key details and requesting clarification if something is not understood.

R.7.A Use the illustrations and details in a text to describe its key ideas (e.g., maps, charts, photographs, political cartoons, etc.).

ELPS: 7. An ELL can adapt language choices to purpose, task, and audience when speaking and writing. 10. An ELL can demonstrate command of the conventions of standard English to communicate in level-appropriate speech and writing.

Warm-up and Review
10–15 minutes (books closed)

Ask students to tell you some of the class rules for your classroom or for other classes they have had. Write two or three of them on the board using *should* and *shouldn't*. Then ask students to desribe the consequences of not following these rules.

Introduction
5–10 minutes

1. Restate the consequences from the warm-up using *might* and write sentences on the board next to the corresponding rule. For example: *Students shouldn't eat in class. They might have trouble practicing pronunciation.*

2. State the objective: *Today we're going to explore how to use* might *and* should.

1 Explore talking about possibility using *might* and *might not*

Presentation I
20–25 minutes

 2-07 1. Direct students to look at the illustration of Martin and Hiroko. Ask: *Where are Martin and Hiroko? What do you think is the work relationship between them?* [Hiroko is a supervisor and Marco is her employee.]

2. Read the questions aloud. Play the audio. Have students answer the questions.

3. Discuss the meaning of *might*: *What might happen if the floor is wet? Will it definitely happen or maybe happen?*

Answers
put up a warning sign; put the cleaning products in the closet

B 1. Read the dialogue in 1A aloud, slowly. Have students raise their hand every time they hear *might* or *might not*.

2. Read the instructions aloud and have students underline the words that follow *might* and *might not*.

3. Students may ask about the difference between *might* and *maybe*. The meaning is the same, but the grammar is very different. *Might* is an auxiliary that comes before a verb: *He might be angry. Maybe* is followed by a clause with a subject and a verb: *Maybe he will be angry.* Encourage students to use *might* for this lesson. Point out that *should* is also an auxiliary and is used in the same way as *might*.

C 1. Demonstrate how to read the grammar charts as complete sentences. Read through the charts sentence by sentence. Then read them again and have students repeat after you.

2. Read the *Grammar Note* aloud. Use the dialogue in 1A to illustrate points in the grammar charts. *Someone might slip and fall. They might be dangerous.*

Guided Practice I
15–20 minutes

D 1. Read the instructions aloud. Give students a few minutes to silently review the charts in 1C again and fill in the blanks.

2. Ask volunteers to write the sentences on the board. Have other students read the sentences aloud.

3. Assess students' comprehension of the charts. Ask: *What words follow* might *or* might not? [verbs] Ask questions to have students respond with *might*: *What might happen if you don't study for a test? What might happen if the floor is wet? What might happen if you forget your work uniform?*

Answers	
1. might fall	4. might not see
2. might break in	5. might have
3. might get hurt	6. might not hear

2 Practice *should* and *should not*

Presentation II and Guided Practice II
20–25 minutes

A **2-08** Demonstrate how to read the grammar charts as complete sentences. Read through the charts sentence by sentence. Play the audio and have students repeat. Read the *Grammar Note* aloud.

B 1. Read the instructions aloud. Give students time to silently review the charts again and fill in the blanks.

2. Ask volunteers to write the sentences on the board. Have students read the sentences aloud.

3. Assess students' comprehension of the charts. Ask: *What words follow* should *or* should not? [verbs, phrases that offer advice] Ask questions to have students respond with *should*: *What should you do if the floor is wet? What should you do if you feel sick?*

Answers	
1. should	4. shouldn't
2. should	5. should
3. shouldn't	6. should

3 Practice using *might* and *should*

Presentation III and Guided Practice III
15–20 minutes

A 1. Write some sentence frames on the board and ask students to choose *should* or *might*: *We don't want hair in the food. You _____ wear a hairnet.*; *He's not at his desk. He _____ be at lunch.*; *She is very sick. She _____ call the doctor.*

2. Direct students' attention to the illustrations. Have volunteers say what they think each sign means.

3. Have students complete the sentences individually and then read them with a partner. Review the answers as a class.

Answers
1. shouldn't, might fall
2. shouldn't, might breathe in
3. should, might get injured
4. should, might get burned
5. shouldn't, might get dirty

TIP

For more practice with *might*, write situations on the board and have students guess what will happen next. *A woman leaves her purse in her car. A boy forgets to bring his lunch to school. A cook puts salt in the cake instead of sugar.* Have students work with a partner to brainstorm as many possibilities as they can before you elicit their ideas.

B 1. Read the instructions aloud. As a class, discuss what students see in the photos. Read the sample conversation with a volunteer.

2. Have students discuss what might happen and what each person should do. Circulate and monitor.

3. Have students share their responses with the class.

Possible Answers
1. Someone might get hurt / slip / fall over. The man should put up a safety sign. The man should clean up the floor.
2. The tangled wires might be dangerous. They might start a fire. Someone might trip over them. The woman should untangle the wires. The woman should call an electrician / a technician.

C Have students write two sentences about each picture, one with *might/might not* and one with *should/should not*. Have volunteers say their sentences.

4 Give and respond to advice at work

Communicative Practice and Application
15–20 minutes

A Read the problems aloud. Read the sample conversation with a volunteer. Set a time limit (ten minutes). Have groups of three to four students discuss each problem.

B Have students share their answers to 4A with the class.

TIP

For more practice with modals, put pictures up around the room of people in different situations. Hang a sheet of paper next to each picture. Divide the class into as many groups as you have pictures and direct each group to stand in front of a picture. Tell the groups to write a sentence about the picture using a modal: *should (not), might (not), will (not)*. After one minute, have groups move to a new picture and write a new sentence using a different modal. Continue until students have moved six times. Correct the sentences together.

MULTILEVEL STRATEGIES

Group same-level students together for 4B.

• **Pre-level** Have these students choose only two or three problems to talk about.

• **Higher-level** Have these students think of one or two additional workplace problems to discuss.

Evaluation

10 minutes

TEST YOURSELF

Ask students to write their two sentences and then tell a partner what would happen if they don't do the things they've written about. Collect and correct their writing.

MULTILEVEL STRATEGIES

Target the *Test Yourself* to the level of your students.

• **Pre-level** Provide these students with sentence frames like the ones in the grammar chart on page 65: (*I _____ in school. I _____ at work.*)

• **Higher-level** Have these students each write a paragraph in response to this prompt: *Write about one thing you should do and explain why you might or might not do it tomorrow.*

EXTENSION ACTIVITY

Write Sentences with Modals

Have students practice writing sentences with *might (not)* and *should (not)*.

1. Bring in pictures and have students make sentences about what might happen next. If you brought in pictures for *will* in Unit 2, you can use the same pictures.

2. When students write their own sentences, you may find confusion about present and future—for example a student may write, *She might walk to school* meaning *She might be walking to school.* To address these problems, encourage students to write about future possibilities if they are using action verbs: *Don't tell me what she might/should be doing now; tell me what she might/should do next.*

Lesson Overview	Lesson Notes
MULTILEVEL OBJECTIVES	
On- and Higher-level: Make and respond to requests in the workplace **Pre-level:** Respond to requests in the workplace	
LANGUAGE FOCUS	
Grammar: Polite questions with *could* (*Could you type this letter for me?*) **Vocabulary:** *Make copies, mail a package, operate a forklift, type a letter, use power tools* For vocabulary support, see these **Oxford Picture Dictionary** topics: Job Skills, page 176; Office Work, pages 188–189	
STRATEGY FOCUS	
Request a job change.	
READINESS CONNECTION	
In this lesson, listen for and clarify job instructions, request a schedule change, and use intonation and word stress to interpret emotions.	
PACING	
To compress this lesson: Skip 4B. **To extend this lesson:** Have students practice polite requests. (See end of lesson.) And/or have students complete **Workbook 2 page 34** and **Multilevel Activities 2 Unit 5 page 61**.	
CORRELATIONS	
CCRS: SL.1.A Participate in collaborative conversations with diverse partners in small and larger groups. SL.2.A Confirm understanding of a text read aloud or information presented orally or through other media by asking and answering questions about key details and requesting clarification if something is not understood.	**ELPS:** 2. An ELL can participate in level-appropriate oral and written exchanges of information, ideas, and analyses, in various social and academic contexts, responding to peer, audience, or reader comments and questions. 9. An ELL can create clear and coherent level-appropriate speech and text.

Warm-up and Review
10–15 minutes (books closed)

Write scrambled workplace instructions on the board: *copies make three Please* [*Please make three copies.*]; *box the on Put shelf* [*Put the box on the shelf.*]; *one Give customer each to coupon* [*Give one coupon to each customer.*]; *mail Please downstairs take the* [*Please take the mail downstairs.*]. Give students a few minutes to work out the answers before you ask volunteers to write the unscrambled sentences on the board. Remind them to add periods.

Introduction
5 minutes

1. Demonstrate how the commands on the board can be made more polite with the use of *could you*. *Could you make three copies, please?*

2. State the objective: *Today we're going to talk about job instructions.*

1 Listen to learn: job instructions

Presentation I and Guided Practice I
25–30 minutes

A 1. Direct students to look at the pictures. Ask: *Where do each of these things happen?*

2. Read the question aloud. Have pairs ask and answer the question with each other and then review the answers as a class.

B 🔊 **2-09** 1. Read the instructions aloud. Have students put down their pencils before they listen. Play the audio and ask them to listen for key words in each conversation. Key words indicate an action that gives a clue about where each conversation is taking place. Replay the audio and have them write where each conversation is taking place.

2. Ask students to compare their answers with a partner. Circulate and monitor to ensure students understand the audio.

Possible Answers
They are at work. They are in an office.

C 🔊 **2-09** 1. Read the instructions aloud. Suggest to students that they take brief notes about the information they hear to help them complete the task.

2. Play the audio again. Have students write their answers individually before comparing answers with a partner. Check answers as a class.

Answers
1. write an email
2. mail a package
3. put copies in the file cabinet

D Read the question aloud. Have students discuss the question in groups of three to four and write down their answers in correct request form. Have groups share their requests with the class and write them on the board. Keep the requests on the board for students to use in 2A.

---

2 Practice your pronunciation

Pronunciation Extension
10–15 minutes

A 🔊 **2-10** 1. Ask a volunteer to make one of the requests from 1D. Reply to this student with a grudging *Sure*. Have another student make a request and reply to that student with an enthusiastic *Sure!* Point out that how you say something can be just as important as what you say. Tell students: *In these two recordings, Simon will say the same thing, but his tone of voice will change.* Read the *Need help?* box aloud.

2. Have students listen and check the correct box. Ask for a show of hands to see how many students chose Conversation 1 and how many chose Conversation 2. If some students chose Conversation 1, play the audio again, so they can hear the difference.

Answer
Conversation 2

B 🔊 **2-11** Have students listen and then practice the conversation with a partner. Circulate and compliment students for sounding helpful.

3 Practice making requests with *can* and *could*

Presentation II and Guided Practice II
20–25 minutes

A 🔊 **2-12** 1. Write the words *instruction* and *request* on the board. Have students give you examples of each. Write them on the board. Have a volunteer give a definition of each.

2. Ask students to read along silently, and then play the audio.

---

3. Have students work in pairs and identify one instruction and one request. Discuss answers as a class.

B **2-13** 1. Read the instructions aloud. Have students read the answer choices silently to themselves.

2. Play the audio and have students circle the correct answers. Replay if necessary.

Answers
1. b
2. b
3. a
4. b

C 1. Introduce the new grammar. Write sentences on the board. *1. Can I open the window? 2. Can you open the window?* Ask a student the first question and prompt a *yes* answer. Open the window or mime opening the window. Then ask the second question to a student and have them open the window. Underline the *I* and the *you* in the requests on the board.

2. Demonstrate how to read the grammar chart as complete sentences. Read the additional information at the bottom of the chart. Read through the chart sentence by sentence and have students repeat after you.

3. Ask a volunteer to say when to use *can I?* and when to use *can you?*

D 1. Direct students' attention to the *Need help?* box. Read the information aloud. Emphasize that intonation is important to speaking politely. Read each response again and have students repeat with the correct intonation. Then ask students the questions in the chart in 3C and have them respond using one of the phrases from the *Need help?* box.

2. Read the instructions and the list of situations aloud. Check for student understanding. Model the sample conversation with a volunteer.

TIP

If necessary, brainstorm reasons for each request as a class. Then have students work in pairs to complete the activity.

3. Have pairs complete the task. Circulate and monitor.

4. Have pairs say one of their conversations for the class.

MULTILEVEL STRATEGIES

Adapt 3D to the level of your students.

• **Pre-level** Have these students work as a group to write their requests and responses.

• **Higher-level** Direct these students to have a negative as well as an affirmative response to each request and to give reasons for a negative response as well.

4 Make conversation: clarify instructions and make requests

Communicative Practice I
15–20 minutes

A 1. Ask students if they remember what *clarify* means [to ask for information again to make sure you understand it]. Ask: *How do we clarify information?* [ask someone to repeat what they said or to repeat what they said back to them]

2. Draw students' attention to the situations in the boxes and explain that they should use them to create new conversations. Model one conversation with a volunteer. Ask: *What words were used to clarify information?*

3. Have pairs create a conversation for each situation and take turns performing parts.

MULTILEVEL STRATEGIES

Adapt 4A to the level of your students.

• **Pre-level** Have these students choose one situation for the conversation. Provide words/ phrases in mixed up order that they can use for each one of the blanks.

• **Higher-level** Challenge these students to have the conversations without looking at their books.

B 1. Ask pairs to share their conversation with another pair.

2. Have pairs present their conversation to the class.

AT WORK

Requesting a schedule change

Presentation III and Communicative Practice II
20–30 minutes

A 🔊 **2-14** Read the instructions aloud. Play the audio and have students read along silently. Play the audio again and have students repeat.

B Have pairs practice the conversations in A. Circulate and monitor.

C Read the questions aloud. Have students discuss the questions in groups of three to four. Then have groups share their answers with the class.

Evaluation
10–15 minutes

TEST YOURSELF

Have pairs perform the role-play. Circulate and assess students' progress. Take note of any mistakes you hear in intonation, pronunciation, grammar, or vocabulary. When all students have finished the activity, as a class, review the kinds of mistakes you heard, without naming any students who made them.

MULTILEVEL STRATEGIES

For the *Test Yourself*, pair pre-level students.

• **Pre-level** Provide these students with sentence frames.

A: *Could I change my schedule?*

B: *Why do you need a schedule change?*

A: *I need to _____.*

B: *What change do you want?*

A: *I'd like to change from _____ to _____.*

Have partners take turns reading each part.

EXTENSION ACTIVITY

Polite requests

Have students practice making and responding to polite requests.

1. Bring in various small objects that people use in class or at work: rulers, paper clips, small pairs of scissors, etc.

2. As a class, brainstorm the tasks that go with each item, and write them on the board.

3. Give the items to half of the students. Have the students with items stand up and ask someone who doesn't have an item to do something. *Could you please _____?* (*measure the box, clip the pages together, cut this,* etc.) As they make a request, they should hand over the item.

4. The person who receives the item responds appropriately and then finds a new partner without an item and repeats the process.

5. Monitor for correct questions and polite responses.

Lesson Overview	Lesson Notes

MULTILEVEL OBJECTIVES

On- and Higher-level: Read about and discuss job performance skills and job evaluations

Pre-level: Read about job performance skills and job evaluations

LANGUAGE FOCUS

Grammar: *Should* (*You should read the instructions.*)

Vocabulary: *Attitude, complain, cooperate, evaluation, positive, promotion*

For vocabulary support, see these **Oxford Picture Dictionary** topics: Job Skills; page 176; Job Search, pages 168–169

STRATEGY FOCUS

Learn to identify reasons in a text. Understand which paragraph tells you why you should have a positive attitude. Identify how many reasons there are.

READINESS CONNECTION

In this lesson, students read about and analyze job performance skills and attitudes, and read and talk about performance evaluations.

PACING

To compress this lesson: Assign 1E and/or 1F for homework.

To extend this lesson: Have students discuss classroom behavior. (See end of lesson.)

And/or have students complete **Workbook 2 page 35** and **Multilevel Activities 2 Unit 5 page 62**.

CORRELATIONS	
CCRS: L.6.A Use words and phrases acquired through conversations, reading and being read to, and responding to texts, including using frequently occurring conjunctions to signal simple relationships (e.g., *because*). R.1.A Ask and answer questions about key details in the text. R.4.A Ask and answer questions to help determine or clarify the meaning of words and phrases in a text. SL.1.A Participate in collaborative conversations with diverse partners in small and larger groups.	**ELPS:** 1. An ELL can construct meaning from oral presentations and literary and informational text through level-appropriate listening, reading, and viewing. 3. An ELL can speak and write about level-appropriate complex literary and informational texts and topics.

Warm-up and Review
10–15 minutes (books closed)

Write *Positive Attitude* on the board. Tell students that someone who has a positive attitude is someone who sees the good side of most situations. Use some students as examples. *Sara has a positive attitude because she's always smiling. Ramon has a positive attitude because he studies his vocabulary at home.* Ask students to quickly write their ideas about how they show a positive attitude at work, school, or home. Ask volunteers to share their ideas.

Introduction
5 minutes

1. Point out that having a positive attitude is important for both students and employees. Use some of the examples on the board in a work context: *Sara is always smiling, so she makes the customers feel good.*

2. State the objective: *Today we're going to talk about positive attitudes and job performance.*

1 Build reading strategies

Presentation
10–20 minutes

 Read the instructions aloud. Have students complete the task individually and then share their answers with the class.

Answers
cheerful
unhappy
well
better

Guided Practice: Pre-reading
5–10 minutes

 1. Read the instructions and the adjectives aloud. Have students answer the question with a partner and then share their answers with the class.

2. As a class, brainstorm other adjectives or behaviors that can describe someone with a positive attitude.

Answers
excited, friendly

TIP

Expand the discussion of positive attitudes by demonstrating different types of body language and asking students what kind of attitude the body language suggests. Ideas for a negative attitude: slouch, drag your feet, look down at the ground, pout, roll your eyes. For a positive attitude: sit straight, smile, walk briskly, look the person in the eye.

Guided Practice: While Reading
15–20 minutes

 1. Read the instructions aloud. Have students read the article and the information in the *Reader's Note* silently. Make sure students understand the new vocabulary. Ask them to use the glossed words in a sentence.

2. Read the *Reader's Note* aloud. Ask volunteers to answer the questions [third paragraph; three reasons].

3. Ask volunteers when they can use the advice in the reading.

MULTILEVEL STRATEGIES

Adapt 1C to the level of your students.

• **Pre-level** Read the text aloud to these students as they follow along.

• **On- and Higher-level** Pair students and have them read the article aloud to each other, taking turns to read each paragraph.

Guided Practice: Rereading
10–15 minutes

 2-15 1. Have students reread the article and write a summary of the advice.

2. Play the audio again and have students read along silently. As a class, write each piece of advice on the board in shortened list form (e.g., *Be sure you now the rules of the company = know the rules*). Have students tell the class which things they do in their job or at school.

TIP

Have students go online to find other articles that give advice about having a positive attitude at work. Provide possible search terms (*job performance + positive attitude*; *job performance + advice*). Have them share their findings with the class.

Guided Practice: Post-reading
15 minutes

 1. Have students work individually to choose the correct answers and then identify in the reading where they found the answer. Check answers as a class.

2. Check comprehension further. Ask: *Who values people with a positive attitude?* [supervisors and co-workers] *What should you do after you make a mistake?* [show you want to improve] *What should you do if there is a problem?* [look for a solution] *What should you ask your co-workers for?* [feedback]

Answers
1. c
2. b
3. c
4. a

MULTILEVEL STRATEGIES

For 1E, work with pre-level students.

• **Pre-level** Ask these students *yes/no* and short-answer information questions about the reading while other students are completing 1E.

• **Higher-level** Have these students take turns asking and answering comprehension questions about the reading.

 1. Have students work individually to complete the sentences.

2. Have pairs read their sentences to each other and then check answers as a class.

Answers
1. cooperate
2. complain
3. attitude
4. improve

2 Interpret a performance evaluation

Communicative Practice
15–20 minutes

 Direct students to look at the evaluation. Ask: *What is in the left-hand column?* [the points Rosa is evaluated on] *What is in the right-hand column?* [her supervisor's comments] Have students study the chart and answer the question as a class.

B 1. Read the questions aloud. Allow students time to think of their own answers and make notes.

2. Set a time limit (five to ten minutes). Have pairs discuss the questions. Circulate and help as needed.

3. Call "time" and have pairs share their responses with another pair. Have volunteers share their partner's answers with the class.

Application
5–10 minutes

BRING IT TO LIFE

Ask students to record examples of co-workers', classmates', and friends' positive attitudes, problem solving, and cooperation. Have them report their findings to the class. Discuss which behaviors they think are the most helpful/important.

EXTENSION ACTIVITY
Discuss Classroom Behavior
Have students practice classroom behavior vocabulary.
1. Direct students to look at 2A and think about how the categories apply to classroom behavior.
2. Ask pairs or groups to come up with an example of classroom behavior that would fit into each category—for example: *follows instructions – brings the right materials to class; helps others – explains homework to students who missed class.* Tell students to score themselves on each behavior, using *Excellent, Good,* or *Fair.*

Lesson Overview	Lesson Notes

MULTILEVEL OBJECTIVES

On-, Pre-, and Higher-level: Expand upon and review unit grammar and life skills

LANGUAGE FOCUS

Grammar: Modals *might*, *should*, and *could* (*He might get a raise. You should put on a sweater. Could you please mail this letter?*)

Vocabulary: Hotel worker vocabulary

For vocabulary support, see these **Oxford Picture Dictionary** topics: Prepositions, page 25; The Workplace, pages 182–183; Job Skills, page 176; Office Skills, page 177; Job Search, pages 168–169; Job Safety, page 197; Office Work, pages 188–189

READINESS CONNECTION

In this review, students work in teams to explore ways to use their skills at a job, organize tasks, and make a to-do list.

PACING

To extend this review: Have students complete **Workbook 2 page 36**, **Multilevel Activities 2 Unit 5 pages 63–66**, and **Multilevel Grammar Exercises 2 Unit 5**.

CORRELATIONS

CCRS: SL.1.A Participate in collaborative conversations with diverse partners in small and larger groups.

L.1.A Demonstrate command of conventions of standard English grammar and usage when writing or speaking.

R.1.A Ask and answer questions about key details in the text.

ELPS: 5. An ELL can conduct research and evaluate and communicate findings to answer questions or solve problems. 6. An ELL can analyze and critique the arguments of others orally and in writing.

Warm-up and Review
10–15 minutes (books closed)

1. Review the *Bring It to Life* assignment from Lesson 5.

2. Have students who did the activity share what they learned. Students who didn't do the activity can talk about classroom or school behaviors.

3. Discuss the students' findings. Ask: *Where else would these behaviors be important?*

Introduction and Presentation
10 minutes

1. Brainstorm the kinds of jobs that there are in a hotel and an office. Then brainstorm the kind of requests a boss would make to that employee. [secretary: *Could you make copies, please?* hotel desk clerk: *Could make a reservation, please?*]

2. State the objective: *Today we're going to review the language we've learned for talking about jobs.*

Guided Practice
10–15 minutes

A 1. Direct students to work in groups of three to four and look at the picture. Ask: *Where is this? Have you ever worked here?*

2. Set a time limit (five minutes) for groups to answer the questions. Circulate and monitor.

3. Have students from each group share the group's responses with the class. If you have a large class, you may not want all of the groups to report their responses. Instead, have groups share their responses with each other. Call "time" and tell all groups to work with a new group and to repeat their responses. Repeat this process as desired, making sure each group gets to share their responses at least once.

Communicative Practice
30–45 minutes

B 1. Put students in new groups of four and assign roles: manager, researcher, administrative assistant, and reporter. Read the instructions and sample request aloud. Check that students understand the task.

2. Set a time limit (five minutes) to complete the task.

MULTILEVEL STRATEGIES

Adapt B to the level of your students.

• **Pre-level** Provide these students with verb phrases that they can use in their requests: *take their bags; give me some toothpaste; make a reservation; hold the door; have that yellow hat,* etc.

• **Higher-level** Have these students help pre-level students write their requests.

C 1. Read the instructions and sample advice aloud. Check that students understand the task.

2. Set a time limit (five minutes) to complete the task.

3. Have volunteer reporters share their group's responses to B and C.

D 1. Have students work with a partner in their group. Tell them they will role-play the conversation. Set a time limit (five minutes). Have students take turns with each part of the conversation. Circulate and monitor.

2. Have pairs perform their conversations for their group.

3. Provide global feedback once the activity ends.

Answers	
1. Could	4. could
2. should	5. Could
3. might	6. might

E 1. Have students switch partners in their group. Read the instructions aloud. Read the sample conversation with a volunteer.

2. Set a time limit (five minutes) to complete the task.

3. Check answers as a class. Have students give reasons for their order.

F 1. Read the instructions aloud. Suggest that students list their tasks for the week before putting them in order.

2. Set a time limit (five minutes) to complete the task.

G 1. Read the instructions and questions aloud. Have groups discuss their to-do lists.

2. Have volunteers share their lists with the class. Discuss the tasks that are the most common.

3. Answer the questions in a class discussion.

PROBLEM SOLVING AT WORK
10–15 minutes

A 1. Ask: *What things at your job or in school make you nervous? Do you ask questions? What might keep a person from asking questions at their job?* Tell students they will read a story about a person who is having some problems at work. Direct students to read Jamal's story silently.

B 1. Elicit answers to question 1. Guide students to a class consensus on the answer.

2. As a class, brainstorm answers to questions 2 and 3. Ask students if they know someone who has this problem and has overcome it, or what they have done themselves to overcome the same problem.

To help students better understand Jamal's problem, show the illustration on pages 86–87 of *The Oxford Picture Dictionary* or use chalkboard drawings to depict a ticket collector at a movie theater. Describe and use the pictures to set the scene: *This is Jamal. He works at the movie theater as a ticket collector. He is a good employee, but he doesn't understand the manager. Let's read about Jamal's problem.*

Evaluation
20–25 minutes

To test students' understanding of the unit language and content, have them take the Unit 5 Test, available on the Teacher Resource Center.

6 On the Phone

Unit Overview

This unit explores phone bills, using phones, apologizing, and making excuses, and using the present continuous and verbs with indirect and direct objects.

KEY OBJECTIVES	
Lesson 1	Interpret a phone bill; identify different uses for phones
Lesson 2	Identify reasons for being absent from work or school; write an absence note
Lesson 3	Use the present continuous and simple present
Lesson 4	Take, interpret, and leave phone messages
Lesson 5	Identify community services; interpret data about volunteering
Teamwork & Language Review	Review unit language

UNIT FEATURES	
Academic Vocabulary	*contribute, volunteer*
Employability Skills	• Interpret information on a phone bill • Interpret a bar chart • Resolve childcare problems due to illness • Understand teamwork • Communicate information • Cooperate with others • Communicate verbally

Resources	**Class Audio** CD2, Tracks 17–34
	Workbook Unit 6, pages 37–43
	Teacher Resource Center
	    Multilevel Activities 2 Unit 6
	    Multilevel Grammar Exercises 2 Unit 6
	    Unit 6 Test
	Oxford Picture Dictionary The Telephone, Office Skills, A Bad Day at Work, Internet Research

Lesson Overview	Lesson Notes
MULTILEVEL OBJECTIVES	
On-level: Identify phone-bill and phone-call vocabulary **Pre-level:** Recognize phone-bill and phone-call vocabulary **Higher-level:** Talk and write about phone bills and phone calls	
LANGUAGE FOCUS	
Grammar: Simple present (*I usually make local calls.*); Present continuous (*She's calling her mother.*) **Vocabulary:** Phone bills, phones, and phone calls For vocabulary support, see this **Oxford Picture Dictionary** topic: The Telephone, pages 14–15	
READINESS CONNECTION	
In this lesson, students talk about the telephone and explore identifying and reading a phone bill.	
PACING	
To compress this lesson: Conduct 2A as a whole-class activity. **To extend this lesson:** Have students discuss features of phone bills or cell phones. (See end of lesson.) And/or have students complete **Workbook 2 page 37** and **Multilevel Activities 2 Unit 6 page 68**.	
CORRELATIONS	
CCRS: L.6.A Use words and phrases acquired through conversations, reading and being read to, and responding to texts, including using frequently occurring conjunctions to signal simple relationships (e.g., *because*). R.7.A Use the illustrations and details in a text to describe its key ideas (e.g., maps, charts, photographs, political cartoons, etc.). SL.1.A Participate in collaborative conversations with diverse partners in small and larger groups.	**ELPS:** 8. An ELL can determine the meaning of words and phrases in oral presentations and literary and informational text.

Warm-up and Review
10–15 minutes

Play "Telephone." Divide the class into groups of eight to ten. Whisper a sentence to one student in the first group and have that student whisper it to the next until the message has passed through all members of the group. Start another message on the other side of the room. Call on the final student in each group to tell the class what he/she heard. Tell students what your original sentences were. Use moderately long sentences with no new vocabulary. *I called my grandmother last Tuesday because it was her birthday. My brother always calls me on Wednesday evenings after dinner.*

Introduction
3 minutes

1. Tell students that the game you played in the warm-up is called "Telephone" and ask them about their phone habits: *Do you have a cell phone? Do you make international calls? Are there people you call every month/week/day?*

2. State the objective: *Today we're going to talk about the telephone, or phone, and learn how to read a phone bill.*

1 Learn about phone bills

Presentation
20–25 minutes

A 1. Ask: *Do you look at your phone bill? Do you understand all the parts of it?* Direct students to look at the phone bill in 1B. Ask: *How much is the bill?* [$86.60] *Is that expensive? What does the bill tell you about Walter?*

2. Read the words aloud. Ask students to circle the words they know.

B 🔊 **2-17** 1. Have students listen to the audio. Ask them to point to the correct section of the bill as they listen. Circulate and monitor.

2. Read the question aloud. Ask students to say where they can find the answers. Check comprehension by making *true/false* statements about the phone bill. *The bill is for two months of service.* [false] *Walter has 4GB of data.* [true] Have students hold up one finger for *true* and two for *false* in order to get a nonverbal response.

Answers
Charges listed are for previous balance, monthly charge, data, and total monthly.

MULTILEVEL STRATEGIES
After the group comprehension check in 1B, call on volunteers and tailor your questions to the level of your students. • **Pre-level** Ask *yes/no* questions. *Did he call his parents?* [yes] • **On-level** Ask information questions. *How many text messages did he send?* [1,652] • **Higher-level** Ask these students additional questions about what they heard. *How much did he pay last month?* [$78.75] *How does he feel about the phone bill?* [It's too expensive.]

C 🔊 **2-18** 1. Ask students to listen and repeat the words.

2. While students are repeating, circulate and listen for pronunciation difficulties. Provide choral practice as necessary.

TIP
Take some time to review the meaning of the words and terms on the bill: *previous balance, payment received, unlimited messaging, data charges, messaging,* and *voice usage.* Have students work in pairs or small groups and look up the words and terms in dictionaries or online. This can be assigned for homework as well. Have volunteers make a poster using the bill in the book as a guide and label each of the parts. Have them include definitions of each part. Display it in the classroom.

Guided Practice I
15–20 minutes

D 1. Read the information in the *Need help?* box aloud. Have students complete the sentences using the vocabulary. Set a time limit (two minutes).

2. Encourage students to take turns reading the completed sentences with a partner.

Answers	
1. previous charges	4. carrier
2. monthly charges	5. billing period
3. data allowance	6. total due

E Read the instructions aloud. Set a time limit (three minutes). Have students take turns asking and answering the questions with a partner. Circulate and listen for any pronunciation or vocabulary difficulties.

MULTILEVEL STRATEGIES
For 1E, pair same-level students together. • **Pre-level** Work with these students and help them ask and answer questions with you. Turn the questions into *yes/no* questions: *Do you use your phone for many voice calls? Do you mostly use your phone for data?* • **Higher-level** When these students finish, have them use the statements in 1D to make questions to ask and answer in pairs.

2 Talk about using phones

Guided Practice II
35–40 minutes

A 1. Direct students to look at the pictures. Ask: *What do these people all have in common?* [They are all using cell phones.] Introduce the topic: *Now let's look at some different ways to use a phone.*

2. Group students and assign roles: manager, researcher, administrative assistant, and reporter. Have students work with their groups to match the words and pictures.

3. Check comprehension of the exercise: *Who looks up the words in the picture dictionary?* [researcher] *Who writes the numbers in the book?* [administrative assistant] *Who tells the class your answers?* [reporter] *Who helps everyone and manages the group?* [manager]

4. Set a time limit (three minutes) and have students work together to complete the task. While students are working, copy the wordlist onto the board.

5. Call "time" and have the reporters from each group take turns calling out the numbers for the wordlist. Record students' answers on the board. If groups disagree, write each group's choice next to the word.

6. Draw students' attention to the illustrations. Prompt students to use vocabulary not labeled in the art. Ask: *What other items can you name? What is Nadine doing?* [charging the phone] *What is Tom doing?* [reading a text] *What is Carla doing?* [reading a map app]

Answers	
1–phone charger	5–make an emergency call
3–headset	
7–listen to voice mail	8–send a text message
2–call directory assistance	6–leave a message
	4–use an app

> **MULTILEVEL STRATEGIES**
>
> For 2A, use mixed-level groups.
> • **Pre-level** Assign these students the role of administrative assistant.
> • **Higher-level** Assign these students the role of manager.

B 1. Play the audio. Ask students to listen and check their answers to 2A.

2. Have students correct the wordlist on the board as needed and then write the correct numbers in their books.

3. Read the sample conversation with a volunteer. Tell the groups from 2A to split into pairs to practice using the new vocabulary to describe the pictures in 2A. Set a time limit (two minutes).

Communicative Practice and Application
10–15 minutes

C 1. Read the questions aloud. Model a conversation with a volunteer. Have the volunteer ask you the questions, and answer them with your own answers.

2. Have groups of three to four students discuss the questions. Circulate and monitor.

3. Have one student from each group share their group's responses with the class.

Evaluation
10–15 minutes

TEST YOURSELF

1. Make a three-column chart on the board with the headings *Phone charges, Phone equipment,* and *Types of communication.* Have students give you an example for each column.

2. Have students copy the chart into their notebooks.

3. Set a time limit (five to ten minutes). Have students fill out the chart with words from the lesson.

4. Call "time" and have students check their spelling in *The Oxford Picture Dictionary* or another dictionary.

> **MULTILEVEL STRATEGIES**
>
> Target the *Test Yourself* to the level of your students.
> • **Pre-level** Have these students work with their books open.
> • **Higher-level** Have these students complete the chart and then write at least one sentence for each column in the chart.

> **EXTENSION ACTIVITY**
> **Discuss Phone Bills**
>
> Discuss real phone bills. Bring in a real phone bill and compare it to the one in the book. Ask students to find the previous charges, the due date, and so on.
>
> Or discuss cell phone vocabulary. Have students take out their cell phones and write down words from the menus. Make a poster with the words and their meanings.

Lesson Overview	Lesson Notes
MULTILEVEL OBJECTIVES	
On-, Pre-, and Higher-level: Read and write about reasons for missing school or work	
LANGUAGE FOCUS	
Grammar: Simple past *(He called in sick.)* **Vocabulary:** *Call in sick, oversleep* For vocabulary support, see this **Oxford Picture Dictionary** topic: Office Skills, page 177	
STRATEGY FOCUS	
In a formal note, start with *Dear Mr., Mrs.,* or *Ms.* and the last name of the person you are writing to. Finish with *Sincerely,* or *Sincerely yours,* and your name.	
READINESS CONNECTION	
In this lesson, students identify reasons for being absent from work or school, and read, write, and talk about calling in sick and explaining why we are absent.	
PACING	
To compress this lesson: Skip 2B. **To extend this lesson:** Have students do a role-play. (See end of lesson.) And/or have students complete **Workbook 2 page 38** and **Multilevel Activities 2 Unit 6 page 69**.	
CORRELATIONS	
CCRS: SL.1.A Participate in collaborative conversations with diverse partners in small and larger groups. SL.2.A Confirm understanding of a text read aloud or information presented orally or through other media by asking and answering questions about key details and requesting clarification if something is not understood. W.2.A Write informative/explanatory texts in which they name a topic, supply some facts about the topic, and provide some sense of closure.	**ELPS:** 6. An ELL can analyze and critique the arguments of others orally and in writing. 9. An ELL can create clear and coherent level-appropriate speech and text.

Warm-up and Review
10–15 minutes (books closed)

Ask students what kinds of problems might cause them to miss work or school. Write their ideas on the board using this framework: *I miss work if _____. I might miss work if _____.*

Introduction
5 minutes

1. Tell students about a time you missed work. Explain how you reported your absence.

2. State the objective: *Today we're going to read and write about calling in sick and explaining why we are absent.*

1 Prepare to write

Presentation
20–25 minutes

 1. Direct students' attention to the pictures and read the captions aloud. Build students' schema by asking questions about the pictures. Ask: *Who are Jennifer and Joshua?* [Jennifer is Joshua's parent.] *What does Jennifer do?* [She calls the school. She types something on the computer.]

2. Have students match the captions with the pictures. Set a time limit (one to two minutes). Then review the correct answers as a class.

Answers
I called my son's school.–2
I wrote an absence note.–3
I was worried.–1

 2-20 1. Direct students to look at the story and the email. Ask what the email is for and to whom it is written. [It's an absence note written to Joshua's teacher.]

2. Read the *Writer's Note* aloud. Ask: *Why is the email formal?* [Because it's written to the school and not a friend or family member.]

3. Play the audio. Have students read along silently.

4. Check comprehension. Ask: *What happened to Joshua?* [He was sick.] *Who did Jennifer call?* [Joshua's school] *What did she write?* [an absence note]

Guided Practice I
10 minutes

 1. Ask students to work individually to mark the sentences *T* (true) or *F* (false). Set a time limit (three to five minutes). Then review the answers as a class.

Answers	
1. F	4. F
2. T	5. T
3. F	6. F

MULTILEVEL STRATEGIES

For 1C, seat same-level students together.

- **Pre-level** While the other students are completing 1C, have pre-level students look at the pictures in 1A and list the things they see. As you review the answers to 1C, write them on the board so that pre-level students can copy them into their books.

- **On- and Higher-level** Write additional questions on the board for these students. *Who did Jennifer call first? Who usually gets up first, Jennifer or Joshua? What will Jennifer do this weekend? When did Jennifer write the absence note?*

Guided Practice II
10–15 minutes

 2-21 Read the instructions and the questions aloud. Play the audio and have students complete the task individually. Don't check answers yet.

 Have pairs compare their answers. Play the audio again and check answers as a class.

Answers
1. b
2. b
3. a

2 Plan

Communicative Practice I
20–25 minutes

 1. Read the instructions and the questions aloud and draw students' attention to the graphic organizer. Draw the graphic organizer on the board. Tell students to listen to you talk about a time when you had to call in sick to work. Indicate or gesture to each section of the graphic organizer and ask students to say how to fill it in based on your story. Make sure students understand that the number of the question corresponds to the numbered section of the graphic organizer. Leave the graphic organizer on the board for students to refer to.

2. Have students complete the exercise individually. Set a time limit (ten minutes). Circulate and monitor.

MULTILEVEL STRATEGIES

Adapt 2A to the level of your students.

• **Pre-level** Group these students together and have them work together to fill out one graphic organizer.

• **Higher-level** Ask these students to include two or three more steps in their graphic organizer.

B Read the instructions aloud. Have students share their graphic organizers with a partner.

TIP

You can provide questions for students to ask each other to get more details: *What did you do after you ____? What did your boss/your child's teacher say? Were they upset? When did you write the email/talk with your employer/teacher?*

---

3 Write

Communicative Practice II and Application
15–20 minutes

A 1. Read the instructions aloud. Have students look at the paragraph templates as you read them aloud. For each blank, have a volunteer give a sample answer.

2. Set a time limit for writing (five minutes). Remind students to use their graphic organizers from 2A to write their descriptions and emails. Have students complete the template paragraphs with their own information.

B 1. Ask students to read their description and email to a partner. Call on volunteers to share one thing they liked about their partner's description and email, and also the ways that their own situation was the same or different than their partner's.

2. Have a class discussion about how students feel when they have to call in sick.

MULTILEVEL STRATEGIES

For 3A, target the writing to the level of your students.

• **Pre-level** Write a wordlist on the board for these students to use to complete their descriptions and emails. Then work with these students to write a group description and email, using their graphic organizer as a guide. Read through the template. At each blank, stop and elicit completions. Decide as a group what to write. Have these students copy the group description and email into their notebooks.

• **Higher-level** Ask these students to write a description and an email without using the template as a guide.

Evaluation
10 minutes

TEST YOURSELF

1. Read the instructions aloud. Assign a time limit (five minutes) and have students work individually.

2. Before collecting student work, invite two or three volunteers to share their sentences. Ask students to raise their hands if they wrote similar answers.

EXTENSION ACTIVITY

Role-play

Have students work in pairs to create a role-play calling in sick with good or bad excuses. Ask volunteers to perform their role-play for the class. As a class, students decide if the excuses are appropriate or not appropriate reasons to call in sick.

Lesson Overview

| Lesson Notes |

MULTILEVEL OBJECTIVES

On- and Higher-level: Ask and answer questions about activities in the simple present and present continuous

Pre-level: Answer questions about activities in the simple present and present continuous

LANGUAGE FOCUS

Grammar: Present continuous and simple present (*He works every day. He is working right now.*) (*I was driving to school.*)

Vocabulary: Everyday activities

For vocabulary support, see this **Oxford Picture Dictionary** topic: Office Skills, page 177

STRATEGY FOCUS

Learn spelling rules for *-ing* verbs: For words that end in *-e*, change the *-e* to *-ing*: *live → living*

READINESS CONNECTION

In this lesson, students use the simple present and present continuous to communicate verbally about daily activities and activities that are happening now.

PACING

To compress this lesson: Assign 2B and/or 3B as homework.

To extend this lesson: Have students describe pictures. (See end of lesson.)

And/or have students complete **Workbook 2 pages 39–40, Multilevel Activities 2 Unit 6 page 70,** and **Multilevel Grammar Exercises 2 Unit 6.**

CORRELATIONS

CCRS: L.1.A Demonstrate command of the conventions of standard English grammar and usage when writing or speaking. e. Use verbs to convey a sense of past, present, and future (e.g., *Yesterday I walked home; Today I walk home; Tomorrow I will walk home.*) j. Use frequently occurring prepositions (e.g., *during, beyond, toward*).

SL.2.A Confirm understanding of a text read aloud or information presented orally or through other media by asking and answering questions about key details and requesting clarification if something is not understood.

SL.4.A Describe people, places, things, and events with relevant details, expressing ideas and feelings clearly.

ELPS: 7. An ELL can adapt language choices to purpose, task, and audience when speaking and writing. 10. An ELL can demonstrate command of the conventions of standard English to communicate in level-appropriate speech and writing.

Warm-up and Review
10–15 minutes (books closed)

Write a series of times on the board: *6 a.m., 10 a.m., 1 p.m., 6 p.m., 9 p.m.,* and *11 p.m.* Ask students about what they are usually doing at that time of day on a weekend day and on a weekday. Write the verbs they use on the board in simple form.

Introduction
5–10 minutes

1. Use the verbs on the board to say sentences about your students. *At 9 a.m., Sunny drinks coffee.*

2. State the objective: *Today we're going to talk about our activities in the present continuous tense and the simple present tense.*

1 Contrast the present continuous and the simple present

Presentation I
20–25 minutes

 A 🔊 **2-22** Ask: *What is something you do every day? What is something you are doing now?* Write some of the students' responses on the board: *Jun cooks dinner every evening. Maria is learning English now.*

2. Play the audio and have students read along silently. Have them answer and then compare answers in pairs and check answers as a class. [Tania (left) is jogging. Stan (right) is eating dinner.]

B 1. Read the conversations in 1A aloud, slowly. Have students raise their hand every time they hear a verb.

2. Read the instructions aloud and have students underline the verbs that describe a regular activity and circle the ones that show something happening now. Check answers as a class.

C 1. Demonstrate how to read the grammar charts as complete sentences. Read through the charts sentence by sentence. Then read them again and have students repeat after you.

2. Read the information in the *Grammar Note* aloud. Use the conversations in 1A to illustrate points in the grammar charts. *I'm jogging right now. We always eat early on Fridays.*

3. Ask: *When do we use* be *and when do we use* do? [*be* – in affirmative and negative statements in the present continuous; *do* – in negative statements in the simple present]

Guided Practice I
10–15 minutes

D 1. Read the instructions aloud. Give students time (2 minutes) to silently review the charts again. Then have them work with a partner to make sentences.

2. Ask volunteers to write their sentences on the board. Have other students read the sentences aloud.

3. Assess students' comprehension of the charts in 1C. Write other daily activity verbs on the board (e.g., *drink water, read the newspaper, walk the dog, wash dishes*) and the time phrases *right now* and *every day*. Point to one of the verbs and one of the time phrases and call on volunteers to say a sentence using these.

MULTILEVEL STRATEGIES

For 1C, Seat pre-level students together.

• **Pre-level** While other students are completing 1C, ask pre-level students to copy the sentences from 1C.

• **On- and Higher-level** Have these students write three to five additional sentences using the present continuous.

---

2 Practice: information questions in the present

Presentation II and Guided Practice II
20–25 minutes

 A 🔊 **2-23** 1. Give students time to silently read the chart. Play the audio and have students repeat.

2. Read the *Spelling Note* aloud. Brainstorm other verbs that will follow the rule [*give, save, bake, smile*, etc.].

3. Write the terms *usually, at the moment, always, now, sometimes*, and *right now* on the board. Ask: *Which words are used in a question with the present continuous? Which are in a question with the simple present?*

 B 1. Read the instructions aloud. Have students complete the sentences individually.

2. Have students compare their answers with a partner. Check answers as a class.

Answers	
1. do they talk	4. are we studying
2. are you talking	5. is he living
3. does she get up	6. does she sleep

3 Practice: *Yes/no* questions in the present

Presentation III and Guided Practice III
15–20 minutes

A 🔊2-24 1. Give students time to silently read the chart. Play the audio and have students repeat.

2. Ask: *What verb is used is a simple present question?* [do] *What verb is used in a present continuous question?* [be] Ask students *yes/no* questions: *Are you learning English right now? Are you eating dinner right now? Do you study every night? Do you get up early every morning?*

B 1. Read the instructions aloud. Have students complete the sentences individually.

2. Have students compare their answers with a partner. Check answers as a class.

Answers
1 Is she talking / Yes, she is.
2 Is she exercising / No, she isn't.
3 Are they eating / Yes, they are.
4 Are they watching / No, they aren't.

MULTILEVEL STRATEGIES

Have same-level students work together to complete 3B.

• **Pre-level** Work with these students to determine the correct tense to use in each sentence.

• **Higher-level** Challenge these students to change the sentence to simple present if it is present continuous and vice versa.

4 Ask and answer questions in the present

Communicative Practice and Application
25–30 minutes

A 1. Read the instructions aloud. Model the sample conversation with a volunteer. Ask: *Which question is in the simple present?* [*What does he do?*] *Which is in the present continuous?* [*Is he using a saw right now?*]

2. Direct students' attention to the pictures. Ask students to identify the occupations and items in each picture. Write vocabulary on the board for students' reference.

3. Set a time limit (ten minutes). Have pairs complete the task. Circulate and monitor.

B 🔊2-25 1. Read the instructions aloud. Play the audio and have students fill in the chart individually.

2. Have students compare their charts with a partner. Play the audio again and check answers as a class.

TIP

Tell students that you will play the conversations twice. The first time they should listen to what the person usually does and fill in the chart. The second time they should listen to what the person is doing "now" and fill in the chart.

Answers	Barry	Cindy	Andrew	Lianne
now	is driving to work	is cooking dinner	is finishing homework	is watching TV
usually	starts work at 10 o'clock	has dinner at 6 o'clock	goes to bed at 10 p.m.	watches the news at six

C 1. Read the instructions aloud. Explain that students should use their charts from 4B to ask and answer questions with a partner. Circulate and monitor.

2. Check for the correct use of the tenses. Have pairs say one or two of their questions and answers to the class.

MULTILEVEL STRATEGIES

For 4C, work with pre-level students.

• **Pre-level** Work with these students and guide them in writing the questions: *In number 2, what tense would you use? What verb will you use to begin the question,* do *or* be? *What time phrase will you use?*

D 1. Read the instructions and the sample questions aloud. Have students work in groups of three to four to complete the task. Circulate and monitor.

2. Mix up the groups and have them take turns asking and answering the questions. Suggest that they take brief notes of their classmates' answers to use in the next task.

E Read the sample sentences aloud. Have students work individually to complete the task. Have students share their sentences with the class.

> **TIP**
>
> Write students' sentences on the board, but include one mistake in each one (e.g., *Tim is walking every day*.). Have students rewrite the sentences correctly in their notebooks, or have volunteers come to the board to correct the sentence (e.g., cross out *is walking* and write *walks*).

Evaluation
10 minutes

TEST YOURSELF

Ask students to write their four sentences about their friend's activities. Collect and correct their writing.

> **MULTILEVEL STRATEGIES**
>
> Target the *Test Yourself* to the level of your students.
>
> • **Pre-level** Have these students write only first-person sentences.
>
> • **Higher-level** Have these write two additional sentences about themselves and their partners.

> **EXTENSION ACTIVITY**
> **Describe Pictures**
> Bring in pictures of people doing common actions or use the pictures of daily routines or housework in *The Oxford Picture Dictionary*. Have students practice asking and answering present continuous questions based on the pictures. *What is he doing at now? He is picking up the children from school.*

Lesson Overview	Lesson Notes
MULTILEVEL OBJECTIVES	
On- and Higher-level: Leave and take messages **Pre-level:** Take messages	
LANGUAGE FOCUS	
Grammar: Simple present (*I don't feel well. She has a cold.*) **Vocabulary:** *Apology, call in sick, excuse, out sick* For vocabulary support, see this **Oxford Picture Dictionary** topic: The Telephone, pages 14–15	
STRATEGY FOCUS	
Practice apologizing and making an excuse.	
READINESS CONNECTION	
In this lesson, students communicate verbally in teams to explore how to take and leave a phone message that makes an excuse.	
PACING	
To compress this lesson: Skip 4B. **To extend this lesson:** Have students practice taking messages. (See end of lesson.) And/or have students complete **Workbook 2 page 41** and **Multilevel Activities 2 Unit 6 page 71**.	

CORRELATIONS	
CCRS: SL.1.A Participate in collaborative conversations with diverse partners in small and larger groups. SL.2.A Confirm understanding of a text read aloud or information presented orally or through other media by asking and answering questions about key details and requesting clarification if something is not understood. RF.2.A Demonstrate understanding of spoken words, syllables, and sounds (phonemes). RF.4.A Read with sufficient accuracy and fluency to support comprehension.	**ELPS:** 2. An ELL can participate in level-appropriate oral and written exchanges of information, ideas, and analyses, in various social and academic contexts, responding to peer, audience, or reader comments and questions. 9. An ELL can create clear and coherent level-appropriate speech and text.

Warm-up and Review
10–15 minutes (books closed)

Encourage students to think about their telephone habits. Ask: *Do you ever make phone calls in English? What was the last one? Did you ever leave a message in English?*

Introduction
5 minutes

1. Discuss the information you learned about your students.

2. State the objective: *Today we're going to learn how to leave and take messages in English.*

1 Listen to learn: leaving and taking messages

Presentation I and Guided Practice I
20–30 minutes

A Direct students to look at the phone message. Ask: *Did someone write this message at home or at work?* Read questions 1–3 aloud and give everyone time to write or say the answers. Review as a class.

Answers
1. Rita Gonzalez
2. Ms. Mendoza
3. out sick / has a bad cold

B 🔊 **2-26** 1. Tell students that they will listen to three messages. Have students put down their pencils before they listen. Ask them to listen for key words in each conversation that match the information in the message form, and then play the audio. Replay the audio and have them complete the messages.

2. Ask students to compare their answers with a partner. Circulate and monitor to ensure students understand the audio.

Answers
1. For: Mr. Jackson
From: Linda Gomez/Santoro Cleaning Agency
Message: They have a special promotion this week/are offering a 10% discount.
2. For: Mrs. Andrews
From: Matthew Novak/Lane's Hardware Store
Message: Her delivery arrived.
3. For: Mr. Green
From: Maria Costanza
Message: She has a cold and can't come to class.

C 🔊 **2-26** 1. Read the three different kinds of messages aloud. Play the audio and have students listen silently.

2. Play the audio again. Have students write their answers individually before comparing answers with a partner. Check answers as a class.

Answers
speak, there
give, leave
take, give

2 Practice your pronunciation

Pronunciation Extension
10–15 minutes

A 🔊 **2-27** Play the audio and have students listen to the two sentences. Illustrate the tongue position of the vowels in *live* and *leave*, or show students diagrams of these vowels.

B 🔊 **2-28** 1. Play the audio. Ask students to circle the words they hear.

2. Play the audio again and review answers as a class.

Answers
1. live
2. his
3. feel
4. we'll

TIP

For further practice, have students write the words from 2C in mixed up order in a numbered list but not show it to anyone. Pairs sit back to back and pronounce the first word on their list. The other student writes the word they hear. They continue saying a word and writing it down until each of them has said all the words on their lists. Then they check each other's lists to see if they wrote down the words in the correct order.

C 🔊 **2-29** Play the audio and have students listen and repeat the sentences. Then ask volunteers to pronounce them.

D Have students repeat the sentences after you. Then have them repeat to a partner. Monitor and provide feedback on pronunciation.

3 Practice using indirect objects

Presentation II and Guided Practice II
20–25 minutes

A 🔊 **2-30** 1. Direct students' attention to the photos. Ask them to say what they think is happening.

2. Read the questions aloud. Play the audio. Ask students to read along silently.

3. Ask volunteers to answer the questions.

Answer
She will give a message to Mr. Reed.

B

🔊 **2-31** Read the instructions aloud. Play the audio and have students circle the correct answers. Replay if necessary. Play the audio again, stopping after each sentence for students to check answers.

Answers
1. a
2. b
3. a
4. b

C

1. Introduce the new grammar in 3D. On the board write the words *direct* and *indirect*. Discuss their meanings. [*Direct* means that something goes from *A* to *B* in a straight line. *Indirect* means something goes from *A* to *B* but not in a straight line; there is a step in between.]

2. Read the instructions aloud. Give students time (one or two minutes) to look at the conversation and answer the questions. Have students compare their answers with a partner. Then check answers as a class.

Answer
1. I'll give him your message.
2. Direct object = message; indirect object = him

D

Check comprehension of the grammar in the chart. Write two or three more sentences on the board with direct and indirect objects. Have volunteers come to the board and label them as *DO* (direct object) or *IO* (indirect object).

E

1. Read the instructions aloud and model the sample conversation with a volunteer. Allow time for students to write their questions first individually, if necessary.

2. Have students work in pairs, taking turns asking and answering each other's questions. Circulate and monitor.

MULTILEVEL STRATEGIES
Adapt 3E to the level of your students.
• **Pre-level** Provide frames for students to write their questions and answers. Leave the objects blank for students to practice the position. *Can you send _____ to _____? / Yes, I'll send _____ an _____.*
• **Higher-level** Challenge these students to refuse a request and give a reason.

4 Make conversation: leaving a message and making an excuse

Communicative Practice I
15–20 minutes

A

1. Read the instructions and the phrases in the *Need help?* box aloud.

2. Have students work in pairs to create a conversation and take turns performing parts. Tell them to also use the phrases in the *Need help?* box.

B

1. Set a time limit (ten minutes). Ask pairs to share their conversation with another pair and write the excuse that the other pair used.

2. Have pairs present their conversation to the class.

TIP
You can challenge students to use their imaginations and use silly or far-fetched excuses in their conversations.

AT WORK

Apologizing and making an excuse

Presentation III and Communicative Practice II
20–30 minutes

A

🔊 **2-32** 1. Direct students to look at the photos. Ask them to describe what is happening.

2. Play the audio and have students identify the apologies and the excuses. Ask how they are different. Lead a class discussion about different situations in which different kinds of apologies are needed and when the response might be more angry or more calm.

Answer
Sorry I'm late. I apologize for mixing up the orders.
My flight was delayed. It was a mistake.

B 1. Read the instructions aloud. Have students practice the conversations with a partner. Circulate and help as needed.

2. Have pairs share their conversations with the class.

MULTILEVEL STRATEGIES

Adapt *At Work* B to the level of your students.

• **Pre-level** Instead of having these students continue the conversations, provide them with two new part *As* and have them practice all four conversations. For the first conversation — *A: I'm sorry I'm late for class. My alarm didn't go off.* For the second conversation — *A: I apologize for breaking the plates. I was carrying too many.*

• **Higher-level** Direct these students to write a new conversation for a different situation.

C Read the instructions aloud. Have pairs discuss the question. Circulate and monitor.

Evaluation
10–15 minutes

TEST YOURSELF

Have pairs perform the role-play. Circulate and assess students' progress. Take note of any mistakes you hear in intonation, pronunciation, grammar, or vocabulary. When all students have finished the activity, as a class, review the kinds of mistakes you heard (without naming any students who made them).

EXTENSION ACTIVITY

Practice Messages

Have students practice leaving and taking messages.

1. As a class, brainstorm information that students might have to leave on a voicemail system (name, number, reason for calling, time available).

2. Have them write and practice leaving a phone message. Remind them that they need to speak slowly.

3. If you have tape recorders or recording computers available, have students leave their messages, then exchange machines (or tapes), and listen to each other's messages. Listeners can write down the information they hear.

Lesson Overview	Lesson Notes
MULTILEVEL OBJECTIVES	
On- and Higher-level: Read about and discuss community services **Pre-level:** Read about community services	
LANGUAGE FOCUS	
Grammar: Simple present (*A volunteer works without pay.*) **Vocabulary:** *Counselor, senior, volunteer* For vocabulary support, see this **Oxford Picture Dictionary** topic: Internet Research, pages 212–213	
STRATEGY FOCUS	
Understand that links that end in *.com* are private organizations that usually charge money for their services. Links that end in *.org* are usually non-profit organizations.	
READINESS CONNECTION	
In this lesson, students communicate information about different community services and volunteer opportunities.	
PACING	
To compress this lesson: Assign 1F and/or 1G for homework. **To extend this lesson:** Have students do a role-play. (See end of lesson.) And/or have students complete **Workbook 2 page 42** and **Multilevel Activities 2 Unit 6 page 72**.	

CORRELATIONS	
CCRS: L.4.A Determine or clarify the meaning of unknown and multiple-meaning words and phrases, choosing flexibly from an array of strategies. R.1.A Ask and answer questions about key details in the text. R.4.A Ask and answer questions to help determine or clarify the meaning of words and phrases in a text. R.7.A Use the illustrations and details in a text to describe its key ideas (e.g., maps, charts, photographs, political cartoons, etc.).	**ELPS:** 1. An ELL can construct meaning from oral presentations and literary and informational text through level-appropriate listening, reading, and viewing. 3. An ELL can speak and write about level-appropriate complex literary and informational texts and topics.

Warm-up and Review
10–15 minutes (books closed)

Bring in pictures of community places or have students look at the pictures of city streets in *The Oxford Picture Dictionary*. Ask students which places they go and how often, which places they never go, and which places they want to go.

Introduction
3–5 minutes

1. Refer to the places from the warm-up and mention services that are provided in these places. You can use the computer in the library.

2. State the objective: *Today we're going to discuss where to go for services in our community.*

1 Build reading strategies

Presentation
10–20 minutes

A Read the instructions aloud. Have students answer the questions individually and then share their answers with the class.

B 1. Read the instructions aloud. Tell students that the root is the main part of the word, and in the word *counselor*, *counsel* is the root word and *-or* is the suffix. Explain that the suffix of a word has a meaning and can give a clue to the meaning of an unfamiliar word. In this case, *-or* means *someone who*.

2. As a class, brainstorm other job names that end in *-or* [actor, professor, advisor, author].

Guided Practice: Pre-reading
5–10 minutes

C 1. Read the instructions aloud. Remind students that to preview a text means to read it quickly and not worry about understanding every word. When we preview a text, we are looking for the general idea.

2. Set a time limit (one minute) for students to preview the article. Then discuss the question as a class.

3. Direct students to look at the footnotes. Ask them to look for where the words appear in the text.

Answers
Food bank and literacy volunteer groups need help; the others offer help.

Guided Practice: While Reading
15–20 minutes

D Read the instructions and the information in the *Reader's Note* aloud. Have students read the web page silently. Discuss the question as a class.

Answers
Counseling service, Job advice center, Senior center

Guided Practice: Rereading
15–20 minutes

E 1. Provide an opportunity for students to extract evidence from the web page. Have students reread the web page and write a one-sentence description of each place.

2. Play the audio again and have students read along silently. Discuss the question as a class. Ask additional questions: *Which places do you think are the most important for this neighborhood? What tasks do you think volunteers do at each place? Are you interested in volunteering at any of these places?* If students do not feel comfortable discussing which organizations they are interested in, you can ask them which organizations they think would benefit their neighborhood.

TIP

Have students go online to find out about these kinds of service in their area. Decide which device(s) students might use and elicit search terms (e.g., *food bank* + your city).

Guided Practice: Post-reading
15 minutes

F 1. Have students work individually to choose the correct answers and identify in the reading where they found the answer. Check answers as a class.

2. Check comprehension further. Ask: *Who is usually a caregiver?* [an adult] *Which places use fewer volunteers? Why?* [counseling service and job advice center; The people there have special training/education.] *What does* seek *mean?* [to look for]

Answers
1. a
2. c
3. c
4. b

MULTILEVEL STRATEGIES

For 1F, work with pre-level students.

• **Pre-level** Ask these students *yes/no* and short-answer information questions about the reading while other students are completing 1F.

• **Higher-level** Have these students take turns asking and answering comprehension questions about the reading.

1. Have students work individually to complete the sentences.

2. Have students work in pairs to read each other their sentences before checking answers as a class.

Answers
1. senior
2. contribute
3. volunteer
4. offer

2 Read a bar chart about volunteering

Communicative Practice
15–20 minutes

A

1. Direct students to look at the chart. Ask: *What do the numbers down the left side show?* [the percent of population that volunteers] *What do the numbers across the bottom show?* [age ranges]

2. Read the questions aloud. Have pairs discuss the chart. Circulate and help as needed.

3. Call on pairs to say their answers for the class.

Answers
1. red = men, blue = women
2. different age groups
3. women volunteer more often than men
4. seniors volunteer more than other age groups

B

1. Read the questions aloud. Allow students time to think of their own answers and make notes.

2. Set a time limit (ten minutes). Have students work in pairs to discuss the questions. Circulate and help as needed.

3. Have pairs share their responses with another pair. Have volunteers share their partner's answers with the class.

Application
5–10 minutes

BRING IT TO LIFE

1. If your city has a website, it can be an excellent source of the information listed. If your class has access to computers, assign a different community service to each group of students and have them research the information on the Internet. Have one group or pair of students be the recorders, who can type all the information on one sheet of paper to distribute to the class.

2. If students are conducting the research on their own, provide them with references such as phone directories, community brochures, URLs, and web page printouts.

EXTENSION ACTIVITY

Community Services Role-play

Have students learn about a service in your community.

1. Bring in brochures from community-service centers.

2. Divide the class into groups and give one brochure to each group.

3. Have each group report to the class about some of the services offered at the place in its brochure, or have the group make a poster advertising the place that includes the name, address, and one of the available services.

4. Have students write and perform a role-play of a phone call to one of the services.

Lesson Overview	Lesson Notes
MULTILEVEL OBJECTIVES	
On-, Pre-, and Higher-level: Expand upon and review unit grammar and life skills	
LANGUAGE FOCUS	
Grammar: Present continuous (*What is Sam doing? Who is calling in sick?*) **Vocabulary:** *Get a taxi, order take-out food, play games, read email, send texts, take photos/videos, use a GPS app* For vocabulary support, see this **Oxford Picture Dictionary** topic: A Bad Day at Work, pages 198–199	
READINESS CONNECTION	
In this review, students work in teams to explore ways to deal with calling in sick to work and all the ways to use a phone.	
PACING	
To extend this review: Have students complete **Workbook 2 page 43**, **Multilevel Activities 2 Unit 6 pages 73–76**, and **Multilevel Grammar Exercises 2 Unit 6**.	

CORRELATIONS	
CCRS: R.1.A Ask and answer questions about key details in the text. R.7.A Use the illustrations and details in a text to describe its key ideas (e.g., maps, charts, photographs, political cartoons, etc.). SL.1.A Participate in collaborative conversations with diverse partners in small and larger groups. W.2.A Write informative/explanatory texts in which they name a topic, supply some facts about the topic, and provide some sense of closure.	**ELPS:** 5. An ELL can conduct research and evaluate and communicate findings to answer questions or solve problems. 6. An ELL can analyze and critique the arguments of others orally and in writing.

Warm-up and Review
10–15 minutes (books closed)

1. Review the *Bring It to Life* assignment from Lesson 5. Have students who did the exercise share what they learned. Have a telephone directory or other resource(s) available for students who didn't do the exercise.

2. If students worked individually, have them share their results. If students worked in groups, ask reporters to share the compiled information. Discuss the results.

Introduction and Presentation
5 minutes

1. Write two sentences on the board: *He works every day. He is working now.* Elicit the verbs and their tenses. Elicit the negative form of each sentence. Ask if students recall the two parts that make up the present continuous (*is/are* and the *-ing* form of the verb).

2. State the objective: *Today we're going to review the present continuous and taking and leaving phone messages.*

Guided Practice

15–20 minutes

A 1. Direct students to work in groups of three to four and look at the picture. Read the questions aloud.

2. Set a time limit (five minutes) for groups to answer the questions. Circulate and monitor.

3. Have volunteers from each group share the group's responses with the class. If you have a large class, you may not want all of the groups to report their responses. Instead, have groups share their responses with each other. Call "time" and tell all groups to work with a new group and to repeat their responses. Repeat this process as desired, making sure each group gets to share their responses at least once.

Communicative Practice

30–45 minutes

B 1. Group students as needed and assign roles: manager, researcher, administrative assistant, and reporter. Read the instructions aloud.

2. Set a time limit (five minutes) to complete the task.

C Have teams ask each other their questions. Circulate and help as needed.

D 1. Read the instructions aloud. Tell students they will write a new conversation in their group.

2. Ask students to read the model conversation in their groups and then extend it and/or write a new conversation. Set a time limit (five to ten minutes).

3. Have groups perform their new conversations for another group.

MULTILEVEL STRATEGIES

Adapt D to the level of your students.

• **Pre- and On-level** Pair these students. Write a conversation on the board with blanks for students to fill in.

A: Hello. This is _____. Is this _____.

B: Hi, Jack. Yes, it is.

A: Can I _____ for Sam?

B: Of course. _____ the message?

A: I'm _____ today. I can't _____.

B: Oh, no! I'm _____.

A: Tell Sam I _____.

B: Sure. I'll _____ him _____.

• **Higher-level** Have these students include additional lines in their conversation.

E 1. Read the sample sentence stem aloud. Call on volunteers to come to the board one by one and write a sentence that talks about Sam's bad day. Remind students about how to write a good paragraph. Before they write their sentence, ask: *Does this sentence follow the sentence before it, or is it about something very different? Is there a sequence word you can use?*

2. As a class, discuss how the paragraph can be improved and what is good about the paragraph.

F 1. Tell students to work in new teams of three to four. Read the instructions aloud.

2. Set a time limit (five minutes) to complete the task. Circulate and monitor.

3. Have groups share their responses with the class.

G 1. Read the instructions aloud. Set a time limit (five minutes) and have students complete the task individually.

2. Have students share their responses with their team from F.

3. If time allows, have volunteers share their responses with the class.

PROBLEM SOLVING AT WORK

10–15 minutes

A 2-34 1. Ask: *Do you have experience with trying to get childcare, or know someone who does? Is it difficult?* Tell students they will read a story about a woman who has a problem with childcare. Direct students to read Janet's story silently.

2. Play the audio and have students read along silently again.

B 1. Elicit answers to question 1. Guide students to a class consensus on the answer.

2. As a class, brainstorm answers to question 2. Ask students if they know someone who has this problem and has overcome it, or what they have done themselves to overcome the same problem.

Evaluation

20–25 minutes

To test students' understanding of the unit language and content, have them take the Unit 6 Test, available on the Teacher Resource Center.

Unit Overview

This unit explores food containers, food measurements, and offering and asking for help.

KEY OBJECTIVES	
Lesson 1	Identify product containers; interpret weights and measurements
Lesson 2	Identify and compare product price information
Lesson 3	Use count and noncount nouns to describe quantities of food
Lesson 4	Ask for and give the location of merchandise
Lesson 5	Interpret nutritional information; interpret food labels
Teamwork & Language Review	Review unit language

UNIT FEATURES	
Academic Vocabulary	*conversion, equivalent*
Employability Skills	• Interpret product price information • Compare and contrast weights and measurements • Examine the relationship between food and good health • Analyze values on nutrition labels • Find solutions to an unhealthy diet • Work with others • Understand teamwork • Communicate information • Communicate verbally • Use math to solve problems and communicate

Resources	**Class Audio** CD2, Tracks 35–49
	Workbook Unit 7, pages 44–50
	Teacher Resource Center
	    Multilevel Activities 2 Unit 7
	    Multilevel Grammar Exercises 2 Unit 7
	    Unit 7 Test
	Oxford Picture Dictionary Back from the Market, A Grocery Store, Containers and Packaging, Weights and Measurements

Lesson Overview	Lesson Notes
MULTILEVEL OBJECTIVES	
On-level: Identify containers and quantities **Pre-level:** Recognize containers and quantities **Higher-level:** Talk and write about containers and quantities	
LANGUAGE FOCUS	
Grammar: *There are* (*There are 16 ounces in one pound.*) **Vocabulary:** Container words; *weights, measurements, equivalents* For vocabulary support, see these **Oxford Picture Dictionary** topics: Containers and Packaging, page 74; Weights and Measurements, page 75	
READINESS CONNECTION	
In this lesson, students communicate information about food containers and measurements and interpret product price information.	
PACING	
To compress this lesson: Conduct 2A as a whole-class activity. **To extend this lesson:** Have students talk about food containers. (See end of lesson.) And/or have students complete **Workbook 2 page 44** and **Multilevel Activities 2 Unit 7 page 78**.	

CORRELATIONS	
CCRS: L.6.A Use words and phrases acquired through conversations, reading and being read to, and responding to texts, including using frequently occurring conjunctions to signal simple relationships (e.g., *because*). R.7.A Use the illustrations and details in a text to describe its key ideas (e.g., maps, charts, photographs, political cartoons, etc.). SL.1.A Participate in collaborative conversations with diverse partners in small and larger groups.	**ELPS:** 8. An ELL can determine the meaning of words and phrases in oral presentations and literary and informational text.

Warm-up and Review
10–15 minutes (books closed)

Bring in packaged food items: a small and a large box of cereal, a small bottle of iced tea and a liter bottle of the same drink, and so on. Create a list with a price for each item and keep it to yourself. Set the items at the front of the room and have students guess the prices. Reveal the true prices and congratulate the students who made the closest guesses.

Introduction
3 minutes

1. Review the real prices from the warm-up, using various container names and measurements. *A small bottle of iced tea is $1.99. A liter of the same drink is $2.99.*

2. Show the students the packages from the items you brought in and say: *Each one of these is a container.* State the objective: *Today we're going to explore the names of containers and measurements.*

1 Learn container words

Presentation
20–25 minutes

A 1. Direct students' attention to the pictures. Build students' schema by asking questions about the pictures. Ask: *Do you buy any of these foods?*

2. Read the words aloud. Ask students to circle the words they use and/or know.

B **◆)) 2-35** 1. Play the audio. Ask students to point to the items as they listen. Circulate and monitor.

2. Check comprehension by making *true/false* statements about the prices. *The peanut butter is $1.46.* [false] *The bananas are $1.59.* [true] Have students hold up one finger for *true* and two for *false* in order to get a nonverbal response.

Answers
loaf, bunch

MULTILEVEL STRATEGIES

After the group comprehension check in 1B, call on volunteers and tailor your questions to the level of your students.

• **Pre-level** Ask *or* questions. *Is it a bottle of oil or a box of oil?* [a bottle]

• **On-level** Ask information questions. *How much is the bottle of oil?* [$6.09] *What can I buy for $5.00?*

• **Higher-level** Ask these students to compare the prices of the items to the prices where they shop. *How much does a box of spaghetti cost where you shop?*

C **◆)) 2-36** 1. Ask students to listen and repeat the words.

2. While students are repeating, circulate and listen for pronunciation difficulties. Provide choral practice as necessary.

TIP

Take some time to talk about how to say prices. In the audio, students hear the pattern *X dollar(s) and X cents.* Tell students that many times at a store, they will not hear the words *dollar(s)* or *cents,* but only the numbers, such as *two fifty-nine* rather than *two dollars and fifty-nine cents.* Explain that either way is correct. If time allows, have students practice saying the prices in 1A both ways.

Guided Practice I
15–20 minutes

D 1. Have students complete the sentences using the new vocabulary. Set a time limit (two to three minutes).

2. Have students take turns reading the completed sentences with a partner.

Answers	
1. carton	6. bunch
2. bottle	7. can
3. jar	8. box
4. bag	9. package
5. loaf	10. six-pack

E Read the instructions aloud. Set a time limit (three minutes). Have students take turns asking and answering the questions with a partner. Circulate and listen for any pronunciation or vocabulary difficulties.

MULTILEVEL STRATEGIES

For 1E, pair same-level students together.

• **Pre-level** Work with these students and help them ask and answer questions with you. Turn the questions into *yes/no* questions: *Do you buy boxes of spaghetti? Do you pay more than $1.49 for it at your store?*

• **Higher-level** When these students finish, have them use the words in 1D and make questions to ask and answer in pairs.

2 Talk about weights and measurements

Guided Practice II
35–40 minutes

A 1. Ask: *Who buys a lot of rice? How much do you buy?* Introduce the new topic: *Now let's look at the weights and measurements of the food we buy.*

2. Group students and assign roles: manager, researcher, administrative assistant, and reporter. Explain that students work with their groups to match the words and pictures.

3. Check comprehension of the exercise. Ask: *Who looks up the words in the picture dictionary?* [researcher] *Who writes the numbers in the book?* [administrative assistant] *Who tells the class your answers?* [reporter] *Who helps everyone and manages the group?* [manager]

4. Set a time limit (two minutes) and have students work together to complete the task. While students are working, copy the wordlist onto the board.

5. Call "time" and have the reporters from each group take turns calling out the numbers for the wordlist. Record students' answers on the board. If groups disagree, write each group's choice next to the word.

6. Draw students' attention to the illustrations. Prompt students to use vocabulary not labeled in the art. Ask: *What other items can you name?* [countertop, handle, bag (of flour), plastic bottle, etc.] *What kind of oil is in the picture?* [canola] *How many ounces of sugar are in the bag?* [80]

MULTILEVEL STRATEGIES

For 2A, use mixed-level groups.

• **Pre-level** Assign these students the role of administrative assistant.

• **Higher-level** Assign these students the role of manager.

Answers

2–one cup of flour	7–one tablespoon of sugar
6–one gallon of water	
4–one pint of milk	5–one teaspoon of salt
3–one quart of milk	8–twelve ounces of oil
	1–two pounds of flour

B 1. Play the audio. Ask students to listen and check their answers.

2. Have students correct the wordlist on the board and then write the correct numbers in their books.

3. Have the groups from 2A split into pairs to practice the words. Set a time limit (two minutes).

C 1. Ask: *What does* equivalent *mean?* [the same] Ask students to work individually to complete the sentences. Have volunteers write the answers on the board.

Answers

1. ounces
2. pints
3. gallon
4. teaspoons
5. ounces

Communicative Practice and Application
10–15 minutes

D 1. Read the questions aloud. Have a volunteer ask you a question, and answer with your own information.

2. Set a time limit (five minutes). Have students work in groups of three to four to discuss the questions. Circulate and monitor.

3. Have one student from each group share their group's responses with the class.

Evaluation
10–15 minutes

TEST YOURSELF

1. Make a four-column chart on the board with the headings on page 89. Have students give you an example for each column.

2. Have students copy the chart into their notebooks.

3. Set a time limit (five to ten minutes). Have students fill out the chart with words from the lesson.

4. Call "time" and have students check their spelling in *The Oxford Picture Dictionary* or another dictionary.

MULTILEVEL STRATEGIES

Target the *Test Yourself* to the level of your students.

• **Pre-level** Have these students work with their books open.

• **Higher-level** Have these students write sentences about items in their kitchens. *There are two gallons of milk in my refrigerator.*

EXTENSION ACTIVITY

Talk about Containers

Put a list of foods on the board and ask students to name the containers in which they come: *mayonnaise, jam, potatoes, nuts,* and so on. Have them ask and answer questions with a partner: *Do you have _____ (a jar of jam) in your _____ (kitchen cabinet/refrigerator)?*

Lesson Overview	Lesson Notes
MULTILEVEL OBJECTIVES	
On-, Pre-, and Higher-level: Name and write about ways to save money, compare prices, and identify better buys	
LANGUAGE FOCUS	
Grammar: Comparatives (*Half a gallon of milk is cheaper than a whole gallon.*) **Vocabulary:** *Coupon, flyer, unit price, store brand* For vocabulary support, see these **Oxford Picture Dictionary** topics: Weights and Measurements, page 75; Back from the Market, pages 66–67	
STRATEGY FOCUS	
Use a topic sentence at the beginning of a paragraph to introduce the main topic.	
READINESS CONNECTION	
In this lesson, students interpret product price information and communicate ways to save money at a supermarket.	
PACING	
To compress this lesson: Have students do 2A with a partner and skip 2B. Shorten the warm-up by using one store flyer and leading a whole-class discussion. **To extend this lesson:** Have students complete a comparison shopping activity. (See end of lesson.) And/or have students complete **Workbook 2 page 45** and **Multilevel Activities 2 Unit 7 page 79**.	

CORRELATIONS	
CCRS: SL.2.A Confirm understanding of a text read aloud or information presented orally or through other media by asking and answering questions about key details and requesting clarification if something is not understood. SL.6.A Speak audibly and express thoughts, feelings, and ideas clearly. Produce complete sentences when appropriate to task and situation. R.1.A Ask and answer questions about key details in the text. W.2.A Write informative/explanatory texts in which they name a topic, supply some facts about the topic, and provide some sense of closure.	**ELPS:** 6. An ELL can analyze and critique the arguments of others orally and in writing. 9. An ELL can create clear and coherent level-appropriate speech and text.

Warm-up and Review
10–15 minutes (books closed)

Bring in different grocery-store flyers. Give one to each group. Have them ask and answer these questions: *What is the store name? Do you shop there? Do you eat the kinds of food they sell? Are the products expensive or cheap there?* Ask volunteers from each group to share what they learned.

Introduction
5 minutes

1. Hold up two flyers from different stores, as used in the warm-up, and tell students: *When you look at prices for the same item at two or more stores, that's comparison shopping.*

2. State the objective: *Today we're going to read and write about comparison shopping and how we can use it to save money.*

1 Prepare to write

Presentation
20–25 minutes

A 1. Direct students to look at the pictures in 1B. Give them one minute to think of answers to the questions. Review the answers as a class.

2. Have students work in pairs. Give them time (one or two minutes) to discuss their responses to the questions.

3. Ask questions so students understand what the unit-price label is: *Does the tuna cost $0.28? What costs $0.28? How many ounces are in the can? What is the total price for the tuna?* Discuss answers as a class.

B 🔊 **2-38** Direct students to look at the pictures as they listen to the blog post. Tell them to point to the pictures as they are named in the audio. Play the audio. Circulate and monitor.

C 🔊 **2-38** 1. Play the audio again. Have students read along silently.

2. Read the *Writer's Note* aloud. Ask: *Why does the topic sentence usually come first?* [so the reader knows what they will be reading about]

3. Check comprehension. Ask: *What is a brand? What are some examples of a name brand? What is a store brand?*

MULTILEVEL STRATEGIES

After the group comprehension check in 1C, call on volunteers and tailor your questions to the level of your students.

• **Pre-level** Ask *or* questions. *Does Mrs. Kim have four or five children?*

• **On-level** Ask information questions. *Why does Mrs. Kim often buy store brands?*

• **Higher-level** Ask these students to expand on the reading. *What makes it difficult to comparison shop?*

Guided Practice I
5–10 minutes

D 1. Ask students to work individually to mark the sentences *T* (true) or *F* (false). Set a time limit (three to five minutes). Review the answers as a class.

Answers
1. F
2. T
3. T
4. F
5. T

Guided Practice II
10–15 minutes

E 🔊 **2-39** Read the instructions and the sentences aloud. Play the audio and have students complete the task individually. Don't check answers yet, but check comprehension of the vocabulary. Ask: *Are there any special offers at your supermarket now? What is a typical special offer? Do you have a rewards card? To what store? What does it do?*

Answers
Checks beside "Get the special offers," "Buy larger quantities," and "Use coupons."

F 🔊 **2-39** 1. Read the instructions and the phrases aloud. Play the audio again and have students complete the task individually.

2. Have pairs compare their answers for 1E and 1F. Play the audio again and check answers for 1E and 1F as a class.

Answers
two jars of jam: $5
one container of yogurt: $1.49
ten pounds of rice: $12

2 Plan

Communicative Practice I
10–15 minutes

A Read the instructions aloud and draw students' attention to the ideas on the right. Have students complete the exercise individually. Set a time limit (three minutes). Circulate and monitor.

MULTILEVEL STRATEGIES

Adapt 2A to the level of your students.

• **Pre-level** Group these students together and have them work together to list money-saving ideas.

• **Higher-level** Ask these students to include some examples of coupons or special offers that they have seen lately.

B Read the instructions aloud. Have students share their lists with a partner

> **TIP**
>
> You can provide questions for students to ask each other to guide their conversation: *Do you _____ (look at supermarket flyers, make a shopping list, etc.)? Where do you usually shop? How often do you shop? Is it difficult to shop when you are hungry?*

3 Write

Communicative Practice II and Application
15–20 minutes

A 1. Read the instructions aloud. Have students look at the template as you read it aloud. For each blank, have a volunteer give a sample answer.

2. Set a time limit for writing (five minutes). Remind students to use their lists from 2A and 2B to write their blog posts. Have students complete the template with their own information.

B 1. Ask students to read their blog post to a partner. Call on volunteers to share one thing they liked about their partner's blog post, and also what was the same or different than their own list.

2. Lead a class discussion about what students think is the most important way to save money.

> **MULTILEVEL STRATEGIES**
>
> In 3A, target the writing to the level of your students.
>
> • **Pre-level** Write a wordlist on the board for these students to use to complete their blog posts. Then work with these students to write a group blog post, using their lists as a guide. Read through the template. At each blank, stop and elicit completions. Decide as a group what to write. Have these students copy the blog post into their notebooks.
>
> • **Higher-level** Ask these students to write a blog post without using the template as a guide.

Evaluation
10 minutes

TEST YOURSELF

1. Read the instructions aloud. Assign a time limit (five minutes) and have students work individually.

2. Before collecting student work, invite two or three volunteers to share their sentences with the class. Ask students to raise their hands if they wrote similar answers.

> **EXTENSION ACTIVITY**
>
> **Comparison Shop**
>
> Use the store flyers from the warm-up to have students make "better buy" decisions. Give two flyers to each group and ask students to make a decision about where to shop and to explain why to the class.

LESSON 3 GRAMMAR

Lesson Overview	Lesson Notes

MULTILEVEL OBJECTIVES

Pre-, On- and Higher-level: Use count and noncount nouns to talk about food

LANGUAGE FOCUS

Grammar: Count and noncount nouns (*How many potatoes do we need? How much cheese?*)

Vocabulary: Count and noncount food items

For vocabulary support, see this **Oxford Picture Dictionary** topic: Containers and Packaging, page 74

READINESS CONNECTION

In this lesson, students use count and noncount nouns to communicate verbally about food inventory.

PACING

To compress this lesson: Assign 2B as homework and/ or skip 3B.

To extend this lesson: Have students practice *How much* and *How many*. (See end of lesson.)

And/or have students complete **Workbook 2 pages 46–47, Multilevel Activities 2 Unit 7 page 80**, and **Multilevel Grammar Exercises 2 Unit 7.**

CORRELATIONS

CCRS: L.1.A Demonstrate command of the conventions of standard English grammar and usage when writing or speaking. i. Use determiners (e.g., articles, demonstratives).

SL.1.A Participate in collaborative conversations with diverse partners in small and larger groups.

SL.2.A Confirm understanding of a text read aloud or information presented orally or through other media by asking and answering questions about key details and requesting clarification if something is not understood.

ELPS: 7. An ELL can adapt language choices to purpose, task, and audience when speaking and writing. 10. An ELL can demonstrate command of the conventions of standard English to communicate in level-appropriate speech and writing.

Warm-up and Review
10–15 minutes (books closed)

Tell students that you are going to write a letter of the alphabet on the board. They need to write food words that begin with that letter. Assign a time limit (one minute). Call "time" and elicit answers. Have other students add any ideas that are not already on the board. Leave this up. Suggested letters: *L, S, C,* and *P.*

Introduction
5 minutes

1. Write sentences using some of the words on the board, contrasting count with noncount nouns. *I'd like some juice. I'd like a strawberry. I'd like some cheese. I'd like one muffin.* Check for students' understanding of *count* and *noncount* as needed.

2. State the objective: *Today we're going to explore how to use count and noncount nouns when we talk about food.*

1 Explore count and noncount nouns

Presentation I
20–25 minutes

  A 🔊 2-40 1. Direct students to look at the recipe card. Ask: *What is a casserole?* Review the abbreviations on the card: *tbsp., tsp¹., oz.,* and *c.*

2. Ask students to find the answers to questions 1, 2, and 3 and raise their hands when they've found all of the answers. Review the answers as a class.

Answers
1. 2 onions
2. 8 ounces of cheese
3. No

B 1. Tell students to look again at the recipe in 1A and point out that measurements with noncount terms have another noun in front of them (e.g., ¼ *cup* of milk, not ¼ *milk*).

2. As a class, add the ingredients from the recipe to the lists of count and noncount terms from the warm-up.

3. Have students repeat the count nouns with a number and the noncount nouns with *some*.

Answers		
Count nouns		**Noncount nouns:**
Singular:	**Plural:**	
vegetable	vegetables	olive oil
onion	onions	flour
potato	potatoes	cheese
mushroom	mushrooms	milk
tomato	tomatoes	salt
		pepper

 C 1. Read and have students repeat the sentences in the chart.

2. Check for comprehension of the chart. Call out a food item and either nod your head to indicate an affirmative sentence, or shake your head to indicate a negative (*not*) sentence. Have volunteers say a sentence using the food item. Say: *onion* and nod your head. Students say: *We need an onion.*

Guided Practice I
15–20 minutes

 D 1. Read the instructions aloud. Give students time to silently review the charts again. Have students work individually to mark the sentences as *T* (true) or *F* (false) and then rewrite the false sentences to make them true.

2. Review the answers as a class. Have volunteers write the corrected sentences on the board.

Answers
1. F, count nouns
2. T
3. F, plural nouns and noncount nouns
4. F, singular nouns
5. T

E Read the instructions aloud. Have students complete the paragraph with a partner before checking answers as a class.

Answers	
1. some	5. a
2. an	6. any
3. some	7. a
4. a	8. any

MULTILEVEL STRATEGIES
For 1E, group same-level students together.
• **Pre-level** Have these students read the paragraph template together and work as a group to decide which word goes in each blank.
• **Higher-level** Challenge these students to substitute different food words into the paragraph.

2 Practice: questions with *How many* and *How much*

Presentation II
10–15 minutes

 A 1. Give students time to silently read the chart. Read and have students repeat the *How many/How much* questions.

2. As a class, use the recipe in 1A to answer the questions in the chart. Use the recipe to ask other questions to illustrate the grammar point: *How many potatoes does she need? How much salt does she need?* Asses students' understanding. Call out a food item and ask students to say *How many* or *How much*.

Guided Practice II
15–20 minutes

 1. Read the instructions aloud. Have students complete the sentences individually.

2. Have students compare their answers with a partner. Check answers as a class.

Answers
1. a
2. b
3. a
4. b

 1. Read the instructions aloud. Model a conversation with a volunteer. Ask: *How many onions does she need?* [*She needs 2 onions.*]

2. Pair students and tell them to take turns asking and answering *How many/How much* questions. Circulate and monitor.

3 Practice: talking about quantities

Presentation III and Guided Practice III
20–25 minutes

 2-41 1. Read the instructions aloud. Ask: *What does* inventory *mean?* [a list of things someone needs to do a job or complete a project] Give students time to silently read the list. Ask: *What is the difference in the two columns?* [The things on the left are the things he already has. The things on the right are the things he must buy.]

2. Play the audio and have students complete the list. Play the audio again if necessary.

B Model the conversation with a volunteer. Have students ask and answer the questions with a partner. Circulate and monitor.

Answers	
1. 10	5. 12
2. 10	6. 10
3. 3	7. 20
4. 5	8. 0

C 1. Read the instructions aloud. Set a time limit (five minutes) for students to think of a recipe and write a list of ingredients. If they don't know a recipe, allow them to look up a recipe on their phones or a computer, or tell them to use the recipe in 1A.

2. Model the sample conversation with a volunteer. Have students work in pairs, taking turns asking each other about their lists. Circulate and monitor.

MULTILEVEL STRATEGIES

For 3C, group same-level students together.

• **Pre-level** Have these students work in pairs or small groups to think of one recipe and make a list.

• **Higher-level** Have these students tell the class about their partner's recipe.

4 Ask and answer questions with *How much* and *How many*

Communicative Practice and Application
20–25 minutes

 1. Read the instructions aloud. Put students in groups of three to four. Have students copy the chart into their notebooks to use as they interview their team.

2. First have teams complete the questions and write one more question in their charts. Set a time limit (10 minutes). Then have students interview the other students in their team. Circulate and monitor.

Answers	
1. How many	5. How much
2. How much	6. How many
3. How much	7. Answers will vary.
4. How many	

B 1. Read the instructions aloud. Read the sample sentences aloud, stopping at each blank for volunteers to give a sample answer.

2. Have students complete the task with their team. Ask one person from each group to share their data with the class. Record the class's summary on the board.

MULTILEVEL STRATEGIES

For 4B, seat pre-level students together.

• **Pre-level** Work with these students and guide them in completing the questions: *Is* apples *a count or noncount word? What question word do you use with count nouns?*

Write students' sentences on the board, but include one mistake (e.g., *Our team has a total of one apples.*). Have students rewrite the sentences correctly in their notebooks, or have volunteers come to the board to correct the sentence (e.g., cross out *apples* and write *apple*, or cross out the *-s* in *apples*).

Evaluation

10 minutes

TEST YOURSELF

Ask students to write their five sentences about the different teams' activities. Collect and correct their writing.

EXTENSION ACTIVITY

How Much/How Many

Have students look at the pictures of fruits, vegetables, containers, and packaged foods (see *The Oxford Picture Dictionary* topics Fruit, Vegetables, Back from the Market, Containers and Packaging) and ask each other *How many/ How much _____ do you have in your kitchen?*

Lesson Overview	Lesson Notes
MULTILEVEL OBJECTIVES	

On- and Higher-level: Ask for and give locations of items in the supermarket

Pre-level: Ask for the location of items in the supermarket

LANGUAGE FOCUS

Grammar: *There is* and *There are* with count and noncount nouns

Vocabulary: Supermarket aisles, count and noncount food items

For vocabulary support, see these **Oxford Picture Dictionary** topics: Back from the Market, pages 66–67; Containers and Packaging, page 74; A Grocery Store, pages 72–73

STRATEGY FOCUS

Practice offering and asking for help.

READINESS CONNECTION

In this lesson, students communicate verbally in teams to explore how to ask and answer questions about the location of items in a supermarket.

PACING

To compress this lesson: Skip 4B.

To extend this lesson: Have students play a memory game. (See end of lesson.)

And/or have students complete **Workbook 2 page 48** and **Multilevel Activities 2 Unit 7 page 81**.

CORRELATIONS

CCRS: L.1.A Demonstrate command of the conventions of standard English grammar and usage when writing or speaking.

SL.1.A Participate in collaborative conversations with diverse partners in small and larger groups.

SL.2.A Confirm understanding of a text read aloud or information presented orally or through other media by asking and answering questions about key details and requesting clarification if something is not understood.

RF.2.A Demonstrate understanding of spoken words, syllables, and sounds (phonemes).

ELPS: 2. An ELL can participate in level-appropriate oral and written exchanges of information, ideas, and analyses, in various social and academic contexts, responding to peer, audience, or reader comments and questions. 9. An ELL can create clear and coherent level-appropriate speech and text.

Warm-up and Review
10–15 minutes (books closed)

Show students the picture of the supermarket in 1A or another picture of a supermarket, such as A Grocery Store in *The Oxford Picture Dictionary*. Let them look at the picture for 30 seconds. Then ask them to write as many words or sentences about the picture as they can from memory. Elicit their ideas and then show the picture again, so students can check their memories.

Introduction
5 minutes

1. Point out that the supermarket is divided into aisles and that different categories of food are located in different aisles.

2. State the objective: *Today we're going to explore how to ask where things are in the market.*

1 Listen to learn about the parts of a supermarket

Presentation I and Guided Practice I
20–30 minutes

A 1. Direct students to look at the picture of supermarket aisles and repeat the words on the signs. Ask about kinds of food they see or expect to find in each aisle.

2. Have students work individually to write the aisle numbers or section names. Review the answers as a class.

Answers
1. Produce
2. Canned goods, aisle 2
3. Dairy
4. Meat

B 🔊 **2-42** 1. Tell students that they will listen to a conversation between two people. Read the questions aloud. Have students put down their pencils before they listen. Play the audio and ask them to listen for key words in each conversation that will help them answer the questions. Replay the audio if necessary.

2. Ask students to compare their answers with a partner. Circulate and monitor to ensure students understand the audio.

Answers
Store manager and sales associate

C 🔊 **2-42** 1. Read the instructions aloud. Have students copy the chart into their notebooks. Play the audio and have students listen silently.

2. Play the audio again. Have students write their answers individually before comparing answers with a partner. Check answers as a class.

Answers
Frozen food: 5, vegetables/meals/pizza/ice cream
Canned food: 8, vegetables/soups/sauces
Beverages: 7, soda/water/juice
Dairy: 10, cheese/yogurt/milk

D Set a time limit (five minutes). Have students work in groups of three to four to discuss the question and make a list. Have volunteers share their group's list with the class.

2 Practice your pronunciation

Pronunciation Extension
10–15 minutes

A **2-43** 1. Tell students: *Sometimes the number of syllables changes from the singular to the plural.*

2. Read the *Need help?* box and pronounce the plurals of *dress*, *box*, *lunch*, and *page*.

3. Tell students: *Read the words and listen for the number of syllables.* Play the audio. Elicit the number of syllables in each word. Ask which one is stressed.

Answers
1. 1, 1
2. 2, 2
3. 1, 2
4. 2, 3

B 🔊 **2-44** 1. Have students write the plural words in the chart. Play the audio, so they can check their answers. Ask two volunteers (one for each column) to copy the words onto the board.

2. Pronounce and have students repeat all of the singular and plural forms.

Answers	
No extra syllable: grapes mushrooms jars cartons	Extra syllable: sausages oranges lunches bunches

3 Review *There is/There are*

Presentation II and Guided Practice II
10–15 minutes

A 🔊 **2-45** 1. Direct students' attention to the pictures. Ask them to say what they think is happening.

2. Read the instructions aloud. Play the audio. Ask students to read along silently. Play the audio again for students to complete the task. Review answers as a class.

Possible Answers
There is fresh bread in the bakery section, next to the cakes.
There are also canned tomatoes on the top shelf in aisle 2.

B ◀))) **2-46** 1. Read the instructions aloud. Make sure students understand that the statements they hear refer to the conversation in 3A.

2. Play the audio and have students circle the correct answers. Replay if necessary. Review answers as a class.

Answers
1. F
2. T
3. F
4. T

C 1. Introduce the new grammar. On the board, write the words *bread* and *onions*. Ask: *Which is a count and which is a noncount noun?* Then ask volunteers to name all of the count and noncount nouns in the conversation in 3A.

2. Read the questions. Give students time (one to two minutes) to look at the conversation and answer the questions. Have students compare their answers with a partner. Then check answers as a class.

4 Make conversation: offer help

Communicative Practice I
15–20 minutes

A Read the instructions aloud. Have students work in pairs to create a conversation and take turns performing parts. Tell them to also use the words and phrases in the box.

B 1. Set a time limit (ten minutes). Ask pairs to share their conversation with another pair and write the count and noncount nouns that the other pair used.

2. Have pairs present their conversation to the class.

> **TIP**
> You can challenge students to use their imaginations and use silly or far-fetched foods in their conversations.

AT WORK

Offering and asking for help

Presentation III and Communicative Practice II
15–20 minutes

A ◀))) **2-47** 1. Direct students to look at the pictures. Ask them to describe what is happening.

2. Play the audio and have students identify the requests for and offers of help. Read the questions and have volunteers answer.

> **TIP**
> Point out to students that using *could* instead of *can* in a request sounds more polite and formal.

B 1. Read the instructions aloud. Have students practice the conversations with a partner. Circulate and help as needed.

2. Read the requests in the *Need help?* box aloud. As a class, brainstorm substitutions. *Can you help me close the window? Can you please show me how to use this computer?*

3. Have pairs take turns offering and asking for help using their new sentences. Circulate and monitor.

C Read the instructions aloud. Have students work in pairs to discuss the questions. Circulate and monitor.

Evaluation
10–15 minutes

TEST YOURSELF

Have students work in pairs to perform the role-play. Circulate and assess students' progress. Take note of any mistakes you hear in intonation, pronunciation, grammar, or vocabulary. When all students have finished the activity, as a class, review the kinds of mistakes you heard (without naming any students who made them).

EXTENSION ACTIVITY

Memory Game

1. Have students stand or sit in a circle and think of an item to buy at the supermarket. Tell them they need to say the quantity or container in which it comes. The containers can be repeated, but the items cannot. For example, if one student says, *I need a box of cookies*, another can say, *I need a box of cereal* but not *I need a package of cookies*.

2. Have each student repeat what the previous students have said: *Marco needs two bags of rice. I need a package of noodles*. The more advanced students should go last.

3. Ask questions with *how much* and *how many* when students forget quantities.

Lesson Overview	Lesson Notes
MULTILEVEL OBJECTIVES	
Pre-, On- and Higher-level: Read about U.S. Department of Agriculture (USDA) dietary guidelines and interpret nutrition labels	
LANGUAGE FOCUS	
Grammar: *How much/How many (How much is one serving? How many servings are there?)* **Vocabulary:** *Calcium, calories, diet, protein* For vocabulary support, see these **Oxford Picture Dictionary** topics: Weights and Measurements, page 75; Back from the Market, pages 66–67	
STRATEGY FOCUS	
Apply information from a reading to real-life problems and tasks so that you will remember it and understand it better.	
READINESS CONNECTION	
In this lesson, students communicate information about food nutrition and how to read food nutrition labels.	
PACING	
To compress this lesson: Assign 1F and 1G for homework. **To extend this lesson:** Have students complete an activity about food labels. (See end of lesson.) And/or have students complete **Workbook 2 page 49** and **Multilevel Activities 2 Unit 7 page 82**.	

CORRELATIONS	
CCRS: SL.1.A Participate in collaborative conversations with diverse partners in small and larger groups. L.4.A Determine or clarify the meaning of unknown and multiple-meaning words and phrases, choosing flexibly from an array of strategies. R.1.A Ask and answer questions about key details in the text. R.4.A Ask and answer questions to help determine or clarify the meaning of words and phrases in a text. R.5.A Know and use various text features (e.g., headings, tables of contents, glossaries, electronic menus, icons) to locate key facts or information in a text. R.7.A Use the illustrations and details in a text to describe its key ideas (e.g., maps, charts, photographs, political cartoons, etc.).	**ELPS:** 1. An ELL can construct meaning from oral presentations and literary and informational text through level-appropriate listening, reading, and viewing. 3. An ELL can speak and write about level-appropriate complex literary and informational texts and topics.

Warm-up and Review
10–15 minutes (books closed)

Bring in food items and set them in front of the class. Ask students to take a minute to rank the items from the most to the least healthy. Discuss their ideas about what is healthy and why.

Introduction
5 minutes

1. Point out to students that there's not always a simple answer to whether a food is healthy or unhealthy—for example, some foods have good nutritional value, but are high in fat or salt.

Peanut butter has a lot of protein, but also a lot of fat, and many soups and other prepared foods have a lot of vegetables, but also a lot of salt or oil.

2. State the objective: *Today we're going to read about nutrition.*

1 Build reading strategies

Presentation
10–20 minutes

A Read the instructions and the definitions aloud. Have students complete the task individually and then share their answers with the class.

B 1. Read the instructions aloud and have students complete the task individually.

2. Have students compare their answers with a partner, and then ask volunteers to share their partner's answers with the class.

MULTILEVEL STRATEGIES

Adapt 1B to the level of your students.

• **Higher-level** Challenge these students to be specific in their answers and specify which fruits and vegetables, brands of foods, and so on.

TIP

Before students write their answers for 1B, ask them to predict which foods are the most popular in the class. Then see if their predictions were correct after they share answers as a class. You can also ask if there are any foods not listed that students think are popular.

Guided Practice: Pre-reading
5–10 minutes

C 1. Read the instructions aloud. Ask: *What is a topic sentence? Where is it usually found?*

2. Set a time limit (one minute) for students to skim the title and the article and think about the purpose of the article. Then have volunteers share their answers.

Guided Practice: While Reading
20–30 minutes

D Read the instructions aloud and confirm that students understand *source*. Have students read the article silently. Discuss the question as a class.

TIP

Preview any unfamiliar vocabulary such as *lifestyle, active, guidelines, pattern, especially, soy, beverage, containing, benefits,* and *moderate*. Write these words, and any others that may be new to students, on the board. Ask volunteers for definitions or examples. Alternatively, let students read the article again and guess the definitions from context. Confirm their answers.

MULTILEVEL STRATEGIES

Adapt 1D to the level of your students.

• **Pre-level** Read the text aloud to these students as they follow along.

• **On- and Higher-level** Pair students and have them read the article aloud to each other, taking turns to read each paragraph.

Guided Practice: Rereading
10–15 minutes

E 🔊 2-48 1. Provide an opportunity for students to extract evidence from the article. Have students reread the article and write two or three comprehension questions and take turns asking and answering them with a partner.

2. Play the audio again and have students read along silently. Discuss the question as a class. Ask: *What do you think it means to have a healthy lifestyle? What can you do to improve your eating and exercise habits?*

TIP

Have students go online to find out about healthy eating and exercise resources in your area. Decide which device(s) students might use and elicit search terms (e.g., *healthy eating + your city*).

Guided Practice: Post-reading
15 minutes

 1. Have students work individually to choose the correct answers, marking them *T* (true) or *F* (false) and then identify in the reading where they found the answer. Check answers as a class. Have students rewrite the false sentences to make them true.

2. Check comprehension further. Ask: *What kinds of vegetables are especially healthy?* [dark green, red, and orange ones] *What does milk contain that is good for health?* [calcium] *What should we eat only small amounts of?* [fat, sugar, salt] *What is an example of high-intensity exercise?* [swimming, jogging]

Answers
1. T
2. T
3. F
4. F

MULTILEVEL STRATEGIES

For 1F, call on volunteers and tailor your questions to the level of your students.

• **Pre-level** Ask *yes/no* questions. *Is it healthy to eat a lot of sugar?* [no]

• **On-level** Ask information questions. *How much do adults need to exercise?* [30 minutes every day]

• **Higher-level** Ask critical-thinking questions. *Are all of these guidelines easy to follow? Why or why not?*

 1. Have students work individually to complete the sentences.

2. Have students read their sentences to a partner. Then check answers as a class.

Answers
1. calcium
2. whole-grain
3. lean
4. vigorous

TIP

Guide a class discussion. Write the words *breakfast, lunch,* and *dinner* on the board. As a class, brainstorm healthy possibilities for each meal. Ask students which meals they'd prefer to eat.

2 Read a nutrition label

Communicative Practice
20–25 minutes

 1. Ask: *Do you read the labels on the packaged food you buy? What do you look for?*

2. Read the questions aloud. Have students discuss the labels with a partner. Circulate and help as needed.

3. Call on volunteers to say their answers for the class.

Answers	Black bean soup	Cream of chicken soup
How much is one serving?	1 cup	½ cup
How many servings are in one package?	2	3
How many calories are in one serving?	110	130
How much salt is in one serving?	920mg	870mg
Which is a better choice according to the article in 1D?	This has less fat, fewer calories, and more calcium per serving.	

B 1. Read the questions and the *Reader's Note* aloud. Allow students time to think of their own answers and make notes.

2. Set a time limit (ten minutes). Have students discuss the questions with a partner. Circulate and help as needed.

3. Have pairs share their responses with another pair. Then have volunteers share their pair's answers with the class.

Application
5–10 minutes

BRING IT TO LIFE

1. To structure this exercise more, divide the class into thirds and assign an ingredient to each group of students: sugar, fat, or salt.

2. Have the groups talk about what food they will bring in (to avoid repeats). Remind them it has to be packaged food with a label. Ask them to predict whether the food they choose will have a lot or a little of their particular group's ingredient.

EXTENSION ACTIVITY

Understand Food Labels

Using the packaged food you brought in for the warm-up, ask students to rank the items from most salty to least salty, highest fat to lowest fat, and most sugar to least sugar. After they have shared their guesses, check answers against the food labels.

Lesson Overview	Lesson Notes
MULTILEVEL OBJECTIVES	
On-, Pre-, and Higher-level: Expand upon and review unit grammar and life skills	
LANGUAGE FOCUS	
Grammar: Count and noncount nouns, *How much, How many* (*How much is in one serving? How many calories are there?*); Simple present with *be* (*The bread is in aisle four.*) **Vocabulary:** Supermarket vocabulary, *diet* For vocabulary support, see these **Oxford Picture Dictionary** topics: A Grocery Store, pages 72–73; Containers and Packaging, page 74; Weights and Measurements, page 75	
READINESS CONNECTION	
In this review, students work in teams to explore ways to ask about the location of items in a supermarket and to talk about healthy eating habits.	
PACING	
To extend this review: Have students complete **Workbook 2 page 50**, **Multilevel Activities 2 Unit 7 pages 83–86**, and **Multilevel Grammar Exercises 2 Unit 7**.	
CORRELATIONS	
CCRS: R.1.A Ask and answer questions about key details in the text. R.7.A Use the illustrations and details in a text to describe its key ideas (e.g., maps, charts, photographs, political cartoons, etc.). SL.1.A Participate in collaborative conversations with diverse partners in small and larger groups. SL.3.A Ask and answer questions in order to seek help, get information, or clarify something that is not understood. W.2.A Write informative/explanatory texts in which they name a topic, supply some facts about the topic, and provide some sense of closure.	**ELPS:** 5. An ELL can conduct research and evaluate and communicate findings to answer questions or solve problems. 6. An ELL can analyze and critique the arguments of others orally and in writing.

Warm-up and Review
10–15 minutes (books closed)

1. Review the *Bring It to Life* assignment from Lesson 5. Bring in cans and packaged food for students who didn't do the exercise.

2. Write the terms *Sugar Content, Salt Content*, and *Fat Content* on the board, and have students come up and write the information for each item about their product.

3. Lead a class discussion about their findings. Ask students if their predictions were close to the actual content or if they were very different.

Introduction and Presentation
10–15 minutes

1. Write *How much _____ is there? How many _____ are there?* Brainstorm different food words that can fill in each blank and write them under each sentence.

2. Ask a student one of the questions and have them answer. [Any answer will do as long as it's grammatically correct.]

3. State the objective: *Today we'll review how to ask questions with count and noncount nouns and how to ask where things are in the supermarket.*

Guided Practice
15–20 minutes

A 1. Direct students to work in groups of three to four and look at the picture. Read the questions aloud.

2. Set a time limit (five to ten minutes) for groups to answer the questions. Circulate and monitor.

3. Have volunteers from each group share the group's responses with the class. If you have a large class, you may not want all of the groups to report their responses. Instead, have groups share their responses with each other. Call "time" and tell all groups to work with a new group and to repeat their responses. Repeat this process as desired, making sure each group gets to share their responses at least once.

Communicative Practice
30–45 minutes

B Put students in new groups of four. Tell them they will role-play supermarket assistants and customers, taking turns asking or answering questions. Read the instructions aloud and model the sample conversation with a volunteer.

C 1. Ask a volunteer to identify the supermarket workers in A. As a class, brainstorm reasons why these workers might ask each other for help [need help finding an item in the store, need help making change for a customer, etc.].

2. Have teams complete the task in their groups from B and again take turns doing different parts. Circulate and help as needed.

D 1. Read the instructions aloud. Set a time limit for writing (three minutes).

2. Have students close their books. Call on volunteers to read one of their sentences to the class. Ask students to hold up one finger if the statement is true, or two fingers if it is false. Ask volunteers to restate false sentences to make them true.

E 1. Have students work in their groups from B. Read the instructions and model completing the sentence frames aloud. Have students copy the chart into their notebooks.

2. Set a time limit (10 minutes) to complete the task. Circulate and monitor.

F 1. Set a time limit (three to five minutes). Have students think about the answers in their surveys and write answers.

2. Have students briefly (for one to two minutes) discuss their responses with their group. Then have volunteers share responses with the class.

G 1. Read the instructions and the sample paragraph aloud. Point out that the writer first describes what they do, and then describes what they don't do.

2. Set a time limit (five minutes) and have students work individually.

3. Have students share their paragraph with their team. Then have volunteers share their group's findings with the class.

PROBLEM SOLVING AT HOME
10–15 minutes

A ◀)) 2-49 1. Ask: *Do you cook for yourself? Do you like cooking? Do you think it is easy or hard for most people to cook healthy foods for themselves?* Tell students they will read a story about a woman who has a problem with eating healthy. Direct students to read Dee's story silently.

2. Play the audio and have students read along silently.

B 1. Elicit answers to question 1. Guide students to a class consensus on the answer.

2. As a class, brainstorm answers to question 2. Ask students if they know someone who has this problem and has overcome it, or what they have done themselves to overcome the same problem.

Evaluation
20–25 minutes

To test students' understanding of the unit language and content, have them take the Unit 7 Test, available on the Teacher Resource Center.

Unit Overview

This unit explores illnesses, symptoms, and clarifying instructions, and the contextualization of the simple past of irregular verbs.

KEY OBJECTIVES	
Lesson 1	Identify and recommend medications; describe symptoms of illnesses
Lesson 2	Identify dental health services; make medical appointments
Lesson 3	Use the simple past of irregular verbs to describe accidents and injuries
Lesson 4	Interpret prescription labels; clarify instructions
Lesson 5	Interpret simple first-aid procedures; interpret a chart about accidents and injuries
Teamwork & Language Review	Review unit language

UNIT FEATURES	
Academic Vocabulary	*injured, instructions, medical*
Employability Skills	• Speculate about the causes of accidents • Analyze prescription label instructions • Interpret a pie chart about workplace injuries • Respond to workplace injuries • Listen actively • Understand teamwork • Communicate information • Work with others • Communicate verbally

Resources	**Class Audio** CD2, Tracks 50–66
	Workbook Unit 8, pages 51–57
	Teacher Resource Center
	    Multilevel Activities 2 Unit 8
	    Multilevel Grammar Exercises 2 Unit 8
	    Unit 8 Test
	Oxford Picture Dictionary Symptoms and Injuries, Illnesses and Medical Conditions, A Pharmacy, First Aid

Lesson Overview	Lesson Notes
MULTILEVEL OBJECTIVES	
On-level: Identify symptoms and medications	
Pre-level: Recognize symptoms and medications	
Higher-level: Talk and write about symptoms and medications	
LANGUAGE FOCUS	
Grammar: Simple present (*She has the flu.*)	
Vocabulary: Medications, Illnesses, and symptoms	
For vocabulary support, see these **Oxford Picture Dictionary** topics: Symptoms and Injuries, page 110; A Pharmacy, pages 114–115	
STRATEGY FOCUS	
Talk about what medications to take for different symptoms and medical problems.	
READINESS CONNECTION	
In this lesson, students listen actively and work with others to talk about illnesses, symptoms, and medications.	
PACING	
To compress this lesson: Conduct 2A as a whole-class activity.	
To extend this lesson: Have students participate in a dictation activity. (See end of lesson.)	
And/or have students complete **Workbook 2 page 51** and **Multilevel Activities 2 Unit 8 page 88**.	

CORRELATIONS	
CCRS: L.6.A Use words and phrases acquired through conversations, reading and being read to, and responding to texts, including using frequently occurring conjunctions to signal simple relationships (e.g., *because*). R.7.A Use the illustrations and details in a text to describe its key ideas (e.g., maps, charts, photographs, political cartoons, etc.). SL.1.A Participate in collaborative conversations with diverse partners in small and larger groups.	**ELPS:** 8. An ELL can determine the meaning of words and phrases in oral presentations and literary and informational text.

Warm-up and Review
10–15 minutes (books closed)

Tell the class they are going to exercise today to warm up, and ask everyone to stand. Give commands to review the parts of the body: *Touch your shoulder. Touch your knee.* If students have difficulty understanding any of the body parts, repeat several times for that part of the body throughout the warm-up.

Introduction
3 minutes

1. Make some humorous complaints about imaginary injuries you incurred during the warm-up. *I'm tired from exercising. Now my knees hurt!* Invite students to complain as well. Ask: *Do your arms hurt? How's your back?*

2. State the objective: *Today we're going to talk about illnesses, symptoms, and medications.*

1 Learn about medications

Presentation
20–25 minutes

 A 1. Ask: *What kind of medications do you buy at the drug store? Which ones do you use most often?* Direct students to look at the pictures. Confirm that students understand *allergy, relief,* and *heartburn.*

2. Read the words aloud. Ask students to circle the words they know.

B ◀) **2-50** 1. Play the audio. Ask students to point to the correct picture in 1A as they listen. Circulate and monitor.

2. Have students work in pairs to answer the question. Check answers as a class.

MULTILEVEL STRATEGIES

After the group comprehension check in 1B, call on individuals and tailor your questions to the level of your students.

• **Pre-level** Ask *yes/no* questions. *Do you take allergy medicine when you have a cold?* [no]

• **On-level** Ask information questions. *What do you use for an earache?* [eardrops]

• **Higher-level** Ask these students to use the vocabulary. *Which of these medicines do you take? Tell me about the last time you took one of these medicines.*

 C ◀) **2-51** 1. Ask students to listen and repeat the words.

2. While students are repeating, circulate and listen for pronunciation difficulties. Provide choral practice as necessary.

TIP

Have students take time to get more information about the treatments and symptoms in 1A and 1D. Have students work in pairs or small groups to look up the words in dictionaries or online and, for example, find out the specific symptoms or body parts affected by an allergy, how a cough syrup works, how long does it take to become a pharmacist, and so on. This can be assigned for homework as well. Have volunteers make a poster about the information they found. Display it in the classroom.

Guided Practice I
15–20 minutes

 D 1. Have students complete the sentences using the new vocabulary. Set a time limit (two to three minutes).

2. Have students take turns reading the completed sentences with a partner.

Answers

1. eardrops	5. antacid
2. cough syrup	6. antihistamine
3. pain reliever	7. pharmacist
4. antibiotic ointment	8. recommends

TIP

The words in 1D are long and may require extra pronunciation practice before students practice individually. Write them on the board and elicit the number of syllables and the stressed syllable for each word. Have students clap out the rhythm as they repeat each word.

E 1. Read the instructions aloud and model the sample conversation with a volunteer.

2. Set a time limit (three minutes). Have students take turns asking and answering questions with a partner. Circulate and listen for any pronunciation or vocabulary difficulties.

MULTILEVEL STRATEGIES

For 1E, pair same-level students together.

• **Pre-level** Assist these students with the exercise.

• **Higher-level** When these students finish, have them use the statements in 1D and make questions to ask and answer in pairs.

2 Talk about illnesses and symptoms

Guided Practice II
35–40 minutes

 A 1. Direct students to look at the pictures. Ask: *When was the last time you were sick?* Introduce the new topic: *Now let's look at illnesses and symptoms.*

2. Group students and assign roles: manager, researcher, administrative assistant, and reporter. Explain that students work with their groups to match the words and pictures.

3. Check comprehension of the exercise: *Who looks up the words in the picture dictionary?* [researcher] *Who writes the numbers in the book?* [administrative assistant] *Who tells the class your answers?* [reporter] *Who helps everyone and manages the group?* [manager]

4. Set a time limit (three minutes) and have students work together to complete the task. While students are working, copy the wordlist onto the board.

5. Call "time" and have the reporters from each group take turns calling out the numbers for the wordlist. Record students' answers on the board. If groups disagree, write each group's choice next to the word.

6. Draw students' attention to the illustrations. Prompt students to use vocabulary not labeled in the art. Ask: *Why is Olivia touching her head?* [to feel if she is warm] *What is Carlos doing?* [sneezing] *What is Emma using?* [a tissue] *What are possible reasons for Abdul feeling sick to his stomach?* [he ate something bad; he has stomach flu] Discuss *ah-choo.* Ask: *How do you say the sound of a sneeze in your first language?*

Answers	
7–feels dizzy	3–has a headache
8–feels nauseous	1–has a rash
9–is swollen	6–has a runny nose
5–has a cough	4–is sneezing
2–has a fever	

TIP

To confirm that students understand the difference between an illness and a symptom, write the words *Illness* and *Symptom* on the board. Call out each word from 2A and have students come to the board and write the word under the correct heading.

MULTILEVEL STRATEGIES

For 2A, use mixed-level groups.

• **Pre-level** Assign these students the role of administrative assistant.

• **Higher-level** Assign these students the role of manager.

B (2-52) 1. Play the audio. Ask students to listen and check their answers to 2A.

2. Have students correct the wordlist on the board and then write the correct numbers in their books as needed.

3. Tell the groups from 2A to split into pairs and practice the words. Set a time limit (two minutes).

C Read the instructions aloud and have students complete the paragraph individually. Check answers as a class.

Answers	
1. fever	5. swollen
2. am sneezing	6. nauseous
3. runny	7. dizzy
4. rash	

MULTILEVEL STRATEGIES

For 2C, seat same-level students together.

• **Pre-level** Have students work in pairs or small groups. Assist those groups.

• **Higher-level** After these students complete the exercise, ask them to write a few sentences about a time when they were sick.

Communicative Practice and Application
10–15 minutes

D 1. Read the instructions aloud and model the sample conversation with a volunteer.

2. Set a time limit (five minutes). Ask students to practice the conversation with several partners.

TIP

For a livelier version of 2D, pass out the pictures of illnesses or use page 94 of Multilevel Activities 2 Unit 8. Have students circulate, practicing the conversation in 2D with the symptoms from the pictures or Multilevel Activities. Assign a time limit (five minutes).

E 1. Read the questions aloud. Have students discuss the questions with a partner. Circulate and monitor.

2. Have volunteers share their or a partner's responses with the class.

Evaluation
10–15 minutes

TEST YOURSELF

1. Make a three-column, two-row chart on the board with the labels from page 103. Have students give you an example for each cell.

2. Have students copy the chart into their notebooks.

3. Set a time limit (five to ten minutes). Have students fill out the chart with words from the lesson.

4. Call "time" and have students check their spelling in the *Oxford Picture Dictionary* or another dictionary.

MULTILEVEL STRATEGIES

Target the *Test Yourself* to the level of your students.

• **Pre-level** Have these students work with their books open.

• **Higher-level** Have these students complete the chart and then write at least one sentence for each cell in the chart.

EXTENSION ACTIVITY

Dictation

Have students practice vocabulary and grammar from this lesson.

1. Dictate sentences with familiar vocabulary and grammar.

2. Tell students to leave their books open to page 103 so they can check spelling.

3. Have volunteers write the sentences on the board.

Lesson Overview

MULTILEVEL OBJECTIVES

On- and Higher-level: Read and write about health-care providers and symptoms

Pre-level: Identify health-care providers and symptoms

LANGUAGE FOCUS

Grammar: Simple present (*I need to see a doctor.*); Simple past (*The dentist cleaned her teeth.*)

Vocabulary: *Cavity, braces, filling, floss, X-ray*

For vocabulary support, see this **Oxford Picture Dictionary** topic: Symptoms and Injuries, page 110

STRATEGY FOCUS

Use the concluding sentences of the review to summarize your opinion and give reasons for the recommendation.

READINESS CONNECTION

In this lesson, students practice communicating verbally about symptoms and health-care providers.

PACING

To compress this lesson: Skip 2B.

To extend this lesson: Have students make a conversation. (See end of lesson.)

And/or have students complete **Workbook 2 page 52** and **Multilevel Activities 2 Unit 8 page 89**.

Lesson Notes

CORRELATIONS

CCRS: SL.2.A Confirm understanding of a text read aloud or information presented orally or through other media by asking and answering questions about key details and requesting clarification if something is not understood.

SL.6.A Speak audibly and express thoughts, feelings, and ideas clearly. Produce complete sentences when appropriate to task and situation.

R.1.A Ask and answer questions about key details in the text.

R.7.A Use the illustrations and details in a text to describe its key ideas (e.g., maps, charts, photographs, political cartoons, etc.).

W.2.A Write informative/explanatory texts in which they name a topic, supply some facts about the topic, and provide some sense of closure.

ELPS: 6. An ELL can analyze and critique the arguments of others orally and in writing. 9. An ELL can create clear and coherent level-appropriate speech and text.

Warm-up and Review
10–15 minutes (books closed)

Write *Do you have ____?* on the board and mime various illness symptoms. Have students ask you what illness you have based on your action: *Do you have a <u>cough</u>?* After students supply the word, write it on the board.

Introduction
5 minutes

1. Ask students if they would go to the doctor for the symptoms listed on the board. *Do you go to the doctor for a cough?*

2. State the objective: *Today we're going to read and write about health-care providers.*

1 Prepare to write

Presentation
20–25 minutes

A 1. Direct students to look at the pictures in 1B. Read the instructions and questions aloud.

2. Have students work with a partner. Give them one minute to discuss their answers to the questions. Elicit answers from the class.

B 🔊 2-53 Direct students' attention to the pictures as well as the title of the review in 1C. Build students' schema by asking questions about the pictures, referring to their work in 1A. Ask: *What is Lina writing about? What do you think her problem was?*

2. Discuss the word *filling*. Tell students how many fillings you have in your teeth. Ask: *Who has more? Who has fewer? Is there anybody who has no fillings?*

3. Play the audio. Have students listen silently.

C 🔊 2-53 1. Introduce the text: *You're going to read an online review of a dental clinic. As you read, look at which parts of the text match the pictures in B. This can help you understand the text better.*

2. Point out the *Writer's Note* and read it aloud. Ask: *What does* summarize *mean? What is the difference between a fact and an opinion?*

3. Play the audio again and have students read along silently.

4. Check comprehension. Ask: *How many times did Lina visit the dental clinic?* [twice] *What did her X-rays show?* [two cavities] *What did the dental hygienist do to Lina's teeth?* [She cleaned them.] *What did the dentist recommend?* [braces for Lina's front teeth]

> **TIP**
>
> Help students define and pronounce new terms, such as *cavity, braces, filling, floss,* and *X-ray*. Help students pronounce new terms in 1C by clapping out the syllables for *dentist* and *orthodontist*. Write each word on the board and underline the stressed syllable.

Guided Practice
10 minutes

D 1. Have students work individually to mark the sentences as *T* (true) or *F* (false).

2. Discuss answers as a class. If students finish the *true/false* exercise early, ask them to rewrite the false sentences to make them true.

Answers	
1. T	4. T
2. F	5. F
3. F	

> **MULTILEVEL STRATEGIES**
>
> For 1D, seat same-level students together.
>
> • **Pre-level** While other students are completing 1D, work with these students to find the answers in the text.
>
> • **On- and Higher-level** Have these students pose additional true/false statements to each other. *Lina got her fillings during her first visit.* [false] *Lina received a new toothbrush.* [true]

Guided Practice II
10–15 minutes

E 🔊 2-54 Read the instructions and chart headings aloud. Play the audio and have students complete the task individually. Don't check answers yet.

F 🔊 2-54 1. Have students compare answers with a partner. Play the audio again and check answers to 1E as a class.

2. Lead a brief class discussion to answer the question.

3. Ask: *Have you ever been to a(n) optometrist/chiropractor/dermatologist? Were they helpful to you?*

Answers			
Name of patient	**Type of health care provider**	**Reason for visit**	**Medications used (if any)**
Omar Mujia	optometrist	eye is very red and swollen	eye drops
Alex Larson	chiropractor	hurt his back	pain reliever
Vicky Kazakis	dermatologist	bad rash on arm	ointment

2 Plan

Communicative Practice I
10–15 minutes

A Read the instructions aloud. Make sure students understand that the numbers in the list match the numbers in the mind map. Have students complete the exercise individually. Circulate and monitor.

B Read the instructions aloud. Have students share and discuss their mind maps with a partner.

3 Write

Communicative Practice II and Application
15–20 minutes

A 1. Read the instructions aloud. Have students look at the template paragraph as you read it aloud. For each blank, have a volunteer give a sample answer.

2. Set a time limit for writing (five minutes). Have students complete the paragraph with their own information.

MULTILEVEL STRATEGIES

In 3A, target the writing to the level of your students.

• **Pre-level** Write a wordlist on the board for these students to use to complete their paragraphs. Then work with these students to write a group review. Read through the template. At each blank, stop and elicit completions. Decide as a group what to write. Have these students copy the group review into their notebooks.

• **Higher-level** Ask these students to write a review without using the template as a guide.

B 1. Ask students to read their review to a partner. Call on volunteers to share one thing they liked about their partner's review.

Evaluation
10 minutes

TEST YOURSELF

1. Read the instructions aloud. Assign a time limit (five minutes) and have students work individually.

2. Before collecting student work, invite two or three volunteers to share their sentences. Ask students to raise their hands if they wrote similar answers.

EXTENSION ACTIVITY

Have a Conversation

Have students look at the pictures of symptoms and injuries in *The Oxford Picture Dictionary* or another picture dictionary and create a conversation to practice with a partner. Pair students and have them practice both conversations.

Lesson Overview	Lesson Notes

MULTILEVEL OBJECTIVES

On- and Higher-level: Use the simple past of irregular verbs to describe accidents

Pre-level: Demonstrate understanding of simple past irregular verbs in descriptions of accidents

LANGUAGE FOCUS

Grammar: Simple past of irregular verbs (*Mario fell and broke his arm.*)

Vocabulary: Irregular past-tense verbs

For vocabulary support, see this **Oxford Picture Dictionary** topic: Symptoms and Injuries, page 110

STRATEGY FOCUS

Study the past tense forms of irregular verbs.

READINESS CONNECTION

In this lesson, students use simple-past irregular verbs to communicate information about accidents and injuries.

PACING

To compress this lesson: Assign 1F and 3B as homework.

To extend this lesson: Have students talk about injuries and accidents. (See end of lesson.)

And/or have students complete **Workbook 2 pages 53–54, Multilevel Activities 2 Unit 8 page 90**, and **Multilevel Grammar Exercises 2 Unit 8**.

CORRELATIONS

CCRS: L.1.A Demonstrate command of the conventions of standard English grammar and usage when writing or speaking. e. Use verbs to convey a sense of past, present, and future (e.g., *Yesterday I walked home; Today I walk home; Tomorrow I will walk home.*) k. Understand and use question words (interrogatives) (e.g., *who, what, where, when, why, how*).

SL.1.A Participate in collaborative conversations with diverse partners in small and larger groups.

SL.2.A Confirm understanding of a text read aloud or information presented orally or through other media by asking and answering questions about key details and requesting clarification if something is not understood.

ELPS: 7. An ELL can adapt language choices to purpose, task, and audience when speaking and writing. 10. An ELL can demonstrate command of the conventions of standard English to communicate in level-appropriate speech and writing.

Warm-up and Review
10–15 minutes (books closed)

Ask for a show of hands: *Did you ever break a bone? Fall down? Cut yourself?* Invite volunteers to share their experiences with the class.

Introduction
5–10 minutes

1. Write sentences about what your students have shared in the warm-up or your own experiences.

Hilda once fell down the stairs. Underline the irregular past tense verb. Explain that for some verbs, the past tense has a different spelling instead of having -*ed* at the end.

2. State the objective: *Today we're going to explore how to use irregular verbs in the simple past to talk about accidents and injuries.*

1 Explore the simple past of irregular verbs

Presentation I
20–25 minutes

A ◀)) **2-55** 1. Direct students to look at the illustrations. Read the instructions and questions aloud. Play the audio and have students read along silently.

2. Have students answer the questions in a class discussion.

B 1. Read the dialogue in 1A aloud, slowly. Have students raise their hand every time they hear a past-tense verb.

2. Read the instructions aloud and have students underline verbs that end in *-ed* and circle the ones that are irregular. Discuss answers as a class.

Answers
1. happened, tried
2. fell, broke, hurt, cut, bled

C 1. Demonstrate how to read the grammar charts as complete sentences. Read through the charts sentence by sentence. Then read them again and have students repeat after you.

2. Read the *Grammar Note* aloud. Ask students if they know any other irregular verbs. Write their present and past tense forms on the board for students to copy into their notebooks.

3. Use the dialogue in 1A to illustrate points in the grammar charts. *She fell off her bicycle and broke her leg. It bled a lot.*

TIP
Explain to students that irregular verbs don't follow any spelling rules; they just have to be memorized. Suggest making flashcards for these, and that spending even just a couple of minutes a day drilling with them will be very helpful! Also, you can spend part of the daily warm-up holding up flashcards and drilling students on the present and past tense of irregular verbs.

Guided Practice I
20–25 minutes

D 1. Read the instructions aloud. Give students time to silently review the charts again and fill in the blanks.

2. Ask volunteers to read the sentences aloud. Then have other volunteers say which verbs are the same in present and past tense.

Answers	
1. had	4. hurt
2. broke	5. cut
3. got	6. bled

E ◀)) **2-56** 1. Read the instructions aloud and direct students to look at the pictures. Play the audio and have students complete the task individually.

2. Play the audio again and have students work in pairs to compare and check their answers.

Answers	
1. T	5. T
2. F	6. T
3. F	7. F
4. F	8. T

F Read the instructions aloud. Have students complete the task individually and check answers with a partner.

Answers	
1. cut, didn't hurt	3. got, got/had
2. didn't hurt, burned	4. didn't break, hurt

G 1. Read the instructions aloud. Model the task with a volunteer: *Jessica hurt her arm. False. She hurt her ankle.*

2. Set a time limit (five minutes). Have students work in pairs to complete the task. Circulate and monitor.

3. Have volunteers say one of their *true/false* sentences to the class and have other students respond. If needed, guide students to a class consensus on their responses.

2 Practice: *Yes/no* questions with irregular verbs in the past

Presentation II and Guided Pratice II
20–25 minutes

A **2-57** Read through the charts sentence by sentence. Play the audio and have students repeat.

B 1. Read the instructions aloud. As a class, talk about what students see in the photos in 1E. Read the sample conversations with a volunteer. Give students time to silently review the charts again.

2. Have students work in pairs to take turns asking and answering questions about the photos. Circulate and monitor.

3 Practice: *Wh-* questions with irregular verbs in the past

Presentation III and Guided Practice III
25–30 minutes

A 🔊 2-58 1. Ask: *What are the* Wh- *question words?* Write them on the board as students call them out [*what, when, where, who, why,* and *how*]. Ask: *What questions might you ask someone who has been in an accident?* Write students' ideas on the board.

2. Read through the charts sentence by sentence. Play the audio and have students repeat.

B 1. Read the instructions and the information in the *Grammar Note* aloud. Write the sentences from the *Grammar Note* on the board. Have volunteers come to the board and label the subject and object in the sentences. Challenge a volunteer to write another sentence on the board that uses a reflexive pronoun.

2. Have students complete the task individually. Set a time limit (five minutes).

3. Check answers as a class. Have volunteers write their questions on the board and label the subject (*S*) and object (*O*) in each question.

Answers
1. How did you cut yourself?
2. How did she hurt her back?
3. Where did they go?/When did they go to the doctor?
4. Where did Dan hurt himself?
5. How did she hurt herself?

C 1. Read the instructions aloud. Model a conversation with a volunteer.

2. Have students work in pairs and take turns role-playing each part. Circulate and monitor.

4 Ask questions about a workplace accident

Communicative Practice and Application
15–20 minutes

A 🔊 2-59 1. Read the instructions aloud and confirm that students understand the information they need to fill in the report.

2. Play the audio and have students fill in the report. Play the audio again if necessary.

Answers
Name of injured person: Mario Salinas
Occupation: truck driver
Date and time: Friday September 10, at 10 a.m.
Location: delivery area
Description of accident: lifted some heavy boxes
Injury: severe backache

B Model the conversation with a volunteer. Have students ask and answer questions about the report with a partner. Have volunteers share their answers with the class.

MULTILEVEL STRATEGIES
Group same-level students together.
• **Pre-level** Work with these students and ask *yes/no* questions about the report.
• **Higher-level** Have these students role-play being Mario and his boss. The boss is asking Mario the questions about the accident.

Evaluation
10 minutes

TEST YOURSELF

Ask students to write their five questions. Collect and correct their writing.

EXTENSION ACTIVITY
Talk about Injuries and Accidents
Bring in pictures of injuries or have students look at the pictures of injuries in *The Oxford Picture Dictionary* or another dictionary. Tell students to imagine how the injury happened and have them create a conversation like the one in 4B.

Lesson Overview	Lesson Notes
MULTILEVEL OBJECTIVES	
On- and Higher-level: Interpret and discuss prescription information **Pre-level:** Interpret basic prescription information	
LANGUAGE FOCUS	
Grammar: Simple-present questions and answers with *have to* (*How many pills do I have to take? Do I have to take them with food? Yes, you do.*) **Vocabulary:** Medical prescription words For vocabulary support, see this **Oxford Picture Dictionary** topic: A Pharmacy, pages 114–115	
STRATEGY FOCUS	
Clarify instructions.	
READINESS CONNECTION	
In this lesson, students communicate verbally about how to read prescriptions and ask clarifying questions about instructions related to them.	
PACING	
To compress this lesson: Skip 4B. **To extend this lesson:** Have students perform a role-play. (See end of lesson.) And/or have students complete **Workbook 2 page 55** and **Multilevel Activities 2 Unit 8 page 91**.	

CORRELATIONS

CCRS: L.1.A Demonstrate command of the conventions of standard English grammar and usage when writing or speaking. SL.1.A Participate in collaborative conversations with diverse partners in small and larger groups. R.7.A Use the illustrations and details in a text to describe its key ideas (e.g., maps, charts, photographs, political cartoons, etc.). RF.2.A Demonstrate understanding of spoken words, syllables, and sounds (phonemes).	**ELPS:** 2. An ELL can participate in level-appropriate oral and written exchanges of information, ideas, and analyses, in various social and academic contexts, responding to peer, audience, or reader comments and questions. 9. An ELL can create clear and coherent level-appropriate speech and text.

Warm-up and Review
10–15 minutes (books closed)

Play "question-answer catch." Say: *I have a headache* and throw a soft ball or a wad of paper to a student. Tell that student to give you advice: *You should take an aspirin.* The student with the ball makes a new statement, stating a different injury or symptom, and throws the ball to another student who gives advice. Continue throwing the ball around the room until most students have spoken.

Introduction
5 minutes

1. Bring in a prescription bottle or draw a label on the board (see 1A for an example). Ask: *What is this? Where do you get a prescription? What information is on the label?*

2. State the objective: *We already studied illnesses and treatments. Today we're going to explore how to read and ask about a prescription.*

1 Listen to learn: reading a prescription label

Presentation I and Guided Practice I
20–30 minutes

A 1. Direct students to look at the prescription label. Ask questions about the information on the label: *Is Tina Kowalski the patient or the doctor? What is the prescription number? What does* dosage *mean? If she finishes the pills, can she get more? When should she throw these pills away?*

2. Discuss what other information is on the label. Review and define any words students are unfamiliar with.

B 🔊 2-60 1. Read the choices aloud. Tell students that they don't have to understand every part of the audio and they should just listen for the overall meaning. Play the audio and have students answer the question as a class.

Answer
b

C 🔊 2-60 1. Tell students they will listen to the audio again and number the parts of the label in A.

2. Play the audio. Have students write their answers individually before comparing answers with a partner. Check answers as a class.

Answers
1. name and address of pharmacy
2. your name and address
3. name of the doctor
4. prescription number
5. name of your medication and the strength of each pill
6. total number of pills in the container
7. number of refills
8. expiration date
9. instructions and dosage
10. warnings

TIP
This audio contains many words that might be new to students. Before playing the audio for 1C, write some of the words on the board and discuss their meanings.

MULTILEVEL STRATEGIES

Adapt 1C to the level of your students.
- **Pre-level** Stop the audio after each numbered section for students to find and number that part of the label.
- **Higher-level** Play the audio once and have students take brief notes as they listen to use when they number the label afterwards.

D Read the question aloud. Have students discuss the question in small groups. Have groups share their responses with the class.

2 Practice your pronunciation

Pronunciation Extension
10–15 minutes

A 🔊 2-61 1. Point out that <u>how</u> you say something can be just as important as what you say: *In these two examples, listen to how* have to *and* has to *are pronounced.*

2. Play the audio a few times and have students repeat.

B 1. Have students work in pairs to practice the sentences using both formal and relaxed pronunciations. Circulate and monitor.

3 Review *have to* and *has to*

Presentation II
10–15 minutes

A 2-62 1. Review *have/has*. Write on the board: *I have a red car. I have to wash my car.* Discuss the difference in the meaning of the verb *have*.

2. Read the question aloud and play the audio. Ask students to read along silently. Suggest they underline the parts of the prescription label in 1A as they hear them.

3. Discuss answers as a class. Ask students to identify the two uses of the verb *have* in the conversation. [*Do you have any questions.../How many pills do I have to take...*]

Answers
dosage and warnings

B 🔊 2-63 Play the audio and have students repeat. Have them work individually to complete the task.

Answers
1. a
2. a
3. b
4. b

Guided Practice II
20–25 minutes

C 1. Read the questions. GIve students time to review the conversation in 1A and answer the questions.

2. Discuss answers as a class.

D 1. Read the instructions and the sample question aloud. Have students complete the task individually.

2. Have students compare questions with a partner. Have volunteers write their questions on the board. Check answers as a class.

Answers
1. When do you have to take the pills?
2. How often does he have to see the doctor?
3. Does she have to avoid dairy products?
4. Does he have to take the pills before meals?
5. How long does she have to take the pills?
6. How much do I have to pay?

MULTILEVEL STRATEGIES
For 2D, pair same-level students together.
• **Pre-level** Have these students work as a group to write their questions.
• **Higher-level** Direct these students to write an answer to each question.

E 1. Read the instructions aloud. Have students work in small groups to complete the task.

2. Have groups share their two best questions with the class and write them on the board to refer to in 3F.

F Guide a class discussion about the question. Ask students why each of the questions on the board is important to ask.

4 Make conversation: clarifying prescription instructions

Communicative Practice I
15–20 minutes

A 1. Ask students if they remember what *clarify* means [to ask for information again in order to make sure you understand it]. Ask: *How do we clarify information?* [ask someone to repeat what they said; repeat what they said back to them]

2. Draw students' attention to the *Need help?* box and read the phrases aloud. As a class, brainstorm ways to complete the question and how to use the time phrases in an answer.

3. Have students work in pairs to create a conversation and take turns performing parts.

MULTILEVEL STRATEGIES
Target your instruction for the level of your students.
• **Pre-level** Work with students to fill in the blanks.
• **Higher-level** Challenge these students to have the conversations without looking at their books.

B 1. Ask pairs to share their conversation with another pair. Circulate and monitor.

2. Have volunteer pairs present their conversation to the class.

▶ AT WORK

Clarifying instructions

Presentation III and Communicative Practice II
15–25 minutes

A 🔊 2-64 1. Read the instructions and the questions aloud.

2. Play the audio and have students read along silently.

3. Answer the questions as a class.

B Have pairs practice the conversations in At Work A and use their own ideas in similar conversations. Circulate and monitor.

C Read the question aloud. Have students discuss the question in small groups. Then have groups share their answers with the class.

Evaluation

10–15 minutes

TEST YOURSELF

Have students perform the role-play with a partner. Circulate and assess students' progress. Take note of any mistakes you hear in intonation, pronunciation, grammar, or vocabulary. When all students have finished the activity, as a class, review the kinds of mistakes you heard (without naming any students who made them).

EXTENSION ACTIVITY

Role-play

Have students work in pairs to write and perform a role-play following these instructions.

1. A patient explains an injury or symptom and tells what he/she was doing when the injury or symptom first occurred.

2. The doctor prescribes a medication and gives the patient directions for its use.

Example:

> Patient: *I have a sore throat. I was shouting at my son's soccer match last night when my throat got sore.*

> Doctor: *Take these lozenges. Put one in your mouth every four hours.*

3. Have pairs perform their role-plays for each other.

Lesson Overview	Lesson Notes

MULTILEVEL OBJECTIVES

On- and Higher-level: Read about and discuss first-aid kits and materials

Pre-level: Read about first-aid kit and materials

LANGUAGE FOCUS

Grammar: *Should (Where should you put your first-aid kit?)*

Vocabulary: *Antibiotic ointment, bandages, first aid, gloves, injured, scissors, serious emergency, supplies*

For vocabulary support, see this **Oxford Picture Dictionary** topic: First Aid, page 119

STRATEGY FOCUS

Understand that the navigation bar at the top of the web page includes links to different topics on the site.

READINESS CONNECTION

In this lesson, students work with others to explore the uses and contents of first-aid kits.

PACING

To compress this lesson: Assign 1F and/or 1G for homework.

To extend this lesson: Have students make a poster. (See end of lesson.)

And/or have students complete **Workbook 2 page 56** and **Multilevel Activities 2 Unit 8 page 92**.

CORRELATIONS

CCRS: SL.1.A Participate in collaborative conversations with diverse partners in small and larger groups.

L.4.A Determine or clarify the meaning of unknown and multiple-meaning words and phrases, choosing flexibly from an array of strategies.

R.1.A Ask and answer questions about key details in the text.

R.4.A Ask and answer questions to help determine or clarify the meaning of words and phrases in a text.

R.5.A Know and use various text features (e.g., headings, tables of contents, glossaries, electronic menus, icons) to locate key facts or information in a text.

R.7.A Use the illustrations and details in a text to describe its key ideas (e.g., maps, charts, photographs, political cartoons, etc.).

ELPS: 1. An ELL can construct meaning from oral presentations and literary and informational text through level-appropriate listening, reading, and viewing. 3. An ELL can speak and write about level-appropriate complex literary and informational texts and topics.

Warm-up and Review
10–15 minutes (books closed)

Ask students to brainstorm what items should go into a first-aid kit. Give them two minutes to make a list. Elicit the items they write down and put them on the board. Leave the list on the board.

Introduction
5 minutes

1. Bring in a first-aid kit and have students compare the items in it to the ones on the board. Add any additional items to the list but don't erase any.

2. State the objective: *Today we're going to read about first-aid kits and accident reports.*

1 Build reading strategies

Presentation
15–20 minutes

 Read the words and definitions aloud. Have students complete the task individually and then share answers with the class.

Guided Practice: Pre-reading
5–10 minutes

 Direct students to read the words and look at the picture of the first-aid kit in 1D. Discuss the meaning of *antibiotic ointment*. When students have identified gloves as the item that does not appear in the picture, ask if it might be a good idea to include gloves in a first-aid kit and why [to avoid infection when treating other people's cuts].

Answers
gloves

> **TIP**
>
> Expand the discussion of first-aid kits. Ask students about the times they have had to use a first-aid kit. What are the items that they use the most/least?

C Read the questions and the *Reader's Note* aloud. Give students about one minute to preview the article. Discuss answers as a class.

Guided Practice: While Reading
15–20 minutes

D 1. On the board write any vocabulary you think may be unfamiliar to students or that you want to review (e.g., *disasters, preparing, basic, thermometer, expiration date*). Tell students to pay attention to these words as they read and to try to figure out their meanings from the context.

2. Have students read the article silently. Make sure students understand the vocabulary on the board. Ask them to give a definition or an example, or to use the word in a new sentence, as needed.

> **MULTILEVEL STRATEGIES**
>
> Adapt 1D to the level of your students.
> - **Pre-level** Read the text aloud to these students as they follow along.
> - **On- and Higher-level** Pair students and have them read the article aloud to each other, taking turns to read each paragraph.

Guided Practice: Rereading
10–15 minutes

E 1. Provide an opportunity for students to extract evidence from the article. Have students reread the article and write one sentence about each paragraph, stating what the paragraph is about.

2. Play the audio again and have students read along silently.

> **TIP**
>
> Have students go online to find other articles that give advice about what to have in a first-aid kit or other safety resources in a home. Provide possible search terms (*first aid + home; emergency + home*) Have volunteers share their findings with the class.

Guided Practice: Post-reading
15 minutes

 1. Have students work individually to choose the correct answers and then identify in the reading where they found the answer. Check answers as a class.

2. Check comprehension further. Ask: *Where should you keep a first-aid kit?* [at home and in the car] *What is acetaminophen used for?* [pain] *What should you keep your fist-aid supplies in?* [a plastic box] *What should you check for in your firs-aid kit?* [expiration dates]

Answers
1. a
2. b
3. a
4. a

G 1. Have students work individually to complete the sentences.

2. Have students read their sentences to a partner before checking answers as a class.

Answers
1. thermometer
2. scissors
3. injured
4. serious

MULTILEVEL STRATEGIES
For 1F and 1G, seat pre-level students together.
• **Pre-level** Have these students work together and assist them by highlighting the sentences in the article where they can find the answers.

2 Read a pie chart about injuries at work

Communicative Practice
15–20 minutes

A Read the questions aloud. Have students work in pairs to study the chart and answer the questions before checking answers as a class.

Answers
1. Occupational (workplace) Injuries
2. Sprains
3. Back pain and muscle soreness

B 1. Read the questions aloud. Allow students time to think of their own answers and make notes.

2. Set a time limit (ten minutes). Have students discuss the questions with a partner. Circulate and help as needed.

3. Have pairs share their responses with another pair. Have volunteers share their partner's answers with the class.

TIP
Call the local Red Cross, or another community health agency, and ask if they have a health education outreach program. Ask a speaker to plan a short presentation for your class. Tell him or her in advance what to focus on. Have your students prepare questions to ask before the speaker comes.

Application
5–10 minutes

BRING IT TO LIFE

Ask students to research the questions and report their findings to the class. Lead a class discussion about how they can improve their own first-aid kits.

EXTENSION ACTIVITY
Make a Poster
Have students work in groups of two to three to make a poster about different aspects of first aid and emergencies. One poster should include recommended items for a first-aid kit (recommended for pre-level students). Other posters requiring research can include steps for treatment for common household injuries (on-level students), or pie charts for occupational injuries for a few occupations such as police, firefighters, factory workers, and so on (higher-level students).

Lesson Overview

Lesson Notes

MULTILEVEL OBJECTIVES

On-, Pre-, and Higher-level: Expand upon and review unit grammar and life skills

LANGUAGE FOCUS

Grammar: Simple past tense irregular verbs

Vocabulary: Medications, illnesses, and symptoms

For vocabulary support, see these **Oxford Picture Dictionary** topics: A Pharmacy, pages 114–115; First Aid, page 119

STRATEGY FOCUS

Talk about what to do in different medical situations.

READINESS CONNECTION

In this review, students work with others and understand teamwork as they talk about medications, allergies, and injuries.

PACING

To extend this review: Have students complete **Workbook 2 page 57**, **Multilevel Activities 2 Unit 8 pages 93–96**, and **Multilevel Grammar Exercises 2 Unit 8**.

CORRELATIONS

CCRS: R.1.A Ask and answer questions about key details in the text.

R.7.A Use the illustrations and details in a text to describe its key ideas (e.g., maps, charts, photographs, political cartoons, etc.).

SL.1.A Participate in collaborative conversations with diverse partners in small and larger groups.

SL.3.A Ask and answer questions in order to seek help, get information, or clarify something that is not understood.

W.2.A Write informative/explanatory texts in which they name a topic, supply some facts about the topic, and provide some sense of closure.

ELPS: 5. An ELL can conduct research and evaluate and communicate findings to answer questions or solve problems. 6. An ELL can analyze and critique the arguments of others orally and in writing.

Warm-up and Review
10–15 minutes (books closed)

1. Review the *Bring It to Life* assignment from Lesson 5.

2. Have students who researched first-aid kits share what they learned. Encourage students who didn't complete the activity to ask their classmates questions.

3. As students share their findings, write prices on the board. Discuss which kit (at which store) is the best buy.

Introduction and Presentation
5 minutes

1. Write *allergy* on the board. Ask students if they have any allergies and what the symptoms are.

2. State the objective: *Today we're going to review how to talk about medications, allergies, and injuries.*

Guided Practice
15–20 minutes

A 1. Direct students to work in groups of three to four and look at the picture. Set a time limit (five minutes) for groups to answer the questions. Circulate and monitor.

2. Have students from each group share the group's responses with the class. If you have a large class, you may not want all of the groups to report their responses. Instead, have groups share their responses with each other. Call "time" and tell all groups to work with a new group and to repeat their responses. Repeat this process as desired, making sure each group gets to share their responses at least once.

Communicative Practice
30–45 minutes

B 1. Review the conversation in Lesson 4, 3A.

2. Have students complete the task with their groups from A. Make sure each student has had a turn doing each part of the role-play.

> **MULTILEVEL STRATEGIES**
>
> Adapt B the level of your students.
>
> • **Pre-level** Provide these students with sentence frames to use in their role-play. Use the conversation from Lesson 4, 3A. You might write it on the board, leaving blanks for students to fill in the information on the prescription label in A.
>
> • **Higher-level** Challenge these students to clarify instructions for every piece of information on the prescription label.

C Have students present their conversation to another team. Circulate and monitor.

D 1. Put students in new groups of four and assign roles: manager, researcher, administrative assistant, and reporter. Read the instructions and the questions aloud. Have students copy the chart into their notebooks.

2. Set a time limit (five minutes) to complete the task.

3. Have students take turns interviewing each other. Circulate and monitor. Provide global feedback once the activity ends.

E 1. Tell students they will work in their team from D to create a group summary. Read the instructions and the sample sentences aloud.

2. Set a time limit (five minutes) to complete the task.

3. Have reporters share their group's summary with the class.

F 1. Read the instructions aloud and direct students to look at the pictures. Model the sample conversations with a volunteer.

2. Set a time limit (three minutes). Have students work in pairs within their teams. Circulate and monitor.

G 1. Read the instructions aloud. Have students copy the chart into their notebooks.

2. Set a time limit (five minutes). Have students work in pairs within their teams.

H 1. Have pairs compare their answers with the other pair in their team.

2. Guide a class discussion about teams' answers and first aid. Ask: *Does everyone agree on steps to take for each situation? Has anyone experienced one these situations recently? What did you do?*

3. Have volunteers who made the posters in the Lesson 4 *Extension Activity* review other students' answers.

PROBLEM SOLVING AT WORK
10–15 minutes

> **TIP**
>
> Before doing the activity, review kinds of work injuries from Lesson 5, 2A. Then review what an accident report is: *If you get injured at work, you should fill out an accident report as soon as you can. An accident report includes information about when and how the accident happened. They are used to determine if your employer needs to make the workplace safer and if you are entitled to compensation for your injury.*

A 🔊 **2-66** 1. Ask: *Have you or someone you know ever been injured at work?* Tell students they will read a story about a man who has been injured at work. Play the audio and have students read Julio's story silently.

B 1. Elicit answers to question 1. Guide students to a class consensus on the answer.

2. As a class, brainstorm answers to question 2. Ask students if they know someone who has this problem and has overcome it, or what they have done themselves to overcome the same problem.

Evaluation
20–25 minutes

To test students' understanding of the unit language and content, have them take the Unit 8 Test, available on the Teacher Resource Center.

Unit Overview

This unit explores personal finances and budgets, banking-related safety, shopping procedures, and using *because* and infinitives of purpose.

KEY OBJECTIVES	
Lesson 1	Interpret personal finances; identify ATM instructions
Lesson 2	Estimate personal budgets; identify ways to save money
Lesson 3	Use *because* and infinitives of purpose to give reasons and purpose; use referents
Lesson 4	Make returns or exchanges when shopping
Lesson 5	Identify credit card safety procedures; interpret a pie chart
Teamwork & Language Review	Review unit language

UNIT FEATURES	
Academic Vocabulary	*feature, purchase, percent*
Employability Skills	• Analyze figures on bank statements • Sequence steps when using an ATM • Examine reasons for buying something • Analyze sales receipts and reasons for returns and exchanges • Analyze a pie chart about credit card fraud • Decide on a budget • Analyze spending and manage credit card bills • Understand teamwork • Communicate information • Work with others • Communicate verbally

Resources	**Class Audio** CD3, Tracks 02–18
	Workbook Unit 9, pages 58–64
	Teacher Resource Center
	    Multilevel Activities 2 Unit 9
	    Multilevel Grammar Exercises 2 Unit 9
	    Unit 9 Test
	Oxford Picture Dictionary Shopping, The Bank

Lesson Overview	Lesson Notes
MULTILEVEL OBJECTIVES	
On-level: Identify bank vocabulary **Pre-level:** Recognize bank vocabulary **Higher-level:** Talk and write about banking	
LANGUAGE FOCUS	
Grammar: Simple present (*Peter deposits $100.*) **Vocabulary:** Banking words For vocabulary support, see this **Oxford Picture Dictionary** topic: The Bank, page 134	
STRATEGY FOCUS	
Talk about using an ATM.	
READINESS CONNECTION	
In this lesson, students analyze figures on bank statements and work with others to communicate information about using ATMs.	
PACING	
To compress this lesson: Assign 1D and/or 2C as homework. **To extend this lesson:** Have students retell a story. (See end of lesson.) And/or have students complete **Workbook 2 page 58** and **Multilevel Activities 2 Unit 9 page 98**.	

CORRELATIONS	
CCRS: L.6.A Use words and phrases acquired through conversations, reading and being read to, and responding to texts, including using frequently occurring conjunctions to signal simple relationships (e.g., *because*). SL.1.A Participate in collaborative conversations with diverse partners in small and larger groups.	**ELPS:** 8. An ELL can determine the meaning of words and phrases in oral presentations and literary and informational text.

Warm-up and Review
10–15 minutes (books closed)

1. Write some large dollar amounts on the board: *$5,506.95; $1,302.00.* Say the amounts out loud and ask students to repeat. Dictate some large dollar amounts and have students write them in large print on paper. Tell them to hold up each number as soon as they have finished writing it. Ask volunteers to say the amounts.

Introduction
3 minutes

1. Write *bank* on the board. Ask students to list the names of banks in the community. Elicit banking-related words: *What do you see at a bank? What do you do?*

2. State the objective: *Today we're going to explore bank words.*

1 Learn about banking

Presentation
20–25 minutes

A 1. Ask: *How often do you go to the bank? Do you go to a teller or use the ATM? Do you do any online banking?*

2. Read the instructions, question, and words aloud. Ask students to circle the words they know. Have students say which things they use regularly.

B 🔊 **3-02** 1. Direct students' attention to the pictures in 1A and play the audio. Ask them to point to the correct picture as they listen. Circulate and monitor.

2. Check comprehension by asking *yes/no* questions. Have students hold up one finger for *yes* and two for *no* in order to get a nonverbal response. Ask: *Does Peter have $540.00 in his checking account?* [no] *Did Peter write a check for $350.96?* [yes]

3. Have volunteers say what Peter is doing.

MULTILEVEL STRATEGIES

After the group comprehension check in 1B, call on volunteers and tailor your questions to the level of your students.

• **Pre-level** Ask *yes/no* questions. *Does Peter have a balance on his credit card?* [yes]

• **On-level** Ask information questions. *How much does Peter have in his checking account?* [$850.00]

• **Higher-level** Ask critical-thinking questions. *Can Peter pay his whole credit card balance this month?* [yes]

C 🔊 **3-03** 1. Ask students to listen and repeat the words.

2. While students are repeating, circulate and listen for pronunciation difficulties. Provide choral practice as necessary.

TIP

Take some time to review the meaning of the items, words, and terms on the banking materials: *routing number* and *account number* (on bottom left of check), *debit, balance, payment due date, savings, activity since last statement,* and so on. Have students work in pairs or small groups to look up the words and terms in dictionaries or online. This can be assigned for homework. Have volunteers make a poster using the banking materials in the book as a guide and label each of the parts. Ask them to include definitions of each part. Display it in the classroom.

Guided Practice I
15–20 minutes

D 1. Have students complete the sentences using the new vocabulary. Set a time limit (two to three minutes).

2. Encourage students to take turns reading the completed sentences with a partner.

Answers	
1. cash	5. current balance
2. personal check	6. debit card
3. checking account	7. bank statement
4. credit card bill	8. savings account

E Read the instructions aloud. Have students take turns asking and answering the question with a partner. Set a time limit (five minutes). Circulate and listen for any pronunciation or vocabulary difficulties.

MULTILEVEL STRATEGIES

For 1E, pair same-level students together.

• **Pre-level** Assist these students with the exercise.

• **Higher-level** When these students finish, have them use the statements in 1D and make questions to ask and answer in pairs.

2 Talk about using an ATM

Guided Practice II
35–40 minutes

A 1. Ask: *Is there an ATM near here? Where?* Introduce the new topic: *Now we're going to talk about using an ATM.*

2. Direct students' attention to the pictures. Set a time limit (three minutes) and have students work in pairs to complete the task. While students are working, copy the sentences onto the board.

3. Call "time" and have volunteers take turns calling out the numbers for the wordlist. Record students' answers on the board.

4. Draw students' attention to the illustrations again. Prompt them to use vocabulary not labeled in the art. Ask: *What objects do you see in the first picture?* [keypad, screen, bank name] *What is the man wearing?* [a T-shirt, glasses] *How many of these steps do you do when you use an ATM?* [I usually only withdraw money at an ATM.]

Answers	
5–Enter the amount. 3–Enter your PIN. 4–Insert your deposit now.	1–Insert your debit card for service. 2–Remove your card. 6–Take your cash.

For 2A, use mixed-level groups.

• **Pre-level** Assign these students the role of administrative assistant.

• **Higher-level** Assign these students the role of manager.

B ◀)) 3-04 1. Play the audio. Ask students to listen and check their answers.

2. Have students correct the sentences on the board and then write the correct numbers in their books as needed.

3. Have students practice the sentences with a partner. Set a time limit (two minutes).

C Ask students to work individually to mark the sentences as *T* (true) or *F* (false). Discuss the answers as a class.

Answers
1. F
2. T
3. F
4. F

For 2C, seat same-level students together.

• **Pre-level** Have students work in pairs or small groups. Assist those groups.

• **Higher-level** After students complete the exercise, ask them to write two more true or false statements and exchange with a partner.

Communicative Practice and Application
10–15 minutes

D 1. Read the instructions aloud and model the sample conversation with a volunteer.

2. Set a time limit (three minutes). Have students take turns asking and answering questions with a partner. Circulate and listen for any pronunciation or vocabulary difficulties.

E 1. Read the questions aloud. Have students discuss the questions with a partner. Circulate and monitor.

2. Have volunteers share their or their partner's responses with the class.

3. Ask for a show of hands about question 2: *How many people use cash the most?* Discuss the results.

Evaluation
10–15 minutes

TEST YOURSELF

1. Make a three-column chart on the board with the headings from page 117. Have students give you an example for each column.

2. Have students copy the chart into their notebooks.

3. Set a time limit (five to ten minutes). Have students fill out their chart with words from the lesson.

4. Call "time" and have students check their spelling in *The Oxford Picture Dictionary* or another dictionary.

Target the *Test Yourself* to the level of your students.

• **Pre-level** Have these students work with their books open.

• **Higher-level** Have these students complete the chart and then write at least one complete sentence for each column in the chart.

EXTENSION ACTIVITY

Retell a Story

Read aloud a short story using the vocabulary from the book.

1. Tell students to listen once without writing and to listen again taking only quick notes. *I had $5.25 in my wallet. I went to the bank. I wanted to withdraw $200.00. I only had $195.00 in my account. Now I'm waiting for my paycheck!*

2. Give students two minutes to retell the story to a partner.

3. Tell the story again.

4. Ask students to work with their partners to write the story.

5. Have volunteers write the story on the board (one sentence per person). Elicit corrections from the class.

Lesson Overview	Lesson Notes

MULTILEVEL OBJECTIVES

Pre-, On- and Higher-level: Read and write about budgeting for buying expensive items for home office use

LANGUAGE FOCUS

Grammar: Simple present (*I want to buy a new computer desk.*)

Vocabulary: Home office vocabulary

For vocabulary support, see this **Oxford Picture Dictionary** topic: Shopping, page 27

STRATEGY FOCUS

Use sequence words to show the different steps in a series of actions: *after that, finally, first, next, then.*

READINESS CONNECTION

In this lesson, students communicate information about making a simple budget and examine reasons for buying something.

PACING

To compress this lesson: Skip 2B and/or 3B.

To extend this lesson: Have students make purchase decision. (See end of lesson.)

And/or have students complete **Workbook 2 page 59** and **Multilevel Activities 2 Unit 9 page 99.**

CORRELATIONS

CCRS: SL.2.A Confirm understanding of a text read aloud or information presented orally or through other media by asking and answering questions about key details and requesting clarification if something is not understood.

R.1.A Ask and answer questions about key details in the text.

R.7.A Use the illustrations and details in a text to describe its key ideas (e.g., maps, charts, photographs, political cartoons, etc.).

W.2.A Write informative/explanatory texts in which they name a topic, supply some facts about the topic, and provide some sense of closure.

ELPS: 6. An ELL can analyze and critique the arguments of others orally and in writing. 9. An ELL can create clear and coherent level-appropriate speech and text.

Warm-up and Review
10–15 minutes (books closed)

Ask students if they have made any large purchases for their home recently. Ask if they take a lot of time to think about making a big purchase. Explain comparison shop: *When you comparison shop, you look at two or more examples of the item you want to buy and see which one has the better price.* Ask students if they ever comparison shop.

Introduction
5 minutes

1. Tell students about some expensive items that you would like to buy for your home. Act out and write the vocabulary on the board as you talk. *I want a new computer. I want to replace some doors. I want to buy a high-quality desk chair.* Ask: *What do you need for your home?* Elicit more ideas from students and write them on the board.

2. Referring to the ideas on the board, ask students how much they think each purchase would cost and where they would go for the lowest price.

3. State the objective: *Today we're going to read and write about buying expensive items and make a simple budget.*

1 Prepare to write

Presentation
20–25 minutes

A 1. Read the instructions and list of steps aloud. Ask students to work individually to number the items. Set a time limit (two minutes).

2. Have students share their answers with a partner. Give them one minute to discuss their answers. Elicit answers from the class.

B 🔊 **3-05** 1. Direct students' attention to the pictures as well as the title of the paragraph in 1C. Build students' schema by asking questions about the pictures, referring to their work in 1A. Ask: *What information do you think Jian is going to include in his paragraph about buying a computer? Where is the first picture?* [a computer/electronics store] *What do you think he is doing in the second picture?* [researching prices online]

2. Play the audio. Have students listen silently.

C 🔊 **3-05** 1. Introduce the text: *You're going to read paragraph about what Jian did before buying a new computer. As you read, look at which parts of the text match the pictures in B. This can help you understand the text better.*

2. Point out the *Writer's Note* and read it aloud. Ask: *What does* sequence *mean?* [the order things happen] Give students time to find the sequence words in the paragraph.

3. Play the audio again and have students read along silently.

4. Check comprehension. Ask: *When did Jian decide to buy a new computer?* [last week] *What did he decide first?* [how much to spend] *What features were important for him?* [good graphics card, plenty of memory] *Who did he ask for advice?* [an assistant in a large electronics store]

Guided Practice I
5–10 minutes

D 1. Have students work individually to mark the sentences as *T* (true) or *F* (false). Set a time limit (two to three minutes).

2. Discuss answers as a class. If students finish the *true/false* exercise early, ask them to rewrite the false sentences to make them correct.

Answers
1. T
2. F
3. T
4. T

MULTILEVEL STRATEGIES

For 1D, seat same-level students together.

• **Pre-level** While other students are completing 1D, work with these students to find the answers in the text.

• **On- and Higher-level** Write additional *true/false* statements on the board for these students. *Jian asked the store assistant about how much to spend.* [False] *Jian probably only needs a computer for emails.* [False] *Jian tried out some computers in person.* [True] *He found a good website to help him make a decision.* [True]

Guided Practice II
15–20 minutes

E 🔊 **3-06** 1. Read the instructions and budget items aloud. Explain to students that they will listen to information about Nina's budget. Play the audio. Have students work individually to fill in the budget.

2. Play the audio again in segments. After the answer for each question comes up, stop the audio and check in with students. If necessary, replay the segment. Have students listen again and check their answers.

Answers
desk–$200
chair–$120
computer–$700
printer–$85
lamp–$0

F 1. Read the instructions aloud and model the sample conversation with a volunteer. Circulate and monitor.

2. Have pairs say their conversation for the class.

2 Plan

Communicative Practice I
10–15 minutes

A 1. Read the instructions aloud. Make sure that students understand that the numbers in the list match the numbers in the chart. Have students complete the exercise individually. Set a time limit (five minutes). Circulate and monitor.

2. Help students understand how the chart can help them organize their paragraphs. As a class, discuss each question and identify the matching parts in the sample paragraph in 1C.

MULTILEVEL STRATEGIES

Adapt 2A to the level of your students.

• **Pre-level** Work with these students to assist them with vocabulary.

• **Higher-level** Ask these students to add a section to their chart that talks about what part of their research was the most helpful to them.

B Read the instructions aloud. Have students share their charts with a partner and give each other advice on what they could add.

3 Write

Communicative Practice II and Application
15–20 minutes

A 1. Read the instructions aloud. Have students look at the template paragraph as you read it aloud. For each blank, have a volunteer give a sample answer.

2. Set a time limit for writing (ten minutes). Have students complete the template paragraph with their own information.

B 1. Ask students to read their completed paragraph to a partner. Call on volunteers to share one thing they liked about their partner's paragraph.

2. Have a class discussion about what methods, websites, or stores are the most helpful when making a decision about major purchases.

MULTILEVEL STRATEGIES

In 3A, target the writing to the level of your students.

• **Pre-level** Write a wordlist on the board for these students to use to complete their paragraphs. Then work with these students to write a group paragraph. Read through the template. At each blank, stop and elicit completions. Decide as a group what to write. Have these students copy the group paragraph into their notebooks.

• **Higher-level** Ask these students to write a paragraph without using the template as a guide.

Evaluation
10 minutes

TEST YOURSELF

1. Read the instructions aloud. Assign a time limit (five minutes) and have students work individually.

2. Before collecting student work, invite two or three volunteers to share their sentences. Ask students to raise their hands if they wrote similar answers.

EXTENSION ACTIVITY

Decide What to Purchase

Provide small groups with flyers from an office supply or electronics store. Assign an expensive item to each group and have the group decide what the best price is.

Lesson Overview

MULTILEVEL OBJECTIVES

On- and Pre-level: Use *to* and *because* to ask and answer questions about purchases

Higher-level: Use *to* and *because* to explain reasons for purchases and returns

LANGUAGE FOCUS

Grammar: Reasons with *to* + verb (*He went to the store to buy a printer.*); Reasons with *because* (*He went to the store because he needed a new printer.*)

Vocabulary: Adjectives with *too* and *not...enough* (*This desk is too small. It's not wide enough.*)

For vocabulary support, see this **Oxford Picture Dictionary** topic: Shopping, page 27

STRATEGY FOCUS

Understand the difference between *too* and *very*.

READINESS CONNECTION

In this lesson, students use *to* and *because* to communicate information about making purchases and returns.

PACING

To compress this lesson: Assign 1D, 1E, and/or 2B as homework.

To extend this lesson: Have students talk about reasons. (See end of lesson.)

And/or have students complete **Workbook 2 pages 60–61, Multilevel Activities 2 page 100**, and **Multilevel Grammar Exercises 2 Unit 9.**

Lesson Notes

CORRELATIONS

CCRS: L.1.A Demonstrate command of the conventions of standard English grammar and usage when writing or speaking.

SL.1.A Participate in collaborative conversations with diverse partners in small and larger groups.

SL.2.A Confirm understanding of a text read aloud or information presented orally or through other media by asking and answering questions about key details and requesting clarification if something is not understood.

ELPS: 7. An ELL can adapt language choices to purpose, task, and audience when speaking and writing. 10. An ELL can demonstrate command of the conventions of standard English to communicate in level-appropriate speech and writing.

Warm-up and Review
10–15 minutes (books closed)

Tell the students about something (preferably a home office item or a related piece of furniture) that you returned to a store. Write the name of the item and the reason for returning it on the board. Ask: *Did you ever return something to a store after you bought it? Why?* Write the items and the reasons on the board.

Introduction
5–10 minutes

1. Write a sentence about one of your students using *because* on the board. *Samar returned an expensive pen because it did not work.* Ask the student which store (or what kind of store) he/she went to, and write a sentence with *to*. *Samar went to the department store to return the pen.*

2. State the objective: *Today we will explore two ways to explain why we do things using* because *or* to.

1 Explore purpose and reasons with *to* and *because*

Presentation I
20–25 minutes

 A 🔊 **3-07** 1. Direct students to look at the picture. Ask: *Who are the people? Where are they? Who do you think the woman might be calling?*

2. Have students read along silently while they listen. Ask a volunteer to say why Nina is upset.

Answers
The store sent her the wrong chair.

B Read the instructions aloud. Give students a minute to read the conversation and find the answers. Discuss answers as a class.

Answers
To complain / Because . . .

C 1. Demonstrate how to read the grammar charts as complete sentences. Read through the charts sentence by sentence. Then read them again and have students repeat after you.

2. Use the conversation in 1A to illustrate points in the grammar charts. Ask: *Why did Nina call customer service? Why is she complaining?*

> ### TIP
> Point out to students that Nina's responses to the questions with *why* are incomplete sentences. Explain that in English, we often use incomplete sentences to answer the question *Why?* in speaking, but in writing we use complete sentences.

Guided Practice I
15–20 minutes

D 1. Read the instructions aloud. Give students time to silently review the charts again and fill in the blanks.

2. Have pairs compare answers. Then check answers as a class.

Answers
1. to
2. because
3. because
4. to
5. because

E 1. Read the instructions aloud. Have students complete the task individually.

2. Have students compare answers with a partner. Discuss answers as a class.

Answers
1. they
2. it
3. it
4. they

2 Practice: purpose and reasons with *to* and *because*

Presentation II and Guided Practice II
20–25 minutes

 A 🔊 **3-08** 1. Direct students to look at the photos. Explain that they will hear sentences about the people in the photos and that they should circle *True* or *False* for each statement.

2. Play the audio and have students complete the task.

3. Have students compare answers with a partner. Play the audio again for students to check answers.

Answers	
1. F	4. F
2. T	5. T
3. T	6. F

B Read the instructions aloud. Have students complete the task individually and then check answers with a partner. Check answers as a class if time allows.

Answers
1. make a deposit, got a paycheck
2. buy a suit, is going to a job interview
3. compare prices, wants to buy a computer

C 1. Read the instructions aloud and model the sample conversation with a volunteer.

2. Have students take turns asking and answering questions with a partner. Circulate and monitor.

3. Have pairs share their conversations with the class.

3 Practice using adjectives with *too* and *not...enough*

Presentation III
10–15 minutes

 A **3-09** 1. Write on the board: *It's too small. It's not big enough.* Ask: *Are these sentences the same or different in meaning?* [same]

2. Read through the charts sentence by sentence. Read the information in the *Grammar Note* aloud. Challenge a volunteer to write another pair of sentences on the board that uses *very* and *too*.

3. Play the audio and have students repeat.

Guided Practice III
15–20 minutes

 B 1. Read the instructions aloud. Have students complete the task individually.

2. Check answers as a class. Have volunteers write their sentences on the board.

Answers
1. It's not small enough.
2. They're not low enough.
3. It's not high enough.
4. They're too short.
5. They're too dark.

MULTILEVEL STRATEGIES

For 3B, group same-level students together.

• **Pre-level** Have these students work in pairs to write sentences.

• **Higher-level** Challenge these students to rewrite the sentences using the opposite adjective: for example, in sentence 1, change *small* to *big*.

C 1. Read the instructions aloud. Direct students to look at the pictures and name the items. Model the sample conversation with a volunteer.

2. Have students work in pairs to complete the task. Circulate and monitor.

D 1. Tell students about a time that you had to return an item to a store and give the reasons. Ask: *Why did I return the (printer)?* Have students answer you using *too* or *not enough*.

2. Have students work in pairs to complete the task. Circulate and monitor.

3. Have volunteers tell the class about their partner's story.

4 Practice talking about reasons

Communicative Practice and Application
15–20 minutes

 A 1. Read the instructions aloud and confirm that students understand the information they need to fill out. Have students complete the task individually.

B Have students work in pairs to ask and answer questions about what they want to buy. Circulate and monitor. Have volunteers share their answers with the class.

TIP

For more practice with giving reasons using *to* and *because*, write role-play scenarios on the board: bank teller, customer withdrawing money; office store clerk, customer returning item; electronics store clerk, customer returning item. Ask students to act the scenarios out with a partner and then switch roles. Assign a time limit for each role-play (two minutes). After each role-play, ask volunteers to perform their role-play for the class.

Evaluation
10 minutes

TEST YOURSELF

Ask students to write their five questions. Collect and correct their writing.

EXTENSION ACTIVITY
Talk about Reasons
Bring in pictures of city streets, or have students look at the picture of city streets in *The Oxford Picture Dictionary*.
1. Tell them to ask and answer questions with a partner using *to*: *Why did you go to the post office?* [I went to the post office to buy stamps.]
2. Assign a time limit (five minutes) and then tell students to continue, answering with *because* instead of *to*.
3. Circulate and provide feedback.

Lesson Overview	Lesson Notes
MULTILEVEL OBJECTIVES	
On-level: Request an exchange or a return and give a reason **Pre-level:** Respond to questions when returning an item **Higher-level:** Ask and answer questions about returns and exchanges	
LANGUAGE FOCUS	
Grammar: *Would like* (*I'd like to return this coat.*) **Vocabulary:** Clothing words, *exchange, return* For vocabulary support, see this **Oxford Picture Dictionary** topic: Shopping, page 27	
STRATEGY FOCUS	
Practice language to respond to customer requests.	
READINESS CONNECTION	
In this lesson, students verbally communicate and explore information about making purchases, exchanges, and returns.	
PACING	
To compress this lesson: Skip 4B. **To extend this lesson:** Have students perform a role-play. (See end of lesson.) And/or have students complete **Workbook 2 page 62** and **Multilevel Activities 2 Unit 9 page 101**.	

CORRELATIONS	
CCRS: R.4.A Ask and answer questions to help determine or clarify the meaning of words and phrases in a text. SL.1.A Participate in collaborative conversations with diverse partners in small and larger groups. SL.2.A Confirm understanding of a text read aloud or information presented orally or through other media by asking and answering questions about key details and requesting clarification if something is not understood. RF.2.A Demonstrate understanding of spoken words, syllables, and sounds (phonemes).	**ELPS:** 2. An ELL can participate in level-appropriate oral and written exchanges of information, ideas, and analyses, in various social and academic contexts, responding to peer, audience, or reader comments and questions. 9. An ELL can create clear and coherent level-appropriate speech and text.

Warm-up and Review
10–15 minutes (books closed)

Review students' sentences from the Lesson 3 *Test Yourself*. Have them share with the class purchases they made and the reasons why, using *to* + verb or *because*.

Introduction
5 minutes

1. Bring in articles of clothing that you can pretend you are not happy with. Tell students: *Sometimes we want to return clothing to the store. Why do you think I might want to return these items?* Write their ideas on the board. Write sentences about one of the clothing items. *I'd like to return this skirt. The color does not work with my other clothes.*

2. State the objective: *Today we will explore how to return and exchange items we buy.*

1 Listen to learn: returning items to a store

Presentation I and Guided Practice I
15–20 minutes

 A 1. Direct students to look at the pictures. Ask: *Are these people at a supermarket or a clothing store?* [clothing store] *Who is the cashier?* [the person in the red vest] Pronounce *receipt* and have students repeat. Read the instructions aloud.

2. Give students time to circle the correct answers. Discuss answers as a class.

Answers
1. a
2. b
3. a

B 🔊 **3-10** 1. Read the instructions aloud. Play the audio and have students complete the return forms.

2. Have students compare answers with a partner. Play the audio again for students to check answers.

Answers
1. refund, it's too small / it's not big enough
2. exchange, wrong color
3. exchange, unwanted gift / doesn't wear ties

MULTILEVEL STRATEGIES

Adapt 1B to the level of your students.

• **Pre-level** Stop the audio after each conversation and help students fill out the forms.

• **Higher-level** Play the audio once and have students take brief notes to fill out the forms.

C Share with students a time when you could not return an item to a store. Discuss the question as a class.

2 Practice your pronunciation

Pronunciation Extension
10–15 minutes

 A 🔊 **3-11** 1. Say the first two sentences and ask students to tell you the differences in meaning. Explain that the /d/ sound in *I'd* is important to hear and pronounce because it indicates politeness and clarifies meaning.

2. Play the audio and ask students to read along silently.

 B 🔊 **3-12** 1. Tell students you will play the audio for the exercise twice. If they aren't sure of the answer on the first time around, they can wait and circle it on the second listening.

2. To check answers, play the audio a third time. Tell students to hold up one finger for *a* and two fingers for *b*. Stop after each item and ask students to hold up the correct number of fingers.

Answers	
1. b	4. b
2. a	5. a
3. b	6. b

C 1. Read the instructions aloud. Give students time to write four sentences individually.

2. Have students work in pairs to complete the task. Circulate and monitor.

TIP

If students need more practice with pronunciation, do a dictation using *I'd like* and *I like*. Say: *Number 1, I'd like a smaller jacket. Number 2, I like the new socks. Number 3, I like long skirts. Number 4, I'd like a blue sweater.* Tell students to write the sentences if they can. If they cannot, they should write *a* (for *I'd like*) or *b* (for *I like*).

3 Practice polite requests and questions with *would like*

Presentation II
5–10 minutes

 A 🔊 **3-13** Read the instructions aloud and play the audio. Have a volunteer answer the question [*I'd like*].

Guided Practice II
15–20 minutes

B 🔊 **3-14** 1. Tell students they will hear sentences about the conversation in A and that they will mark each as *True* or *False*.

2. Play the audio and have students complete the task individually. Check answers as a class.

Answers	
1. T	4. T
2. F	5. F
3. F	6. F

C Give students time to read the sentences silently and study the conversation. Check answers as a class.

Answers
1. I'd like
2. Would you like

D 🔊 **3-15** Give students a moment to read the chart. Play the audio and have students repeat.

E 1. Read the situations aloud and model the sample conversation with a volunteer.

2. Have students work in pairs to role-play the situations, taking turns being the customer. Circulate and monitor.

3. Have pairs say one of their conversations for the class.

4 Make conversation: returning and exchanging items

Communicative Practice I
15–20 minutes

A 1. Draw students' attention to the *Need help?* box and read the sentences aloud. As a class, brainstorm ways to complete the conversation.

2. Have students work in pairs to create a conversation and take turns performing parts.

> **MULTILEVEL STRATEGIES**
>
> For 4A, group same-level students together.
> • **Pre-level** Have these students work in a group to fill in the blanks.
> • **Higher-level** Challenge these students to have the conversations without looking at their books.

B 1. Read the instructions and question aloud. Then ask pairs to share their conversation with another pair.

2. Have pairs present their conversation to the class. Have a class discussion about which pairs sounded the most polite.

AT WORK

Responding to customer requests

Presentation III and Communicative Practice II
15–20 minutes

A 🔊 **3-16** 1. Read the instructions and the questions aloud. Play the audio and have students read along silently.

2. Have students fill in the blanks for each conversation. Play the audio again for students to check their answers and have volunteers write the sentences on the board.

Answers
Would you like an earlier date or a later one?
Would you like to change the date?

B 1. Have students work in pairs to practice the conversations in A. Circulate and monitor.

2. Prompt students to create conversations using their own ideas.

> **TIP**
>
> Brainstorm possible ways to continue the conversations as a class, rather than have students do so in pairs.

Evaluation
10–15 minutes

TEST YOURSELF

Have students work in pairs to perform the role-play. Circulate and assess students' progress. Take note of any mistakes you hear in intonation, pronunciation, grammar, or vocabulary. When all students have finished the activity, review the kinds of mistakes you heard (without naming any students who made them).

EXTENSION ACTIVITY

Role-play

Set up a "store" in your classroom. Bring in enough items for most of the students to have something to "return" (clothing, accessories, personal-care items, sports equipment, calculators). Students can also use their own sweaters, backpacks, etc. Assign several higher-level students to the cashier roles, and have the other students stand in line and return their items to the cashier. The cashier can guide the conversation and, if necessary, help "customers" with vocabulary.

Lesson Overview	Lesson Notes
MULTILEVEL OBJECTIVES	
On- and Higher-level: Read about and discuss credit card safety **Pre-level:** Read about credit card safety	
LANGUAGE FOCUS	
Grammar: Simple present (*Julio uses a credit card.*); Imperative (*Put them in a safe place.*) **Vocabulary:** *Fraud, lend, protect, transactions* For vocabulary support, see this **Oxford Picture Dictionary** topic: The Bank, page 134	
STRATEGY FOCUS	
Understand that a bulleted list helps the reader to identify separate points more easily, and that the introductory paragraph contains information to help you understand the context.	
READINESS CONNECTION	
In this lesson, students communicate information about credit card safety and using data in a pie chart.	
PACING	
To compress this lesson: Assign 1E and/or 1F for homework. **To extend this lesson:** Have students make a poster. (See end of lesson.) And/or have students complete **Workbook 2 page 63** and **Multilevel Activities 2 Unit 9 page 102**.	
CORRELATIONS	

CCRS: R.1.A Ask and answer questions about key details in the text. R.4.A Ask and answer questions to help determine or clarify the meaning of words and phrases in a text. R.5.A Know and use various text features (e.g., headings, tables of contents, glossaries, electronic menus, icons) to locate key facts or information in a text. R.7.A Use the illustrations and details in a text to describe its key ideas (e.g., maps, charts, photographs, political cartoons, etc.).	**ELPS:** 1. An ELL can construct meaning from oral presentations and literary and informational text through level-appropriate listening, reading, and viewing. 3. An ELL can speak and write about level-appropriate complex literary and informational texts and topics.

Warm-up and Review
10–15 minutes (books closed)

Write *cash, a check, a credit card,* and *a bank loan* on the board. Ask students how they think people usually make payments for a car, pay household bills, or pay for supermarket food, restaurant food, a sofa, a CD, an Internet purchase, or a snack. Elicit more examples of things that people often buy with a bank loan or charge on a credit card.

Introduction
5 minutes

1. Tell students about some purchases that you typically charge or don't charge on a credit card. Ask them to tell you some of the good things about using a credit card for purchases. Then elicit possible problems with credit cards.

2. State the objective: *Today we're going to read about credit card safety.*

1 Build reading strategies

Presentation
10–15 minutes

 Read the sentences and definitions aloud. Have students complete the task individually and then share their answers with the class.

Answers
4–fraud
3–lend
2–protect
1–transactions

Guided Practice: Pre-reading
5–10 minutes

 1. Direct students to locate the bullet points in the article in 1C. Discuss why a writer might use bullet points [to make a list of specific points that is easy to read].

2. Read the *Reader's Note* aloud. Ask: *Have you read something recently that had bullet points? Do fiction stories have bullet points? Why or why not? What kinds of readings have bullet points?*

Guided Practice: While Reading
15–20 minutes

 1. On the board write any vocabulary you think may be unfamiliar to students, or that you want to review (e.g., *account, expiration date, secure*). Tell students to pay attention to these words as they read and to try and figure out their meaning from the context. If students need additional help understanding vocabulary, provide practice. Ask them to give a definition, give an example, or use a word in a new setence.

2. Have students read the article silently.

3. Discuss the answer as a class. [The information is for anyone with a credit card.]

MULTILEVEL STRATEGIES

Adapt 1C to the level of your students.

• **Pre-level** Read the text aloud to these students as they follow along.

• **On- and Higher-level** Pair students and have them read the article aloud to each other, taking turns to read each paragraph.

Guided Practice: Rereading
10–15 minutes

 3-17 1. Provide an opportunity for students to extract evidence from the article. Have students reread the article and rewrite the first paragraph as bulleted points.

2. Play the audio again and have students read along silently. Have volunteers share what things they do, or don't do, for credit card safety.

TIP

Have students go online to find other articles that give advice about credit card safety. Provide possible search terms (*credit card + safety*). Have them share their findings with the class.

Guided Practice: Post-reading
15 minutes

 1. Have students work individually to choose the correct answers and then identify in the reading where they found each answer. Check answers as a class.

2. Check comprehension further. Ask: *How often does credit card fraud happen?* [every day] *What should you keep a record of?* [account numbers and expiration dates and phone number to report fraud] *What should you do during a transaction?* [keep your eye on your card] *What things should you compare?* [receipts and statement]

Answers
1. b
2. a
3. b
4. a

MULTILEVEL STRATEGIES

Adapt 1E to the level of your students.

• **Pre-level** Ask these students *yes/no* and short-answer information questions about the reading while other students are completing 1E.

• **Higher-level** Have these students take turns asking and answering comprehension questions about the reading.

F 1. Read the instructions aloud. Have students work individually to complete the task.

2. Have students compare their answers with a partner. Check answers as a class and have students say where they found the answers in the text.

Answers
1. Bad idea
2. Good idea
3. Bad idea
4. Good idea

2 Read a pie chart

Communicative Practice
15–20 minutes

A Read the questions aloud. Have students study the chart and answer the questions with a partner before checking answers as a class.

Answers
1. how common different types of credit card fraud are
2. fake credit cards
3. stolen information

B 1. Read the questions aloud. Allow students time to think of their own answers and make notes.

2. Set a time limit (ten minutes). Have students discuss the questions with a partner. Circulate and help as needed.

3. Have pairs share their responses with another pair. Have volunteers share their partner's answers with the class.

Application
5–10 minutes

BRING IT TO LIFE

Ask students to predict what information the application form will request. Ask students to stop at their bank or print out an application from the Internet and bring it to the class. Discuss the things the applications have in common and what is different.

EXTENSION ACTIVITY

Make a Poster

Have students practice credit card vocabulary.

1. Put students in groups of three to four.

2. Ask them to make a poster or perform a "public service announcement" telling people how to protect themselves from credit card theft.

3. When they are finished, have groups share their work with the class.

Lesson Overview	Lesson Notes
MULTILEVEL OBJECTIVES	
On-, Pre-, and Higher-level: Expand upon and review unit grammar and life skills	
LANGUAGE FOCUS	
Grammar: Reasons with *to + verb* and *because* (*I went to the bank to get some money. I went to the bank because I needed some money.*); Would like (*I'd like to return this skirt.*); Comparatives (*Do you have a smaller one?*); Object pronouns (*I can't find them.*) **Vocabulary:** Community places, comparative adjectives For vocabulary support, see these **Oxford Picture Dictionary** topics: Shopping, page 27; The Bank, page 134	
STRATEGY FOCUS	
Plan and budget a party.	
READINESS CONNECTION	
In this review, students practice teamwork, vocabulary associated with returning items to a store, using a budget, and protecting their credit card information.	
PACING	
To extend this review: Have students complete **Workbook 2 page 64**, **Multilevel Activities 2 Unit 9 pages 103–106**, and **Multilevel Grammar Exercises 2 Unit 9**	
CORRELATIONS	
CCRS: R.1.A Ask and answer questions about key details in the text. R.7.A Use the illustrations and details in a text to describe its key ideas (e.g., maps, charts, photographs, political cartoons, etc.). SL.1.A Participate in collaborative conversations with diverse partners in small and larger groups. SL.3.A Ask and answer questions in order to seek help, get information, or clarify something that is not understood. W.2.A Write informative/explanatory texts in which they name a topic, supply some facts about the topic, and provide some sense of closure.	**ELPS:** 5. An ELL can conduct research and evaluate and communicate findings to answer questions or solve problems. 6. An ELL can analyze and critique the arguments of others orally and in writing.

Warm-up and Review
10–15 minutes (books closed)

1. Review the *Bring It to Life* assignment from Lesson 5.

2. Ask students who completed the exercise to present their applications. Have additional applications available for students who didn't complete the exercise.

3. Ask if the applications required any information that was not predicted by the class. Discuss the results.

Introduction and Presentation
5 minutes

1. Write on the board: *Tom went to the shoe store.* Ask: *Why do you think Tom went to the shoe store?*

2. Record students' answers on the board using both *to* and *because*.

3. Say: *When Tom got to the shoe store, what did he say to the clerk?* Write students' answers on the board using *I'd like.*

4. State the objective: *Today we're going to review how to return items to a store.*

Guided Practice
15–20 minutes

A 1. Direct students to work in groups of three to four and look at the picture. Set a time limit (five minutes) for groups to answer the questions. Circulate and monitor.

2. Have volunteers from each group share the group's responses with the class. If you have a large class, you may not want all of the groups to report their responses. Instead, have groups share their responses with each other. Call "time" and tell all groups to work with a new group and to repeat their responses. Repeat this process as desired, making sure each group gets to share their responses at least once.

Communicative Practice
30–45 minutes

B 1. Review the conversation from Lesson 4, 3A.

2. Have students complete the task with their groups from A. Make sure each student has had a turn doing each part of the role-play.

MULTILEVEL STRATEGIES

Adapt B to the level of your students.

• **Pre-level** Provide these students with sentence frames to use in their role-play. Use the conversation from Lesson 4, 3A. Write it on the board, but leave blanks for students to fill in.

• **Higher-level** Challenge these students to write another four to five line exchange between a customer and assistant in another store in the picture.

C Have students present their conversation to another team. Circulate and monitor.

D 1. Put students in new groups of four and assign roles: manager, researcher, administrative assistant, and reporter. Read the instructions and the questions aloud. Tell them to copy the chart into their notebooks.

2. Set a time limit (five minutes) to complete the activity. Direct students to take turns interviewing each other. Circulate and monitor. Provide global feedback once the activity ends.

E 1. Read the instructions aloud. Set a time limit (five minutes) for students to complete the task with their team from D. Circulate and monitor.

2. Have teams present their role-plays to the class.

F 1. Read the instructions aloud. Have students copy the budget planner into their notebooks.

2. Set a time limit (ten minutes). Direct students to work in their teams to plan the budget for the party. Circulate and monitor.

TIP
You may want to present common prices for each of the items on the list in F. Ask students if they have bought any of the items, what the prices were, and if they think it was possible to get it for less somewhere else.

G Read the instructions and the sample summary aloud. Set a time limit (five minutes). Have students work in their teams, with the administrative assistant recording the group summary.

H 1. Have the reporter from each team read the team's summary. Suggest that students take brief notes to remember the details.

2. Have students vote on which team has the best plan. Ask students to give reasons for their vote.

PROBLEM SOLVING
10–15 minutes

A 🔊 3-18 1. Ask: *Do you save all your credit card receipts? Are you careful about what you use credit cards for?* Tell students they will read a story about a man who doesn't manage his credit card use well.

2. Have students read the problem silently to themselves.

B 1. Elicit answers to question 1. Guide students to a class consensus on the answer.

2. As a class, brainstorm answers to question 2. Ask students if they know someone who has this problem and has overcome it, or what they have done themselves to overcome the same problem.

Evaluation
20–25 minutes

To test students' understanding of the unit language and content, have them take the Unit 9 Test, available on the Teacher Resource Center.

10 Steps to Citizenship

Unit Overview

This unit explores community participation, becoming a U.S. citizen, the basic form of the U.S. government, responding to requests from officials, and using *must* to describe rules.

KEY OBJECTIVES	
Lesson 1	Identify citizenship requirements; identify government leaders
Lesson 2	Identify community problems and solutions
Lesson 3	Use *must* for obligation to describe community and transportation rules
Lesson 4	Respond to police and security personnel requests and commands
Lesson 5	Interpret information about the U.S. government
Teamwork & Language Review	Review unit language

UNIT FEATURES	
Academic Vocabulary	*administrative, benefit, community, document, federal, role*
Employability Skills	• Differentiate between federal, state, and local officials • Reflect on ways to resolve community problems • Analyze and calculate term limits for government officials • Determine how to handle traffic violations • Listen actively • Understand teamwork • Communicate information • Work with others • Communicate verbally • Use·math to solve problems and communicate

Resources	**Class Audio** CD3, Tracks 19–33
	Workbook Unit 10, pages 65–71
	Teacher Resource Center
	    Multilevel Activities 2 Unit 10
	    Multilevel Grammar Exercises 2 Unit 10
	    Unit 10 Test
	Oxford Picture Dictionary Government and Military Service, Civic Engagement, Traffic Signs

Lesson Overview	Lesson Notes
MULTILEVEL OBJECTIVES	
On-level: Identify citizenship requirements and levels of government **Pre-level:** Recognize citizenship requirements and levels of government **Higher-level:** Talk and write about citizenship requirements and levels of government	
LANGUAGE FOCUS	
Grammar: Simple present (*The mayor of my city is Jane Smith.*) **Vocabulary:** Citizenship and government words For vocabulary support, see this **Oxford Picture Dictionary** topic: Government and Military Service, pages 140–141	
READINESS CONNECTION	
In this lesson, students work with others and communicate information to differentiate between federal, state, and local officials.	
PACING	
To compress this lesson: Conduct 2A as a whole-class activity. Have students complete 1D for homework. **To extend this lesson:** Have students write a letter to a government official. (See end of lesson.) And/or have students complete **Workbook 2 page 65** and **Multilevel Activities 2 Unit 10 page 108**.	

CORRELATIONS	
CCRS: L.6.A Use words and phrases acquired through conversations, reading and being read to, and responding to texts, including using frequently occurring conjunctions to signal simple relationships (e.g., *because*). SL.1.A Participate in collaborative conversations with diverse partners in small and larger groups. SL.2.A Confirm understanding of a text read aloud or information presented orally or through other media by asking and answering questions about key details and requesting clarification if something is not understood.	**ELPS:** 8. An ELL can determine the meaning of words and phrases in oral presentations and literary and informational text.

Warm-up and Review
10–15 minutes (books closed)

Ask students questions related to immigration: *Do you think it should be difficult or easy for someone to become a citizen of another country? What should a new citizen know about their new country?*

> **TIP**
>
> During the warm-up, be careful to address the questions to the whole class and only call on volunteers. Some students may not want to share their residency status or experiences.

Introduction
5 minutes

1. Write *government* and *citizenship* on the board. Ask students to brainstorm about these topics. Ask: *What ideas and tasks do these words make you think of?* Write their ideas on the board.

2. State the objective: *Today we're going to learn about citizenship requirements and branches of government.*

1 Learn about citizenship

Presentation I
20–25 minutes

A 1. Direct students to look at the pictures. Ask questions: *What is the woman's name? How old do you think she is? Does she look happy?*

2. Ask students to say the dates in the pictures. Discuss the information in the documents and answer the question as a class.

B 1. Have students listen to the audio. Ask them to point to the correct pictures in 1A as they listen. Circulate and monitor.

2. Ask: *How long did it take for Emilia to become a citizen?* [more than five years]

3. Check comprehension by asking *yes/no* questions. Have students hold up one finger for *yes* and two for *no* in order to get a nonverbal response. Ask: *Can you become a citizen if you're 17?* [no] *Is an oath like a promise?* [yes]

MULTILEVEL STRATEGIES

After the group comprehension check in 1B, call on volunteers and tailor your questions to the level of your students.

• **Pre-level** Ask *yes/no* questions. *Do you have to take a test to become a citizen?* [yes]

• **On- and Higher-level** Ask information questions. *What is one requirement for becoming a citizen?* [You must be 18, you must live in the U.S. for five years, and so on.]

C 1. Ask students to listen and repeat the words.

2. While students are repeating, circulate and listen for pronunciation difficulties. Provide choral practice as necessary.

Guided Practice I
10–20 minutes

D 1. Have students complete the sentences using the new vocabulary. Set a time limit (two to three minutes).

2. Encourage students to take turns reading the completed sentences with a partner.

Answers	
1. citizenship requirements 2. green card 3. application for naturalization	4. citizenship test 5. oath of allegiance 6. passport

E Read the instructions and questions aloud. Set a time limit (three to five minutes). Have students take turns asking and answering the questions with a partner. Circulate and listen for any pronunciation or vocabulary difficulties.

2 Talk about government officials

Guided Practice II
35–40 minutes

A 1. Ask: *Who is the governor of the state you live in? Who is the mayor of your city or town?* Introduce the new topic: *Now we're going to talk about government officials.*

2. Group students and assign roles: manager, researcher, administrative assistant, and reporter. Explain that students work with their groups to match the words and pictures.

3. Check comprehension of the exercise. Ask: *Who looks up the words in the picture dictionary?* [researcher] *Who writes the numbers in the book?* [administrative assistant] *Who tells the class your answers?* [reporter] *Who helps everyone and manages the group?* [manager]

4. Set a time limit (two minutes) and have students work together to complete the task. While students are working, copy the wordlist onto the board.

5. Call "time" and have the reporters from each group take turns calling out the numbers for the wordlist. Record students' answers on the board. If groups disagree, write each group's choice next to the word.

6. Draw students' attention to the illustrations. Prompt students to use vocabulary not labeled in the art. Ask: *What are all of the people wearing?* [suits, ties, formal clothes] *What state is in the top right picture?* [California] *What do you call the thing the people are standing behind in the left picture?* [a podium]

Answers	
11–city council	4–U.S. representative
6–Congress	5–U.S. senator
7–governor	2–vice president
8–lieutenant governor	12–City Hall
10–mayor	9–State House
1–president	3–White House

B ◀)) **3-21** 1. Play the audio. Ask students to listen and check their answers to 2A.

2. Have students correct the wordlist on the board and then write the correct numbers in their books as needed.

3. Have the groups from 2A split into pairs to practice the words. Set a time limit (two minutes).

Communicative Practice and Application
20–25 minutes

C Model the sample conversation with a volunteer. Have pairs talk about the pictures in 2A and where the people work. Circulate and monitor.

D 1. Have students complete the sentences using the new vocabulary. Set a time limit (two minutes).

2. Have students take turns reading the completed sentences to a partner and answering the questions they form.

E Read the instructions aloud. Set a time limit (three minutes). Have students take turns asking and answering the questions with a partner. Circulate and listen for any pronunciation or vocabulary difficulties.

TIP

Ask students which search terms they can use to find information about government officials online. If students don't have access to the Internet in class, have them research the questions in 2D and 2E for homework and share their answers in class the next day.

Evaluation
10–15 minutes

TEST YOURSELF

1. Make a two-column chart on the board with the headings from the chart on page 131. Have students give you an example for each column.

2. Have students copy the chart into their notebooks.

3. Set a time limit (five to ten minutes). Have students test themselves by writing the words they recall from the lesson in the chart.

4. Call "time" and have students check their spelling in *The Oxford Picture Dictionary* or another dictionary.

MULTILEVEL STRATEGIES

Target the *Test Yourself* to the level of your students.

• **Pre-level** Have these students work with their books open.

• **Higher-level** Have these students complete the chart and then write at least one sentence for each column in the chart.

EXTENSION ACTIVITY

Write to a Government Official

Write a list of situations on the board and have a class discussion about which government officials students could write to with their concerns: 1) Crime in your city; 2) Events in another country; 3) Problems with the school system; 4) National parks.

Have students work in groups to choose one of the problems and draft a letter to the appropriate government official.

Lesson Overview

Lesson Notes

MULTILEVEL OBJECTIVES

On-, Pre-, and Higher-level: Read and write about a community problem and ways to participate in the community

LANGUAGE FOCUS

Grammar: Simple present (*Our community has a problem.*)

Vocabulary: *Bake sale, budget, city council, PTA, volunteer*

For vocabulary support, see this **Oxford Picture Dictionary** topic: Civic Engagement, pages 142–143

STRATEGY FOCUS

Understand that each paragraph in the story is about a new idea.

READINESS CONNECTION

In this lesson, students listen actively and work with others to find solutions for community problems.

PACING

To compress this lesson: Assign 2A for homework.

To extend this lesson: Have students make a poster. (See end of lesson.)

And/or have students complete **Workbook 2 page 66** and **Multilevel Activities 2 Unit 10 page 109**.

CORRELATIONS

CCRS: SL.1.A Participate in collaborative conversations with diverse partners in small and larger groups.

SL.2.A Confirm understanding of a text read aloud or information presented orally or through other media by asking and answering questions about key details and requesting clarification if something is not understood.

R.1.A Ask and answer questions about key details in the text.

R.7.A Use the illustrations and details in a text to describe its key ideas (e.g., maps, charts, photographs, political cartoons, etc.).

W.3.A Write narratives in which they recount two or more appropriately sequenced events, include some details regarding what happened, use temporal words to signal event order, and provide some sense of closure.

ELPS: 6. An ELL can analyze and critique the arguments of others orally and in writing. 9. An ELL can create clear and coherent level-appropriate speech and text.

Warm-up and Review
10–15 minutes (books closed)

On the board, write names of community locations that are important to your students' lives: schools, parks, streets. Ask students to brainstorm problems these places have and write their ideas on the board. Leave this list on the board.

Introduction
5 minutes

1. Point to the list of problems on the board and ask: *Who can help with this problem?*

2. State the objective: *Today we're going to read and write about community problems and how to get help for those problems.*

1 Prepare to write

Presentation
20–25 minutes

A 1. Direct students' attention to the pictures and read any text from the pictures aloud. Build students' schema by asking questions about the pictures. Ask: *What is the PTA?* [Parent-Teacher Association] *Why do schools have bake sales?* [to raise money for trips, supplies, repairs, and so on]

2. Have students work with a partner. Give them one minute to discuss their answers to the questions. [The people pictured are parent members of the PTA at a school, students, and other parents.] Elicit responses from the class.

B 🔊 3-22 1. Introduce the story: *You're going to read and listen to a story about a school fundraiser.* Draw students' attention to the *Writer's Note* and read the information aloud. Say: *As you read, pay attention to the purpose of each paragraph.*

2. Play the audio and have students look at the pictures in 1A again as they listen.

C 🔊 3-22 1. Play the audio again and have students read along silently.

2. Check comprehension. Ask: *What does the school need?* [new science equipment] *What did the volunteers do?* [made cookies and cakes] *What does* donate *mean?* [to give something for no cost] *Who donated cupcakes?* [a local supermarket] *What did the committee members do?* [Voted Sharma to be treasurer]

MULTILEVEL STRATEGIES

After the group comprehension check in 1C, call on volunteers and tailor your questions to the level of your students.

• **Pre-level** Ask *yes/no* questions. *Did Sharma meet with the mayor?* [no]

• **On-level** Ask information questions. *What is one thing Sharma did to fix this problem?* [She went to a PTA meeting. She organized volunteers.]

• **Higher-level** Ask critical-thinking questions. *Do you think Sharma will be a good treasurer? Why?*

Guided Practice I
5–10 minutes

D 1. Ask students to work individually to mark the sentences *T* (true) or *F* (false). Set a time limit (three to five minutes). Discuss answers as a class.

Answers
1. T
2. F
3. F
4. F

MULTILEVEL STRATEGIES

For 1D, seat same-level students together.

• **Pre-level** While other students are completing 1D, work with these students to find the answers in the text.

• **On- and Higher-level** Have these students pose additional true/false statements to each other. *The PTA is a student organization.* [false] *The bake sale was successful.* [true]

Guided Practice II
10–15 minutes

E 🔊 3-23 Read the instructions aloud. Play the audio and have students complete the task individually. Set a time limit (three to five minutes). Don't check answers yet.

F 🔊 3-23 1. Have students compare answers for 1E with a partner.

2. Play the audio again in segments. After the answer for each item comes up, stop the audio and check in with the students. Check answers as a class.

Answers

The school <u>needed</u> money for new equipment. The PTA <u>held</u> a bake sale. Sharma <u>organized the volunteers</u>.
They <u>raised money</u> for the school. The PTA <u>voted</u> for Sharma to be the treasurer.

2 Plan

Communicative Practice I
15–25 minutes

A Read the instructions and the activities aloud. Have students complete the task individually.

TIP

Brainstorm other community activities that are possible in your area. Or ask students if they can think of activities that they would like to try in other places, whether in the country or in the world.

B 1. Read the instructions and questions aloud. Give students time (one or two minutes) to think of their answers and briefly make some notes.

2. Have students take turns asking and answering the questions with a partner. Have volunteers share their partner's responses with the class.

C 1. Direct students to look at the graphic organizer from 1E and to copy it into their notebooks, leaving each section blank for their own answers.

2. Have students complete their charts with their own answers from 2B. Set a time limit (five minutes).

3 Write

Communicative Practice II Application
20–30 minutes

A 1. Read the instructions aloud. Have students look at the paragraph template as you read it aloud. For each blank, have a volunteer give a sample answer.

2. Set a time limit for writing (five to ten minutes). Have students complete the template with their own information. Remind students they can use their lists from 2A to write their story.

MULTILEVEL STRATEGIES

Adapt 2A to the level of your students.

• **Pre-level** Group these students and work with them to create a paragraph together. Have them copy the paragraph into their notebooks.

• **Higher-level** Ask these students to include answers to these questions: *What other problem would you like to help solve? How will you solve it?*

B 1. Ask students to read their story to a partner. Call on volunteers to share one thing they liked about their partner's story, and also what was the same or different in their story than their partner's.

2. Lead a class discussion about what students think is the most difficult problem to solve in their community and possible solutions they can take part in.

Evaluation
10 minutes

TEST YOURSELF

1. Read the instructions aloud. Assign a time limit (five minutes) and have students work individually.

2. Before collecting student work, invite two or three volunteers to share their sentences with the class. Ask students to raise their hands if they wrote similar answers.

EXTENSION ACTIVITY

Make a Poster

Have students work with a partner to choose one of the activities in 2A and make a poster for an event that would benefit that activity.

Lesson Overview

| Lesson Notes |

MULTILEVEL OBJECTIVES

On-level: Use *must* to state civic rules

Pre-level: Use *must* to recognize civic rules

Higher-level: Use *must* to write civic rules

LANGUAGE FOCUS

Grammar: *Must* and *must not* (*Drivers must stop at red lights.*)

Vocabulary: *Exact change, pedestrian, speed limit, walk signal*

For vocabulary support, see this **Oxford Picture Dictionary** topic: Traffic Signs, page 158

STRATEGY FOCUS

Use adverbs of frequency with *must*.

READINESS CONNECTION

In this lesson, students reflect on ways to resolve community problems.

PACING

To compress this lesson: Skip 3E and/or 4B.

To extend this lesson: Have students make a poster. (See end of lesson.)

And/or have students complete **Workbook 2 pages 67–68, Multilevel Activities 2 Unit 10 page 110**, and **Multilevel Grammar Exercises 2 Unit 10**

CORRELATIONS

CCRS: L.1.A Demonstrate command of the conventions of standard English grammar and usage when writing or speaking.

SL.1.A Participate in collaborative conversations with diverse partners in small and larger groups.

SL.2.A Confirm understanding of a text read aloud or information presented orally or through other media by asking and answering questions about key details and requesting clarification if something is not understood.

SL.6.A Speak audibly and express thoughts, feelings, and ideas clearly. Produce complete sentences when appropriate to task and situation.

ELPS: 7. An ELL can adapt language choices to purpose, task, and audience when speaking and writing. 10. An ELL can demonstrate command of the conventions of standard English to communicate in level-appropriate speech and writing.

Warm-up and Review
10–15 minutes (books closed)

Take a class poll. Ask: *How many people walk to school? How many people drive to school? How many take the bus?* Ask students about some of the rules for each of these situations: *What are some rules for driving? For walking?* Write their ideas on the board.

Introduction
5–10 minutes

1. Restate some of the students' ideas using *must*. Write a sentence with *must* on the board: *Drivers must stop at red lights. Drivers must not speed.*

2. State the objective: *Today we will explore how to use* must.

1 Explore using *must* and *must not*

Presentation I
20–25 minutes

A 1. Direct students to look at the pictures. Pronounce, mime, and have students repeat the word *pedestrians*.

2. Read the sentences aloud and have students repeat. Discuss the answers as a class.

B Read the instructions aloud and have a volunteer say which word means the same as *have to*. [*must*]

> **TIP**
>
> Explain to students that *must* and *must not* are usually used when talking about specific laws, rules, and regulations. In everyday conversation, *have to* and *can't* are much more common and sound less emphatic, or serious, than <u>must</u>.

C 1. Demonstrate how to read the grammar charts as complete sentences. Read through the charts sentence by sentence. Then read them again and have students repeat after you.

2. Refer to the pictures in 1A to illustrate points in the grammar chart. Read each caption aloud, and ask students to repeat the verb. Point out that we do not use *to* after *must* and never put an *-s* on the end of it.

3. Assess students' understanding of the charts. Write on the board: *I must stop at red lights.* Then have students repeat the sentence. Erase *I* and replace it with *He*. Ask: *Do I need to change the verb? How do I make the sentence negative?*

Guided Practice I
15–20 minutes

D 1. Have students work individually to complete the sentences. Ask volunteers to write the completed sentences on the board.

2. Give students time to silently review the charts and, if they haven't already, fill in the blanks.

Answers
1. must stop
2. must not drive
3. must wear
4. must not walk

E Read the instructions aloud. Set a time limit (five minutes) and have students write sentences with a partner. Check answers as a class. To check, consider having students write their sentences on the board.

2 Practice statements with *must* and *must not*

Presentation II and Guided Practice II
15–20 minutes

A 1. Direct students to read the list of passenger rules for the bus, at right. If you have students who take the bus, ask them if they have seen rules like these posted in the bus.

2. Read the first sentence aloud (uncorrected) and ask students if it's true or false. Point out to them that false sentences need to be corrected, as done in the example.

3. Have students work individually to mark the sentences as *T* (true) or *F* (false). Discuss correct answers as a class.

Answers
1. F, must not
2. T
3. F, must not
4. F, must not
5. T

B Have students work individually to write their sentences. Ask volunteers to share their sentences with the class.

TIP

For more practice with *must* and *must not* after 2B, bring in pictures that illustrate rules or use the picture cards on page 114 of Multilevel Activities Level 2 Unit 10. Elicit a *must* or *must not* sentence for each picture. Discuss the situations in which *must* would be appropriate. For example, *You must not smoke* is fine in an adult class, but *You must raise your hand* is likely to sound too strong.

Answers
1. You must not park here.
2. You must not smoke here.
3. You must turn left here.
4. You must not turn right here.

3 Practice using *must* with adverbs of frequency

Presentation III
10–15 minutes

A ◀))) **3-24** 1. Draw students' attention to the graphic and talk about adverbs of frequency. Say sentences about yourself: *I always ride my bike to school. I usually eat dinner at 6:00. I never watch TV during dinner.* Have students give percentages of how often you do each thing.

2. Read through the chart sentence by sentence. Play the audio and have students repeat.

3. Have students identify the adverbs of frequency in the chart. Discuss how the meaning of each rule in the chart would change if you used a different adverb of frequency.

Guided Practice III
20–25 minutes

B 1. Read the instructions aloud. Have students complete the task individually.

2. As a class, discuss the rules in students' own states.

Answers	
1. must always	5. must always
2. must usually	6. must never
3. must always	7. must usually/always
4. must always/usually	8. must never

C 1. Have students discuss their answers with a partner.

2. Have volunteers share their answer to the question with the class.

D ◀))) **3-25** 1. Read the instructions aloud. Play the audio and have students listen silently.

2. Have students fill in the poster individually and then compare answers with a partner. Play the audio again for students to check their answers.

Answers
1. must not eat/have
2. must not use
3. must not talk
4. must keep
5. must keep

E Read the instructions aloud. Set a time limit (five minutes) and have students discuss the questions with a partner. Circulate and monitor.

2. Have volunteers share their answers with the class.

4 Practice talking about rules in your community

Communicative Practice and Application
15–20 minutes

A Read the instructions and the sample sentences aloud. Have students copy the chart into their notebooks. Have students work in pairs to write more rules and reasons. Circulate and monitor.

B 1. Model the sample conversation with a volunteer. Set a time limit (ten minutes) and have students complete the task.

2. Write the chart from 4A on the board. Have students write their sentences in the chart on the board. Guide a class discussion of the different rules and why they are a good idea (or not).

Evaluation

10 minutes

TEST YOURSELF

Ask students to write the sentences individually. Collect and correct their writing.

MULTILEVEL STRATEGIES

Target the *Test Yourself* to the level of your students.

• **Pre-level** Allow these students to use three rules from the lesson.

• **Higher-level** Ask these students to write five new rules.

EXTENSION ACTIVITY

Write Rules

Have students create classroom rules.

1. Ask volunteers to write their ideas for classroom rules on the board.

2. Have the class vote on the five most important rules.

3. Create a class poster with those rules on it.

Lesson Overview	Lesson Notes

MULTILEVEL OBJECTIVES

On-, Pre-, and Higher-level: Respond to police commands and requests

LANGUAGE FOCUS

Grammar: *Must* (*You must wear a seat belt.*); *Should* (*You should check your engine.*)

Vocabulary: *Seat belt, sidewalk*

For vocabulary support, see these **Oxford Picture Dictionary** topics: Government and Military Service, pages 140–141; Civic Engagement, pages 142–143; Traffic Signs, page 158

STRATEGY FOCUS

Make polite commands.

READINESS CONNECTION

In this lesson, students practice using *must* and *should* to communicate how to talk and respond to police officers and other official persons.

PACING

To compress this lesson: Skip 4B and/or assign 3D for homework.

To extend this lesson: Have students work together to make rules. (See end of lesson.)

And/or have students complete **Workbook 2 page 69** and **Multilevel Activities 2 Unit 10 page 111**.

CORRELATIONS

CCRS: SL.1.A Participate in collaborative conversations with diverse partners in small and larger groups.

SL.2.A Confirm understanding of a text read aloud or information presented orally or through other media by asking and answering questions about key details and requesting clarification if something is not understood.

RF.2.A Demonstrate understanding of spoken words, syllables, and sounds (phonemes).

ELPS: 2. An ELL can participate in level-appropriate oral and written exchanges of information, ideas, and analyses, in various social and academic contexts, responding to peer, audience, or reader comments and questions. 9. An ELL can create clear and coherent level-appropriate speech and text.

Warm-up and Review
10–15 minutes (books closed)

Write scrambled words on the board. Tell students all of the words are related to transportation, and give them a few minutes to work on unscrambling the letters: *lcnisee* (license), *esat lbet* (seat belt), *eetstr* (street), *nigeen* (engine), *tiristegnrao* (registration). Ask volunteers to put the correct answers on the board. If students are having difficulty, underline the starting letter for each word.

Introduction
5 minutes

1. Write *ticket* on the board. If you have ever gotten a ticket, tell students the story of what happened. Elicit student ideas about why a person might get a ticket. Leave them on the board.

2. Choose one of the situations on the board—for example, *go over the speed limit*. Ask: *If I go over the speed limit, what will the police officer do? What will the police officer say?*

3. State the objective: *Today we're going to learn how to talk to police officers and other officials.*

1 Learn to listen: forms of ID

Presentation I and Guided Practice I
15–25 minutes

A Direct students to look at the identification cards and answer the question [when you are driving; when you need to show ID]. Read each caption. Ask for a show of hands: *How many people have a driver's license?*

B ◀》 **3-26** 1. Read the instructions and the occupations aloud. Play the audio and have students complete the task individually. Explain that they will listen again to the conversation in the next task, and for this one they only have to listen for who is asking for the ID.

2. Play the audio again, stopping after each conversation and discuss answers as a class.

Answers
2–police officer
4–administrative assistant
1–security guard
3–train ticket inspector

C ◀》 **3-26** 1. Read the instructions and the answer choices aloud. Play the audio and have students complete the task individually.

2. Play the audio again, stopping after each conversation. Discuss answers as a class.

Answers
1. no ID
2. speeding
3. expired
4. wrong card

D 1. Have students discuss the question with a partner. Circulate and monitor. Have volunteers share their responses with the class.

2 Practice your pronunciation

Pronunciation Extension
15–20 minutes

A ◀》 **3-27** 1. Remind students that intonation is how your voice rises and falls when you say something, and that your intonation shows how you feel.

2. Read the instructions aloud and play the audio. As a class, discuss how the intonation is different in each response.

B ◀》 **3-28** 1. Read the instructions aloud and play the audio. Have students complete the task individually.

2. Have students compare answers with a partner. Play the audio for students to check their answers.

Answers
1. upset
2. polite
3. polite
4. upset

C Have students work in pairs to complete the task. Circulate and monitor.

TIP
For an extra challenge, have students sit back to back to complete the task so they can only use their hearing to determine if their partner is being polite or upset.

3 Practice using *must* and *should*

Presentation II and Guided Practice II
15–20 minutes

A ◀》 **3-29** 1. Remind students of the difference between *must* and *should*. On the board write: *You ___ wear a seatbelt. You ___ study one hour per day.* Ask volunteers to fill in the blanks. Write *should* and *must* on the board and brainstorm actions that are appropriate for each one.

2. Play the audio and have students read along silently. Discuss the rules and advice as a class.

TIP
If students don't use *must* or *should* correctly, explain. For example: *You shouldn't speed. This is incorrect because* should *is used for advice and the speed limit is a rule.*

B ◀》 **3-30** Play the audio and have students work individually to circle the answers. Discuss answers as a class.

Answers
1. a
2. b
3. a
4. a

C Read through the chart sentence by sentence. Then read it again and have students repeat after you. Have volunteers answer the question. [You use *should* for advice.]

D Have students complete the sentences using the new vocabulary.

2. Encourage students to take turns reading their completed sentences to a partner.

Answers	
1. should	4. should not
2. must	5. must not
3. must not	6. should

4 Make conversation: responding politely to a police officer

Communicative Practice I
15–20 minutes

A 1. Ask students if they have ever been pulled over by the police for a traffic violation. Ask: *Why is it important to be polite if you get pulled over?*

2. Read the template conversation aloud. Then ask volunteers to suggest a term from the word box to fill each blank.

3. Direct students' attention to the *Need help?* box. Explain that the responses are useful when you are in a situation and you need to be polite to an authority figure. Read the sentences aloud and have students say where they can be substituted into the conversation.

4. Have students work in pairs to create a conversation and take turns performing the parts.

B 1. Set a time limit (ten minutes). Ask pairs to share their conversation with another pair. Circulate and monitor.

2. Have pairs present their conversation to the class.

Making polite commands

Presentation III and Communicative Practice II
15–20 minutes

A 🔊 **3-31** 1. Direct students to look at the pictures. Ask them to describe what they see and what they think the different situations are.

2. Play the audio and have students read along silently. Give students time to study the questions. Answer any questions about vocabulary.

B 1. Have students work in pairs to role-play each situation. Circulate and monitor.

2. Have pairs present their conversation to the class.

MULTILEVEL STRATEGIES
For B, group same-level students together. • **Pre-level** Have students choose only one of the situations to role-play. Provide them with a conversation template to fill in and use in their conversation. • **Higher-level** Have these students think of one additional situation to role-play.

Evaluation
10–15 minutes

TEST YOURSELF

1. Model the role-play with a volunteer. Then switch roles.

2. Pair students. Check comprehension. Ask: *What other officials could Partner A be? Why would an official want to see your ID?*

3. Set a time limit (five minutes) and have the partners perform both roles of the role-play.

4. Circulate and monitor. Encourage pantomime and improvisation.

5. Provide feedback.

MULTILEVEL STRATEGIES

Target the *Test Yourself* to the level of your students.

• **Pre-level** Have these students use the conversation in 4A.

EXTENSION ACTIVITY

Make Rules

Provide more practice with *must* and *should*.

1. Put students into groups and assign each group a "person" category: teachers, students, parents, small children, teenagers, bosses, workers, police officers, and so on.

2. Give each group a piece of poster paper or butcher paper and ask students to write six sentences—three things their "person" should/ should not do and three things he or she must/must not do. *Teachers should be patient. Teachers must come to class on time.*

3. Correct the sentences as a class and encourage discussion about the choice of *must* or *should*.

Lesson Overview	Lesson Notes

MULTILEVEL OBJECTIVES

On- and Higher-level: Read about and discuss the branches of the U.S. government

Pre-level: Read about the branches of the U.S. government

LANGUAGE FOCUS

Grammar: Simple present (*The president signs new laws.*)

Vocabulary: *Judicial, legislative, and executive branches; court, judge, serve, term*

For vocabulary support, see these **Oxford Picture Dictionary** topics: Government and Military Service, pages 140–141; Civic Engagement, pages 142–143

STRATEGY FOCUS

Use the information in a chart to help you understand an article. Combining information from different sources can help you understand it better.

READINESS CONNECTION

In this lesson, students listen actively and communicate information about the U.S. government.

PACING

To compress this lesson: Assign 1E and/or 1F for homework.

To extend this lesson: Have students work together to make a citizenship test. (See end of lesson.)

And/or have students complete **Workbook 2 page 70** and **Multilevel Activities 2 Unit 10 page 112**

CORRELATIONS

CCRS: R.1.A Ask and answer questions about key details in the text.

R.4.A Ask and answer questions to help determine or clarify the meaning of words and phrases in a text.

R.5.A Know and use various text features (e.g., headings, tables of contents, glossaries, electronic menus, icons) to locate key facts or information in a text.

R.7.A Use the illustrations and details in a text to describe its key ideas (e.g., maps, charts, photographs, political cartoons, etc.).

SL.1.A Participate in collaborative conversations with diverse partners in small and larger groups.

SL.6.A Speak audibly and express thoughts, feelings, and ideas clearly. Produce complete sentences when appropriate to task and situation.

ELPS: 1. An ELL can construct meaning from oral presentations and literary and informational text through level-appropriate listening, reading, and viewing. 3. An ELL can speak and write about level-appropriate complex literary and informational texts and topics.

Warm-up and Review
10–15 minutes (books closed)

Write *Job Title* and *Name* on the board as column heads. Tell students you want to review the government officials that were discussed in

Lesson 1. Write *president* under job title and elicit the name of the president. Ask volunteers to provide other government job titles and names.

Introduction
5 minutes

1. Draw a tree on the board with three branches. Write the word *branch* on one branch. Tell students that the U.S. federal government has three branches. The president is part of one branch. If they mentioned senator and/or representative during the warm-up, tell them those officials are part of another branch.

2. State the objective: *Today we're going to read about the three branches of government in the United States.*

1 Build reading strategies

Presentation
10–15 minutes

 1. Read the definitions aloud. Check comprehension. Ask: *Who makes decisions about the law? Where does a judge work?*

2. Have students answer the questions. Check answers as a class.

Answers
organization = branch
person = judge
place = court

Guided Practice: Pre-reading
5–10 minutes

B 1. Read the instructions aloud and remind students that to preview an article means to look at pictures, headings, captions, and so on, but not to read every word for details.

2. Give students a moment to preview the article. Have students answer the questions with a partner. Then check answers as a class. If any students answer incorrectly, ask them to support their answer using the pictures, title, and headers. Establish the correct answer as a class. [The pictures and headings give information about different parts of the U.S. government.]

Guided Practice: While Reading
15–20 minutes

C 1. Ask students to read the article silently and think about their answer to the question. Answer any questions about unfamiliar vocabulary.

2. Have students compare and discuss their answers with a partner. Then check answers as a class.

3. Check comprehension. Ask: *Who signs new laws?* [the president] *How many senators are there?* [100] *How many Supreme Court judges are there?* [nine]

Guided Practice: Rereading
10–15 minutes

 🔊 3-32 1. Play the audio and have students listen and read along silently.

2. Provide an opportunity for students to extract evidence from the article. Have students reread the article and underline any words or phrases that tell what each branch of government does.

3. Have students discuss their answers to the question with a partner. Circulate and monitor. Have volunteers share their own or their partner's responses with the class.

4. Ask additional comprehension questions: *Does the president sign new laws?* [yes] *Are the senators part of the executive branch?* [no] *What branch are the federal courts in?* [judicial]

TIP
Have students share with the class any other facts that they know about the three branches of government.

Guided Practice: Post-reading
15 minutes

E Have students work individually to complete the task and identify in the reading where they found each answer.

Answers
1. The president is the leader of the country.
2. Congress makes new laws for the country.
3. The Cabinet is part of the executive branch.
4. There are 435 representatives in the House of Representatives.
5. There are nine judges on the Supreme Court.

MULTILEVEL STRATEGIES

For 1E, call on volunteers and tailor your questions to the level of your students.

• **Pre-level** Ask *yes/no* questions. *Does Congress have two parts?* [yes]

• **On-level** Ask information questions. *Who makes the laws for the U.S.?* [Congress]

• **Higher-level** Ask critical-thinking questions. *Why do we have three branches of government? Why doesn't the president make, sign, and explain the laws?*

F 1. Have students work individually to complete the sentences.

2. Have students read each of their sentences to a partner before checking answers as a class.

Answers
1. leader
2. laws
3. judges
4. composed
5. branches

2 Read about government officials

Communicative Practice
20–25 minutes

A 1. Ask students to read the chart. Read the information in the *Reader's Note* aloud. Check comprehension. Ask: *How long is a president's term?* [four years] *How many terms can a senator serve?* [no limit]

2. Have students complete the task individually before comparing answers with a partner.

3. Check answers as a class.

TIP

After 3A, encourage students to share information about their countries of origin. *Who is the leader? What is his/her name? Is the leader elected? How long is the term? Do people vote for a party or for a person? Do most people vote?*

Answers
1. 2016
2. 2018
3. 2016

B 1. Read the questions aloud. Allow students time to think of their own answers and make notes.

2. Set a time limit (ten minutes). Have students discuss the questions with a partner. Circulate and help as needed.

3. Have pairs share their responses with another pair. Have volunteers share their partner's answers with the class.

TIP

As a follow-up to your discussion of the U.S. government in 3B, talk about the flag. Tell students the meaning of the stars and stripes. On the Internet, find and print copies of the flags representing your students' countries of origin. Ask students to describe the flags, including colors and symbols. Ask them to share what they know about the meanings of the symbols.

Application
5–10 minutes

BRING IT TO LIFE

1. As students brainstorm questions, write them on poster paper or butcher paper, leaving enough space for the answer.

2. Assign different questions to different students.

TIP

The federal government has a large number of websites with comprehensive information about the government that could help students with the *Bring It to Life* activity. Students can access all of the government websites through the U.S. government web portal. Several sites are written for K–12 students and have different levels of simplified language. Remind students that all official government sites end in *.gov* (not *.com*).

EXTENSION ACTIVITY

Write a Citizenship Test

Have students work in groups to create their own "U.S. citizenship test."

1. Instruct them to write questions they think every U.S. citizen should know the answers to.

2. Have a reporter "administer" the test to the class to see if his/her classmates can pass the test.

Lesson Overview	Lesson Notes

MULTILEVEL OBJECTIVES

On-, Pre-, and Higher-level: Expand upon and review unit grammar and life skills

LANGUAGE FOCUS

Grammar: *Must, should, have to, could,* and *may* (*Do I have to take the test? May I see your passport, please?*)

Vocabulary: *Application, green card, naturalization, oath of allegiance, requirements*

For vocabulary support, see these **Oxford Picture Dictionary** topics: Government and Military Service, pages 140–141; Civic Engagement, pages 142–143; Traffic Signs, page 158

READINESS CONNECTION

In this review, students work with others to explore the use of *must*, *should*, and *have to* with different intonations and communicate information about community rules.

PACING

To extend this review: Have students complete **Workbook 2 page 71**, **Multilevel Activities 2 Unit 10 pages 113–116**, and **Multilevel Grammar Exercises 2 Unit 10.**

CORRELATIONS

CCRS: R.1.A Ask and answer questions about key details in the text.

R.7.A Use the illustrations and details in a text to describe its key ideas (e.g., maps, charts, photographs, political cartoons, etc.).

SL.1.A Participate in collaborative conversations with diverse partners in small and larger groups.

SL.3.A Ask and answer questions in order to seek help, get information, or clarify something that is not understood.

ELPS: 5. An ELL can conduct research and evaluate and communicate findings to answer questions or solve problems. 6. An ELL can analyze and critique the arguments of others orally and in writing.

Warm-up and Review
10–15 minutes (books closed)

1. Review the *Bring It to Life* assignment from Lesson 5.

2. Have students present their answers to the class and write them on the poster paper or butcher paper under the correct questions. Ask students who didn't complete the assignment to write down any unanswered questions. Provide the answers if you know them. If not, encourage students to try to find the answers and report back the next day. Encourage students to make observations and discuss conclusions about the questions and answers.

Introduction and Presentation
5 minutes

1. Ask students to keep their books closed. Review *should* and *must*. Write one negative and one positive classroom rule on the board: *No eating in class. Speak English.* Ask students to state these rules as complete sentences using *must* and write them on the board.

2. Write a piece of advice on the board that you have given students in the past, such as *Practice your pronunciation in front of the mirror.* Ask: *Is that something you* must *do or something you* should *do?* Write the sentence using *should* on the board.

3. Introduce questions with *have to*. Tell students that we don't usually use *must* in questions. For example, the question form for *You must speak English in class* is *Do we have to speak English in class?* Elicit some other examples of questions students might ask on the first day of class.

4. State the objective: *Today we're going to review the use of* must, should, *and* have to.

Guided Practice
20–25 minutes

A 1. Direct students to work in groups of three to four and look at the pictures. Ask: *How many businesses do you see?* [2] *Which picture is the "before" one?* [the top one]

2. Set a time limit (five minutes) for groups to complete the task. Circulate and answer any questions.

3. Have students from each group share the group's responses with the class. If you have a large class, you may not want all of the groups to report their responses. Instead, have groups share their responses with each other. Call "time" and tell all groups to work with a new group and to repeat their responses. Repeat this process as desired, making sure each group gets to share their responses at least once.

B 1. Have students work in their groups from A. Read the instructions aloud. Model the sample conversation with a volunteer.

2. Set a time limit (five minutes) to complete the task.

3. Have teams share their conversations with the class.

TIP
To make sure that there are not too many duplicate rules, you can assign different categories to different groups, such as transportation, safety, businesses, or parks.

Communicative Practice
30–45 minutes

C 1. Have students work with their group from A. Read the instructions and sample rule aloud. Set a time limit (ten minutes).

2. Ask volunteers to share their group's rules with the class, while other volunteers write them on the board. (Instruct students not to duplicate any rules that are already on the board.)

D 1. Give students time (two minutes) to look at the rules on the board. Ask them to think which five rules they like best.

2. Point to each rule on the board and have students raise their hands to vote for the ones they think are the best. Keep a tally on the board.

3. After the class determines their "best" rules, plan a poster. As a class, list any diagrams or illustrations that might be needed. Supply chart paper and markers and have volunteers each write one of the top ten rules on the poster. Ask other volunteers to add the illustrations or diagrams. Alternatively, have students work in their teams to make smaller posters on notebook paper.

E 1. Ask students to form new groups of three to four. Read the instructions aloud. Have students copy the chart into their notebooks. Model the sample conversation with a volunteer.

2. Set a time limit (ten minutes) to complete the task.

MULTILEVEL STRATEGIES
For E, group same-level students together.
• **Pre-level:** Have these students ask and answer *yes/no* and *Wh-* questions: *Do you volunteer? Where? When do you volunteer?*

F 1. Have volunteers report their findings about one student of their group to the class.

2. Guide a discussion about community participation. Ask: *How do you feel when you volunteer? Can you make friends from participating in the community? What can you learn from participating in the community?*

G Read the instructions and the sample sentence stems aloud. Set a time limit (five minutes) and have students work individually to complete the task. Have volunteers share their answers with the class.

PROBLEM SOLVING

10–15 minutes

A (�))3-33 1. Ask students to read the paragraph silently. Then play the audio and have them read along silently.

2. Check comprehension. Ask: *What is the speed limit around a school? Is it different than in other areas? How much do you think a speeding ticket is?*

B 1. Read the questions aloud. Have students work in small groups to answer the questions. Circulate and monitor.

2. Come to a class consensus of what problem Kemal has. Then have groups share their solutions. Write each one on the board.

3. As a class, discuss the pros and cons of each solution. Have students vote on the top three of each.

C Have students work in pairs to role-play the conversation between Kemal and the judge. Circulate and monitor. Have pairs share their conversation with the class. Ask the class to say who they thought was the most polite.

> **TIP**
>
> As a review of the unit grammar, write *teacher, doctor, police officer, immigration officer,* and *boss* on the board. Ask students to copy the words into their notebooks. Say a series of sentences. Tell students to write the number of the sentence under the correct job title. 1. *You should organize your notebook.* 2. *May I see your driver's license?* 3. *You must wear a hairnet behind the counter.* 4. *You should exercise more.* 5. *May I see your passport?* Read the sentences again, eliciting the correct job titles.

Evaluation

20–25 minutes

To test students' understanding of the unit language and content, have them take the Unit 10 Test, available on the Teacher Resource Center.

11 Deal with Difficulties

Unit Overview

This unit explores emergency situations, practice making 911 calls, being prepared for an emergency, and using the simple past and past continuous together to communicate about past events.

KEY OBJECTIVES	
Lesson 1	Identify crimes, emergencies, and natural disasters
Lesson 2	Identify emergency services; describe and report emergencies
Lesson 3	Use the past continuous to describe emergencies
Lesson 4	Identify and describe emergencies; make emergency calls
Lesson 5	Identify safety procedures for emergencies
Teamwork & Language Review	Review unit language

UNIT FEATURES	
Academic Vocabulary	*occur, medical, injury*
Employability Skills	• Interpret dates and facts about natural disasters • Differentiate between emergencies and non-emergencies • Draw conclusions about emergency kit items • Choose appropriate action during an emergency • Respond appropriately to a hurricane warning • Understand teamwork • Communicate information • Work with others • Communicate verbally • Listen actively

Resources	**Class Audio** CD3, Tracks 34–48
	Workbook Unit 11, pages 72–78
	Teacher Resource Center
	    Multilevel Activities 2 Unit 11
	    Multilevel Grammar Exercises 2 Unit 11
	    Unit 11 Test
	Oxford Picture Dictionary The Telephone, Crime, Emergencies and Natural Disasters, Emergency Procedures

Lesson Overview	Lesson Notes

MULTILEVEL OBJECTIVES

On-level: Identify crimes and emergencies
Pre-level: Recognize crimes and emergencies
Higher-level: Talk and write about crimes and emergencies

LANGUAGE FOCUS

Grammar: Simple past (*There was a tornado.*)

Vocabulary: Crime words, emergency words, natural disaster words

For vocabulary support, see these **Oxford Picture Dictionary** topics: The Telephone, pages 14–15; Crime, page 145; Emergencies and Natural Disasters, pages 148–149; Emergency Procedures, pages 150–151

STRATEGY FOCUS

Learn and talk about natural disasters.

READINESS CONNECTION

In this lesson, students communicate information about emergency situations.

PACING

To compress this lesson: Assign 1D and 2C for homework.

To extend this lesson: Have students play Emergency Bingo. (See end of lesson.)

And/or have students complete **Workbook 2 page 72** and **Multilevel Activities 2 Unit 11 page 118.**

CORRELATIONS

CCRS: L.6.A Use words and phrases acquired through conversations, reading and being read to, and responding to texts, including using frequently occurring conjunctions to signal simple relationships (e.g., *because*).

R.7.A Use the illustrations and details in a text to describe its key ideas (e.g., maps, charts, photographs, political cartoons, etc.).

SL.1.A Participate in collaborative conversations with diverse partners in small and larger groups.

SL.2.A Confirm understanding of a text read aloud or information presented orally or through other media by asking and answering questions about key details and requesting clarification if something is not understood.

ELPS: 8. An ELL can determine the meaning of words and phrases in oral presentations and literary and informational text.

Warm-up and Review
10–15 minutes (books closed)

Draw a quick map on the board showing an intersection and several labeled buildings: a mall, a parking lot, a supermarket. Tell students, *There was an accident here* and make an *X* on the map. Elicit the location, prompting students with the correct preposition if necessary.

Introduction
5 minutes

1. Write *911* on the board and ask: *When do people call 911?* As students brainstorm ideas, write them on the board.

2. Pantomime some of the emergencies on the board and have students guess which one you are doing.

3. State the objective: *Today we will explore more words for emergencies and disasters.*

1 Learn about crimes and emergencies

Presentation
20–25 minutes

 1. Write *emergency, crime,* and *natural disaster* on the board and discuss how each is different. [An emergency is an unexpected and usually dangerous situation. A crime is an illegal act that may or may not be dangerous to people. A natural disaster is a sudden and extreme event in nature that may or may not be dangerous to people.] Have students work together and brainstorm in a group. Make a list on the board of emergencies, crimes, and natural disasters that students name.

2. Have students look at the pictures and identify the words they know. Elicit which situations are crimes and which ones are emergencies, and encourage students to explain their reasons.

 3-34 1. Tell students that they will hear six people talking about the pictures and that they should listen for where each situation is happening. Play the audio.

2. Have students compare answers with a partner. Play the audio again and check answers as a class.

> **MULTILEVEL STRATEGIES**
>
> After the group comprehension check in 1B, call on volunteers and tailor your questions to the level of your students.
>
> • **Pre-level** Ask *yes/no* questions. *Do you have light during a power outage?* [no]
>
> • **On-level** Ask information questions. *Who should you call if you see a crime?* [the police]
>
> • **Higher-level** Ask critical-thinking questions. *What do vandals use to commit vandalism? Why is vandalism bad for a neighborhood?*

 3-35 1. Ask students to listen and repeat the words.

2. While students are repeating, circulate and listen for pronunciation difficulties. Provide choral practice as necessary.

Guided Practice I
15–20 minutes

D 1. Have students complete the sentences using the new vocabulary. Set a time limit (two to three minutes).

2. Encourage students to take turns reading the completed sentences with a partner.

Answers	
1. accident	4. explosion
2. robbery	5. mugging
3. vandalism	6. power outage

E 1. Read the instructions aloud and model the sample conversation with a volunteer.

2. Set a time limit (three minutes). Have students take turns asking and answering questions with a partner. Circulate and listen for any pronunciation or vocabulary difficulties.

2 Talk about natural disasters

Guided Practice II
25–30 minutes

A 1. Ask: *Do you remember a recent natural disaster from the news? Or one that happened here?* Introduce the new topic: *Now we're going to talk about natural disasters.*

2. Group students and assign roles: manager, researcher, administrative assistant, and reporter. Explain that students work with their groups to match the words and pictures.

3. Check comprehension of the exercise. Ask: *Who looks up the words in the picture dictionary?* [researcher] *Who writes the numbers in the book?* [administrative assistant] *Who tells the class your answers?* [reporter] *Who helps everyone and manages the group?* [manager]

4. Set a time limit (two minutes) and have students work together to complete the task. While students are working, copy the wordlist onto the board.

5. Call "time" and have the reporters from each group take turns calling out the numbers for the wordlist. Record students' answers on the board. If groups disagree, write each group's choice next to the word.

6. Draw students' attention to the illustrations. Prompt students to use vocabulary not labeled in the art. Ask: *What other items can you name in the picture?* [map of the U.S., smoke, rain, cracks in the ground/street, plant, etc.] *Where else in the world do (droughts, blizzards, earthquakes, etc.) happen?* [Earthquakes happen in Japan, etc.] *What does a town look like after a tornado?* [Houses are gone, items are everywhere, trees are pulled out of the ground.]

Answers	
4–blizzard 6–drought 8–earthquake 3–flood	7–wildfire 5–hurricane 2–tornado 1–volcanic eruption

MULTILEVEL STRATEGIES

For 2A, use mixed-level groups.

• **Pre-level** Assign these students the role of administrative assistant.

• **Higher-level** Assign these students the role of manager.

B 3-36 1. Play the audio. Ask students to listen and check their answers.

2. Have students correct the wordlist on the board and then write the correct numbers in their books.

3. Have the groups from 2A split into pairs to practice the words. Set a time limit (two minutes).

Communicative Practice and Application

15–20 minutes

C Have students read through all of the sentences before they fill in the blanks. Tell them to complete as many sentences as they can and then check their answers with a partner. Discuss answers as a class.

TIP

Ask students if they know of any other natural disasters that have happened in theirs state, home country, or other places in the world. Encourage them to give whatever details they can.

Answers	
1. earthquake 2. drought 3. volcanic eruption 4. hurricane	5. blizzard 6. flood 7. wildfires 8. tornadoes

D 1. Read the instructions aloud.

2. Set a time limit (three minutes). Have students take turns asking and answering questions with a partner. Circulate and listen for any pronunciation or vocabulary difficulties.

3. Have volunteers share their answers and ideas in a class discussion.

Evaluation

10–15 minutes

TEST YOURSELF

1. Make a three-column chart on the board with the headings *Crimes, Emergencies,* and *Natural disasters*. Have students give you an example for each column.

2. Have students copy the chart into their notebooks. Set a time limit (five to ten minutes). Have students test themselves by writing the words they recall from the lesson in their chart.

3. Call "time" and have students check their spelling in *The Oxford Picture Dictionary* or another dictionary.

MULTILEVEL STRATEGIES

Target the *Test Yourself* to the level of your students.

• **Pre-level** Have these students work with their books open.

• **Higher-level** Ask these students to complete the chart and then write at least one sentence for each column in the chart.

EXTENSION ACTIVITY

Emergency Bingo

1. Have students draw a three-by-three grid in their notebooks and write in nine of the vocabulary words from 1A and 2A.

2. Describe each situation (*Help! The earth is shaking!* or *Someone broke into my car!*). Tell students to put an *X* through the word corresponding to the situation if they wrote it in their grid. The first person to get three in a row wins.

3. Have students draw new grids and repeat the game using different words.

Lesson Overview	Lesson Notes
MULTILEVEL OBJECTIVES	
On-, Pre, and Higher-level: Read and write about emergencies	
LANGUAGE FOCUS	
Grammar: Simple past (*I saw a fire.*); past continuous (*He was doing yard work.*)	
Vocabulary: Emergency words	
For vocabulary support, see these **Oxford Picture Dictionary** topics: The Telephone, pages 14–15; Emergencies and Natural Disasters, pages 148–149; Emergency Procedures, pages 150–151	
STRATEGY FOCUS	
Add details to make your description more vivid.	
READINESS CONNECTION	
In this lesson, students listen actively, read, and write about appropriate actions during an emergency situation.	
PACING	
To compress this lesson: Do 1D as a whole class activity.	
To extend this lesson: Have students do a dictation activity. (See end of lesson.)	
And/or have students complete **Workbook 2 page 73** and **Multilevel Activities 2 Unit 11 page 119**	

CORRELATIONS	
CCRS: SL.1.A Participate in collaborative conversations with diverse partners in small and larger groups.	**ELPS:** 6. An ELL can analyze and critique the arguments of others orally and in writing. 9. An ELL can create clear and coherent level-appropriate speech and text.
SL.2.A Confirm understanding of a text read aloud or information presented orally or through other media by asking and answering questions about key details and requesting clarification if something is not understood.	
R.1.A Ask and answer questions about key details in the text.	
R.7.A Use the illustrations and details in a text to describe its key ideas (e.g., maps, charts, photographs, political cartoons, etc.).	
W.3.A Write narratives in which they recount two or more appropriately sequenced events, include some details regarding what happened, use temporal words to signal event order, and provide some sense of closure.	

Warm-up and Review
10–15 minutes (books closed)

Ask students to say all of the words they remember for emergencies and natural disasters. Write them on the board. Describe any experiences you have had with emergencies. Then ask volunteers to share their experiences. You might prompt them with questions to elaborate: *Where were you? What did you see? What did you do?*

TIP

In the warm-up, call on volunteers only. Some students may not want to share their experiences.

Introduction

5 minutes

1. Write *fire* on the board. Ask students to brainstorm any words they can think of that are associated with fire. Write their ideas on the board.

2. State the objective: *Today we will read and write about a fire and other emergencies.*

1 Prepare to write

Presentation

20–25 minutes

A Direct students' attention to the pictures in 1B and circle words they can connect to the pictures. Build students' schema by asking questions about the words and the pictures. Ask: *Where was the fire?* [in the kitchen] *What is the firefighter wearing?* [a yellow suit that protects from fire and smoke]

B **3-37** 1. Direct students to look at the pictures again. Ask: *What objects are in the pictures that were not named in A or during the warm-up?*

2. Play the audio and have students listen silently. Ask them to point to the correct picture as they listen. Circulate and monitor.

3. Check students' comprehension. Ask: *Was the smoke coming out of the kitchen door?* [no] *Did Lisa's neighbor call 911?* [no]

MULTILEVEL STRATEGIES

After the group comprehension check in 1B, call on volunteers and tailor your questions to the level of your students.

• **Pre-level** Ask *yes/no* questions. *Did the fire truck arrive quickly?* [yes]

• **On-level** Ask information questions. *What did the fire do to the kitchen?* [It made the walls black.]

• **Higher-level** Ask critical-thinking questions. *What kind of person is Lisa? What kind of person is her neighbor?*

C **3-37** 1. Introduce the model text and its purpose: *You're going to read a story about an emergency at someone's home. As you read, look at which parts of the text match the pictures in B. This can help you understand the text better.* Play the audio again and have students read along silently.

2. Check comprehension. Ask: *How did Lisa try to get her neighbor's attention?* [She banged on the back door.] *How did Lisa feel when she couldn't find her neighbor?* [worried] *How did the firefighters get in the house?* [They broke the kitchen window.] *What was Lisa's neighbor doing at the same time?* [cooking and doing yard work]

3. Point out the *Writer's Note* and read it aloud. Ask: *What kind of words help to describe nouns and actions?* [adjective and adverb] Point out how there are two adjectives used to describe the smoke. Do a quick brainstorming session and have students call out any adjectives or adverbs they know. Write them on the board for students to refer to later when they write their own stories.

Guided Practice I

5–10 minutes

D Have students work individually to write numbers to indicate the order of the sentences. Set a time limit (three to five minutes). Discuss answers as a class.

Answers
5, 3, 2, 4, 1

TIP

For more practice after 1C, bring in pictures of emergencies and disasters or use the picture cards on page 124 of Multilevel Activities Level 2 Unit 11. Group students and give each group a set of pictures or cards. Have students test each other on the vocabulary by asking: *What happened?* Encourage more-verbal students to try these questions as well: *Where did it happen? What did the people do?*

Guided Practice II

15–20 minutes

E **3-38** 1. Explain to students that they will hear three conversations about people who had accidents. Ask them to look at the emergency reports and confirm that they understand what information they have to fill out. Play the audio and have students complete the task individually.

2. Play the audio again in segments. After the answer for each item comes up, stop the audio and give students a few seconds to edit or add to their answers. Don't check answers yet.

F Have students compare answers with a partner. Play the audio again to check answers as a class.

Answers
1. car accident, outside his home
2. mugging, in the subway station
3. gas explosion, hotel kitchen

MULTILEVEL STRATEGIES

For 1E and 1F, have same-level students sit together.

• **Pre-level** Stop the tape after each answer is given for students to fill in the blanks.

• **On-level** Play the audio through once and have students complete the forms.

• **Higher-level** Challenge these students to write one more piece of information from each conversation.

2 Plan

Communicative Practice I
15–20 minutes

A 1. Read the directions aloud and explain the meaning of *imagine. I can imagine that I am a bird flying in the sky, but it's not true.* Tell students: *You need to imagine you really saw this emergency.*

2. Review question words and brainstorm some questions that students can ask each other about the scenarios.

3. Have students work in pairs to take turns asking and answering questions about one of the scenarios. Set a time limit (five to eight minutes). Suggest that they take notes to use in the next task. Circulate and monitor.

B 1. Read the instructions and the questions aloud. Confirm that students understand that they should answer their questions based on the accident they worked on in 2A.

2. Have students write their answers individually.

3 Write

Communicative Practice II and Application
20–25 minutes

A 1. Read the instructions aloud. Have students look at the paragraph template as you read it aloud. For each blank, have a volunteer give a sample answer.

2. Set a time limit for writing (ten minutes). Remind students to use their responses from 2B to help them complete their paragraph with their own information.

B 1. Ask students to read their story to a partner. Call on volunteers to share one thing they liked about their partner's story, and also what was the same or different than their partner's story.

2. Lead a class discussion about what you should or should not do if you see an emergency.

MULTILEVEL STRATEGIES

Adapt 2A to the level of your students.

• **Pre-level** Work with these students to write a group story and ask them to copy it into their notebooks.

• **Higher-level** Ask these students to include adjectives and adverbs in their stories to make them more descriptive. If they finish early, have these students share with their partners while you are working with the pre-level students.

Evaluation
10 minutes

TEST YOURSELF

1. Read the instructions aloud. Assign a time limit (five minutes) and have students work individually.

2. Before collecting student work, invite two or three volunteers to share their sentences with the class. Ask students to raise their hands if they wrote similar answers.

EXTENSION ACTIVITY

Dictation

Dictate sentences about emergencies and have students, depending on their levels, write each sentence or just the emergency words. For example: *There was a robbery on Third Street last night.*

Lesson Overview	Lesson Notes
MULTILEVEL OBJECTIVES	
On- and Higher-level: Ask and answer questions about emergencies in the past **Pre-level:** Answer questions about emergencies in the past	
LANGUAGE FOCUS	
Grammar: Simple past (*Yesterday, I drove to work.*); Past continuous (*I was driving to work.*) **Vocabulary:** Past continuous verb forms For vocabulary support, see these **Oxford Picture Dictionary** topics: Crime, page 145; Emergencies and Natural Disasters, pages 148–149; Emergency Procedures, pages 150–151	
STRATEGY FOCUS	
Learn spelling rules for verbs in the past continuous tense.	
READINESS CONNECTION	
In this lesson, students practice using the simple past and past continuous together to communicate about events in their lives.	
PACING	
To compress this lesson: Assign 3B and 3C for homework. **To extend this lesson:** Have students write a story. (See end of lesson.) And/or have students complete **Workbook 2 pages 74–75, Multilevel Activities 2 Unit 11 page 120** and **Multilevel Grammar Exercises 2 Unit 11.**	

CORRELATIONS	
CCRS: L.1.A Demonstrate command of the conventions of standard English grammar and usage when writing or speaking. e. Use verbs to convey a sense of past, present, and future (e.g., *Yesterday I walked home; Today I walk home; Tomorrow I will walk home.*) j. Use frequently occurring prepositions (e.g., *during, beyond, toward*). SL.1.A Participate in collaborative conversations with diverse partners in small and larger groups. SL.2.A Confirm understanding of a text read aloud or information presented orally or through other media by asking and answering questions about key details and requesting clarification if something is not understood.	**ELPS:** 7. An ELL can adapt language choices to purpose, task, and audience when speaking and writing. 10. An ELL can demonstrate command of the conventions of standard English to communicate in level-appropriate speech and writing.

Warm-up and Review
10–15 minutes (books closed)

Review the past tense. Say two sentences about events that happened in the past and at the same time. (*I was reading a book. The doorbell rang.; Saul was driving. It started to snow.*) Ask them about similar experiences. As they speak, write some of their sentences on the board.

Introduction
5–10 minutes

1. Choose one or two pairs of the sentences on the board and show students the combined sentence: *I was reading a book when the doorbell rang. Saul was driving when it started to snow.*

2. State the objective: *Today we'll talk about the simple past and past continuous and practice using them together to describe events in our lives.*

1 Explore the past continuous

Presentation I
20–25 minutes

A 1. Direct students to look at the picture. Read the questions aloud.

2. Read the paragraph aloud while students read along silently.

B 1. Tell students you will read the story in 1A again, and ask them to raise their hand every time they hear a past tense verb. Then read the story aloud again, slowly.

2. Read the instructions aloud and have students work individually to underline actions that continued for some time and circle actions that describe a single, short event. Discuss answers as a class.

Answers
past continuous: was raining, was driving, was standing, wasn't driving
simple past: left, saw, stopped, told, was

C 1. Read through the charts sentence by sentence. Then read them again and have students repeat after you.

2. Assess student understanding of the charts and text. Ask: *Did it start raining after Ramiro left the house? What happened at the same time as he was driving to work? Is there usually a flood under the bridge?*

Guided Practice I
10–15 minutes

D Have students work individually to complete the sentences. Ask volunteers to say their sentences aloud or write them on the board.

Answers	
1. was driving	4. weren't sitting
2. wasn't raining	5. were eating
3. was having	

TIP

Before doing 2A, check for tense recognition. Put students in groups of three to four. Give each person in a group a card with one of the tenses on it: past, present, past continuous. Ask questions and make statements. Have students hold up the correct card. After a few sentences, have group members exchange cards.

2 Practice using the past continuous and the simple past

Presentation II and Guided Practice II
20–25 minutes

A 🔊 **3-39** 1. Direct students to look at the pictures and discuss what they see and what they think is happening. Play the audio and have students listen silently.

2. Read the first sentence aloud (uncorrected), and ask students if it's true or false. Remind them that false sentences need to be corrected, and point out the example.

3. Have students work individually to mark each statement as *T* (*true*) or *F* (*false*). Discuss answers and corrections as a class.

Answers
1. F, fixing old pipes
2. T
3. F, main water supply
4. F, didn't flood
5. F, a meeting
6. F, alarm
7. T
8. F, fire department

B 1. Read the instructions aloud. Have students complete the sentences individually.

2. Have students compare their answers with a partner. Check answers as a class.

Answers
1. was fixing, broke, turned, didn't flood
2. were having, went, ran, waited

C 1. Read the instructions aloud and then model the sample conversation with a volunteer.

2. Have students work in pairs to complete the task. Circulate and monitor.

3. Have volunteer pairs say one of their conversations to the class. Have the class say if it is true or false, and correct it if it is false.

3 Practice using questions in the past

Presentation III
10–15 minutes

 3-40 1. Read the questions in the chart aloud and ask students to repeat.

2. Copy the questions onto the board and underline the verb and auxiliary in each question. Ask: *Is* did *used with simple past tense questions or past continuous questions?* [simple past] *In which question does the main verb stay in the simple present?* [simple past] *Do I use a simple verb or an* -ing *verb with* was *and* were*?* [-ing]

3. Play the audio and have students repeat.

Guided Practice III
10–15 minutes

 1. Ask students to work individually to match the questions and answers.

2. Have students compare answers with a partner and then check answers as a class.

Answers
1. c
2. d
3. a
4. b

 1. Have students work individually to complete the conversations.

2. Have two volunteers read a conversation aloud. Write the correct answers on the board and give students time to correct their work.

Answers
1. were, doing
did, do
2. Was, doing
did, go

4 Practice talking about an emergency

Communicative Practice and Application
20–25 minutes

 1. Read the instructions and the situations in the box aloud. Confirm that students understand *blizzard* and *hurricane*.

2. Model the sample conversation with two volunteers.

3. Brainstorm questions that students can ask in their conversations: *Who was there? Where did it happen? How did he/she feel?*

4. Have students complete the task in groups of three.

MULTILEVEL STRATEGIES
For 4A, have students work in same-level groups.
• **Pre-level** Provide these students with questions and answer frames to ask each other.
• **Higher-level** Challenge these students to use five *Wh-* questions and five *Did/Was/Were* questions in their conversation.

B 1. Read the instructions and questions aloud and allow students to have a few minutes to think of their emergency and make some brief notes.

2. Have students work in their groups from 4A and take turns asking and answering questions. Remind them that they can use the same questions that they used in 4A for this new conversation. Circulate and monitor.

Evaluation

10 minutes

TEST YOURSELF

Have students work in pairs. Give students a set time (two minutes) to think or make notes about a recent crime or an emergency before they tell their partner about it. Circulate and evaluate students' command of the lesson goals.

MULTILEVEL STRATEGIES

Target the *Test Yourself* to the level of your students.

• **Pre-level** Write *Wh-* questions for students to answer: *What happened? Who did it happen to? When did it happen? Where did it happen?* Have students write one sentence for each question and each answer. Have them use the questions and answers to talk with their partner.

• **Higher-level** Have these students write a paragraph with details about the crime or emergency. Challenge them to use at least three sentences that use both the simple past and the past continuous.

EXTENSION ACTIVITY

Write a Story

Have students write stories in groups of three to four.

1. Give each group a picture of a person, or give them a magazine and allow them two minutes to find a picture of a person they want to write about.

2. Tell groups to make up a story about something that happened to the person at the time that they were doing something else.

3. Pass out poster or butcher paper and have the groups write their stories. Display the stories and correct them as a class.

Lesson Overview	Lesson Notes
MULTILEVEL OBJECTIVES	
On-, Pre-, and Higher-level: Make a 911 call	
LANGUAGE FOCUS	
Grammar: Simple past (*He fell and hurt his leg.*) **Vocabulary:** Emergency words, *ambulance, crashed, intersection, on the way, operator* For vocabulary support, see these **Oxford Picture Dictionary** topics: The Telephone, pages 14–15; Emergencies and Natural Disasters, pages 148–149; Emergency Procedures, pages 150–151	
STRATEGY FOCUS	
Make an emergency call.	
READINESS CONNECTION	
In this lesson, students verbally communicate about and practice how to make a 911 call.	
PACING	
To compress this lesson: Skip 3E. **To extend this lesson:** Have students practice making a 911 call. (See end of lesson.) And/or have students complete **Workbook 2 page 76** and **Multilevel Activities 2 Unit 11 page 121**.	

CORRELATIONS	
CCRS: SL.1.A Participate in collaborative conversations with diverse partners in small and larger groups. SL.2.A Confirm understanding of a text read aloud or information presented orally or through other media by asking and answering questions about key details and requesting clarification if something is not understood. RF.2.A Demonstrate understanding of spoken words, syllables, and sounds (phonemes). L.1.A Demonstrate command of the conventions of standard English grammar and usage when writing or speaking. g. Use frequently occurring nouns and verbs. k. Understand and use question words (interrogatives) (e.g., *who, what, where, when, why, how*).	**ELPS:** 2. An ELL can participate in level-appropriate oral and written exchanges of information, ideas, and analyses, in various social and academic contexts, responding to peer, audience, or reader comments and questions. 9. An ELL can create clear and coherent level-appropriate speech and text.

Warm-up and Review
10–15 minutes (books closed)

Write *emergency* on the board and ask students to recall words for emergencies. Write the words on the board. Pantomime medical emergencies and have students call out guesses. Write the words on the board.

Introduction
5 minutes

1. Ask students if they would call 911 for all of the emergencies on the board. In some cases, such as an accident, flood, or tornado, they wouldn't call 911 unless someone was injured.

2. State the objective: *Today we're going to learn how to make a 911 call.*

1 Listen to learn: making a 911 call

Presentation I and Guided Practice I
15–25 minutes

A 1. Direct students to look at the pictures. Ask: *When should you call 911?* [in an emergency] *What is a 911 operator?* [the person who answers a 911 call] Discuss any vocabulary that students are unfamiliar with.

B 🔊 3-41 Read the questions aloud and play the audio. Have students answer the questions. [The 911 operator is not speaking. It is a person talking about when to call 911 and when not to call 911.]

C 🔊 3-41 1. Read the instructions aloud. Have students work individually to mark each situation as an emergency (*E*) or non-emergency (*NE*).

2. Play the audio and have students check their answers. Discuss answers as a class.

Answers
1. NE, E
2. E, NE
3. NE, E

Communicative Practice
10–15 minutes

D 1. Set a time limit (10 minutes). Have groups of three to four discuss other reasons to call 911 and make a list. Have groups share their lists with the class. Write students' ideas on the board.

2. Lead a class discussion to determine if all the students agree with each reason to call 911 written on the board.

2 Practice your pronunciation

Pronunciation Extension
10–15 minutes

A 🔊 3-42 1. Read the *Need help?* box aloud. Tell students: *If you put stress on the wrong syllable, it might be difficult for the listener to understand what you are saying. This is especially true for longer words.*

2. Don't read the words aloud. Tell students to read the information about each word and then call on volunteers to pronounce each word aloud. Don't make any corrections.

3. Play the audio and have students repeat.

B 🔊 3-43 1. Read the instructions aloud. Play the audio and have students repeat.

2. Play the audio again and have students write the numbers of syllables for each word and complete the task individually. Check answers as a class.

Answers		
Words	**Syllables**	**Stressed syllable**
1. operator	4	first
2. ambulance	3	first
3. medication	4	third
4. emergency	4	second

3 Practice making an emergency call

Presentation II and Guided Practice II
20–30 minutes

A 🔊 3-44 1. Read the instructions aloud. Play the audio and have students read along silently. Check students' understanding of *ambulance, intersection, crashed,* and *on the way.*

2. Have volunteers answer the question. [*Where are you? What happened? Is he hurt?*]

B 🔊 3-45 Play the audio. Have students work individually to complete the task. Discuss answers as a class.

Answers
1. b
2. b
3. a
4. a

C Read the instructions aloud. Give students time (one to two minutes) to look at the conversation in A again and answer the questions. Discuss answers as a class. [three *Wh-* questions; one *yes/no* question]

D 1. Write on the board: *Right now, there is a blizzard in New York City. Yesterday, ___ ___ a blizzard in New York City. ___ ___ a blizzard in New York City yesterday? Yes, ___ ___.* Underline *yesterday* and *is* and ask a volunteer how to fill in the blanks in the second sentence. [*there was*] Point to the question mark in the third sentence and have volunteers fill in the blanks in the question and the answer. [*Was there, there was*] Write on the board: *Right now, there are rain storms in Chicago and Boston.* Have volunteers come to the board and write the past tense statement, question, and answer.

2. Read through the questions and answers and have students repeat. Then have students practice them with a partner. Circulate and monitor.

E Read the instructions aloud and model the sample conversation with a volunteer. Have students ask and answer new questions with a partner.

> **MULTILEVEL STRATEGIES**
>
> For 3E, have same-level students sit together.
>
> • **Pre-level** Work with these students and help them think of new questions. Model making a question from the man's statements. (*There's a medical emergency = Is there a medical emergency?*) Have them work together to make three new questions from three statements and practice asking and answering them.
>
> • **Higher-level** Have these students make a completely new conversation by substituting new details.

4 Make conversation: asking for help

Communicative Practice I
15–20 minutes

A 1. Read the template conversation aloud. Ask volunteers to give an example for each blank. Model completing the conversation with a volunteer.

2. Direct students' attention to the *Need help?* box. Read the sentences aloud and have volunteers say examples of an emergency for which people would need the police, ambulance, or fire department.

3. Have students work in pairs to create a conversation and take turns performing the parts.

> **MULTILEVEL STRATEGIES**
>
> For 4A, group same-level students together.
>
> • **Pre-level** Work with students to fill in the blanks.
>
> • **Higher-level** Challenge these students to have the conversations without looking at their books.

B 1. Set a time limit (ten minutes). Ask pairs to share their conversation with another pair. Circulate and monitor.

2. Have pairs present their conversation to the class.

AT WORK

Making an emergency call

Presentation III and Communicative Practice II
15–20 minutes

A 🔊 3-46 1. Direct students to look at the pictures. Ask them to describe what is happening.

2. Play the audio and have students identify what is happening and who Karl is talking to. Have volunteers answer. [*There's a pipe leaking and dripping water all over the boxes.; the supervisor, Ms. Fuentes*]

B 1. Read the instructions aloud. Have students practice the conversations with a partner. Circulate and help as needed.

2. Have pairs share one of their conversations with the class.

> **MULTILEVEL STRATEGIES**
>
> For At Work B, have same-level students sit together in pairs.
>
> • **Pre-level** Write the conversation from A on the board for students to use as a guide for their new conversations.
>
> • **Higher-level** Have these students think of more situations and have a conversation.

Evaluation
10–15 minutes

TEST YOURSELF

Have students work in pairs to perform the role-play. Circulate and assess students' progress. Take note of any mistakes you hear in intonation, pronunciation, grammar, or vocabulary. When all students have finished the activity, as a class, review the kinds of mistakes you heard (without naming any students who made them).

EXTENSION ACTIVITY

Call 911

Have students create maps to practice emergency vocabulary.

1. Pass out one copy of a simple street map to each pair of students, or have students draw a simple grid map with First, Second, Third, and Fourth Streets running north and south and A, B, C, and D Streets running east and west.

2. Describe emergencies and tell students to write the emergency name on the correct part of the map. *There was a robbery on B Street between First and Second. Did you hear about the accident at the comer of Fourth and D?*

3. Have students use their maps to talk about the emergencies and their locations.

Lesson Overview	Lesson Notes

MULTILEVEL OBJECTIVES

On- and Higher-level: Read about and discuss emergency safety procedures

Pre-level: Read about emergency safety procedures

LANGUAGE FOCUS

Grammar: *Should* (*You should prepare an emergency kit.*)

Vocabulary: *Evacuate, hot water bottle, prepare, rescue, valuables*

For vocabulary support, see these **Oxford Picture Dictionary** topics: Emergencies and Natural Disasters, pages 148–149; Emergency Procedures, pages 150–151

STRATEGY FOCUS

Before you start reading an article, read the headings first. They can help you decide if this article is the one you need or not.

READINESS CONNECTION

In this lesson, students verbally communicate information about emergency preparedness.

PACING

To compress this lesson: Assign 1F and 1G for homework or do either as a whole-class activity.

To extend this lesson: Have students practice making an emergency announcement. (See end of lesson.)

And/or have students complete **Workbook 2 page 77** and **Multilevel Activities 2 Unit 11 pages 122**.

CORRELATIONS

CCRS: R.1.A Ask and answer questions about key details in the text.

R.4.A Ask and answer questions to help determine or clarify the meaning of words and phrases in a text.

R.5.A Know and use various text features (e.g., headings, tables of contents, glossaries, electronic menus, icons) to locate key facts or information in a text.

R.7.A Use the illustrations and details in a text to describe its key ideas (e.g., maps, charts, photographs, political cartoons, etc.).

SL.1.A Participate in collaborative conversations with diverse partners in small and larger groups.

SL.6.A Speak audibly and express thoughts, feelings, and ideas clearly. Produce complete sentences when appropriate to task and situation.

ELPS: 1. An ELL can construct meaning from oral presentations and literary and informational text through level-appropriate listening, reading, and viewing. 3. An ELL can speak and write about level-appropriate complex literary and informational texts and topics.

Warm-up and Review
10–15 minutes (books closed)

Write *Before an Emergency* and *During an Emergency* on the board. Elicit students' ideas for what to do before and during a fire, an earthquake, or a tornado.

Introduction
5 minutes

1. Ask students if they are prepared for the emergencies discussed in the warm-up.

2. State the objective: *Today we're going to read about preparing for emergencies. At the end of the lesson, you'll know what you need to do if there is a fire or a flood.*

> **TIP**
>
> Before reading about emergency preparedness in 1A and 1B, pass out copies of a map of the United States. A simple blackline map with only the names of the states labeled works well. (You can find these at geography websites on the Internet.) Read aloud these news headlines: *January 14, 1994: California had a major earthquake. May 3, 1999: Oklahoma had big tornadoes. August 29, 2005: Hurricane Katrina hit Mississippi and Louisiana.* Have students write the name of the disaster and the date (or month) on the map. Have students ask and answer with a partner. *What happened in _____? When did it happen? Where were you that year/month? What were you doing?*

1 Build reading strategies

Presentation I
10–15 minutes

A 1. Read the words and definitions aloud. Give students an example of each word, using familiar situations if possible: *They evacuated the building because of a fire. You prepare for school by getting your materials together. The firefighters rescued the people from the burning building.*

2. Have students complete the activity individually. Check answers as a class.

Answers
1. rescue
2. prepare
3. evacuate

B 1. Read the instructions and actions aloud. Have students talk with a partner about the things they do to prepare for an emergency.

2. Have students share their partner's answers with the class. Ask: *Does anyone do all of the actions? Does anyone do none of them?*

Guided Practice: Pre-reading
5–10 minutes

C 1. Direct students to look at the title in 1D and read the *Reader's Note* aloud. Ask: *What kind of information is usually in a heading?* [the main idea of the paragraph or section]

2. Tell students that the web article focuses on two particular emergencies. Ask them to scan or look quickly through the article to find out what the emergencies are. Ask them to raise their hands when they've found the two emergencies. When most of the students have their hands up, elicit the answer to the question.

Guided Practice: While Reading
20–30 minutes

D 1. Ask students to read the article silently and think about their answer to the question. Answer any questions about unfamiliar vocabulary.

2. Have students work in pairs to compare and discuss their answers, and then check answers as a class.

3. Check comprehension. Ask: *What should you prepare before an emergency? What should you put on your face if there is smoke? What should you turn off if there is a flood?*

> **MULTILEVEL STRATEGIES**
>
> Adapt 1D to the level of your students.
>
> • **Pre-level** Read the text aloud to these students as they follow along.
>
> • **On- and Higher-level** Pair students and have them read the article aloud to each other, taking turns to read each paragraph.

Guided Practice: Rereading
10–15 minutes

E 1. Play the audio and have students listen and read along silently.

2. Provide an opportunity for students to extract evidence from the article. Have students underline any words or phrases that they already knew.

3. Have students discuss their answers to the question with a partner. Circulate and monitor. Have volunteers report their partner's responses to the class.

Guided Practice: Post-reading
15 minutes

F Have students work individually to choose the correct answers and then identify in the reading where they found the answers. Check answers as a class.

2. Check comprehension further. Ask: *Where should you go if there's a fire?* [the nearest emergency exit] *Should you stand up or stay close to the floor?* [stay close to the floor]

Answers
1. b
2. a
3. b
4. a

MULTILEVEL STRATEGIES

After the group comprehension check in 1F, call on volunteers and tailor your questions to the level of your students.

• **Pre-level** Ask *yes/no* questions. *Should you put a wet towel over your mouth and nose?* [yes]

• **On-level** Ask information questions. *What should you do before an emergency?* [prepare a kit, learn where emergency exits are, talk to your family about what to do during an emergency]

• **Higher-level** Ask critical-thinking questions. *Why do some people not prepare for emergencies? What are the costs to the community if people don't prepare?*

G 1. Have students work individually to complete the sentences.

2. Have students read their sentences to a partner, before checking answers as a class.

Answers
1. prepare
2. valuables
3. evacuate
4. rescue

2 Read an emergency checklist

Communicative Practice
20–30 minutes

TIP

Bring an emergency kit to class. Before completing 2A, ask students to name the items in your kit if they can. Ask them to brainstorm other items you might add to the kit.

A 1. Direct students to look at the emergency kit checklist. Say and have students repeat the words in the checklist. Ask students to check off the items they have at home.

B 1. Read the questions aloud. Allow students time to think of their own answers and make notes.

2. Set a time limit (ten minutes). Have students discuss the questions with a partner. Circulate and help as needed.

3. Have pairs share their responses with another pair. Have volunteers share their partner's answers with the class.

Application
5–10 minutes

BRING IT TO LIFE

As a class, discuss which emergencies are most likely to happen in your state. If there are several choices, ask students to choose which emergency they're going to focus on before they leave class, and make sure the number of students researching each emergency is fairly even.

EXTENSION ACTIVITY

Emergency Announcement

Have students compose and perform a short announcement that tells people what to do in an emergency.

1. Put them into groups of three to four and assign an emergency to each group.

2. Tell groups to write and perform a short announcement to raise public awareness about that emergency.

TEAMWORK & LANGUAGE REVIEW

Lesson Overview	Lesson Notes
MULTILEVEL OBJECTIVES	
On-, Pre-, and Higher-level: Expand upon and review unit grammar and life skills	
LANGUAGE FOCUS	
Grammar: Simple past and past continuous (*It was raining when I looked out the window.*) **Vocabulary:** Weather words For vocabulary support, see these **Oxford Picture Dictionary** topics: The Telephone, pages 14–15; Emergencies and Natural Disasters, pages 148–149; Emergency Procedures, pages 150–151	
READINESS CONNECTION	
In this review, students work in a team to review what to do in and how to prepare for an emergency.	
PACING	
To extend this review: Have students complete **Workbook 2 page 78**, **Multilevel Activities 2 Unit 11 pages 123–126**, and **Multilevel Grammar Exercises 2 Unit 11.**	
CORRELATIONS	

CCRS: R.1.A Ask and answer questions about key details in the text. R.7.A Use the illustrations and details in a text to describe its key ideas (e.g., maps, charts, photographs, political cartoons, etc.). SL.1.A Participate in collaborative conversations with diverse partners in small and larger groups. SL.3.A Ask and answer questions in order to seek help, get information, or clarify something that is not understood. SL.6.A Speak audibly and express thoughts, feelings, and ideas clearly. Produce complete sentences when appropriate to task and situation. W.2.A Write informative/explanatory texts in which they name a topic, supply some facts about the topic, and provide some sense of closure. W.8.A With guidance and support, recall information from experiences or gather information from provided sources to answer a question.	**ELPS:** 5. An ELL can conduct research and evaluate and communicate findings to answer questions or solve problems. 6. An ELL can analyze and critique the arguments of others orally and in writing.

Warm-up and Review
10–15 minutes (books closed)

1. Review the *Bring It to Life* assignment from Lesson 5.

2. Have students who did the exercise tell about what they learned. Encourage students who didn't do the exercise to ask their classmates questions about what they learned.

3. Write the emergencies on the board. As a class, write the important preparation and procedures to follow for each emergency.

4. Ask students if they plan to improve their emergency preparation.

Introduction and Presentation
5 minutes

1. Tell students to leave their books closed. Ask: *Did you ever see a traffic accident?* Choose one volunteer and write a sentence about him/her on the board. *Yumi saw a traffic accident.* Ask the student what he/she was doing when he/she saw the accident. Write the answer as a past continuous sentence. *She was driving home [walking to school, etc.] when she saw the accident.*

2. Ask the student if he/she usually drives home (or walks to school, etc.) and write the present tense question on the board. *Does Yumi usually drive home?*

3. Ask other volunteers about accidents they've witnessed, and write what they were doing at the time in the present continuous: *He/She was _____ when _____.* Elicit the third-person question for each sentence and write the questions above the answers. Underline the verb (and auxiliary) in each question and sentence.

4. State the objective: *Today we're going to review what we learned about preparing for and what to do in an emergency.*

Guided Practice
15–20 minutes

 1. Direct students to work in groups of three to four and look at the picture. Read the questions aloud.

2. Set a time limit (five minutes) for groups to answer the questions. Circulate and monitor.

3. Have students from each group share the group's responses with the class. If you have a large class, you may not want all of the groups to report their responses. Instead, have groups share their responses with each other. Call "time" and tell all groups to work with a new group and to repeat their responses. Repeat this process as desired, making sure each group gets to share their responses at least once.

> **TIP**
> Suggest that students, especially pre-level students, write down the items for their emergency kits to use in B.

Communicative Practice
30–50 minutes

 1. Have students work in their same groups from A. If necessary, have them review the information they discussed for that exercise.

2. Read the instructions aloud and model the sample conversation with a volunteer, inserting vocabulary from A.

3. Tell groups that each student should have a turn to write a line for the conversation. Set a time limit (ten minutes).

C Have teams present their conversation to the rest of the class.

> **TIP**
> As an extra challenge, have students write the items that other teams mention in their conversations and see if the items match their own list.

D 1. Have students continue to work with the same group from A. Read the instructions and have a volunteer read the sample text aloud.

2. Set a time limit (ten minutes) to complete the task. Circulate and assist groups as needed.

E 1. Put students in new teams of three to four. Read the instructions aloud and give teams time (one minute) to choose an emergency.

2. Tell teams to discuss what people need to do to stay safe or help others during their emergency. Set a time limit (three minutes).

F 1. If students will use the Internet for this task, establish what device(s) they'll use: a class computer, tablets, or smartphones. Alternatively, print information from the Internet before class and distribute to groups.

2. Have students copy the chart into their notebooks. As a class, brainstorm search words that students can use for their research (e.g., *blizzard + emergency kit; hurricane + prepare*). Set a time limit (15 minutes) for students to perform their research.

G 1. Have students continue to work in their teams from E. Read the instructions aloud. Set a time limit (five minutes) to complete the task.

2. Have teams share their findings with the class. With each presentation, ask the class, *Are there steps you would add? Is the order correct?*

H Have teams make a poster about what to do in an emergency based on their charts and the class discussion. Display the posters in class.

PROBLEM SOLVING
10–15 minutes

A 🔊 **3-48** 1. Ask students to read the paragraph silently. Then play the audio and have them silently read along again.

2. Check comprehension. Ask: *Where is Min?* [She's at home alone.] *Where is the rest of her family?* [Her husband's in Mexico and her children are at school.] *Why is she worried?* [She is worried about their house.]

B 1. Read the questions aloud. Have students work in groups of three to four to answer the questions. Circulate and monitor.

2. Come to a class consensus of what problem Min has. Then have teams share their solutions. Write each one on the board.

3. As a class, brainstorm answers to question 2. Ask students if they know someone who has this problem and has overcome it, or what they have done themselves to overcome the same problem.

4. As a class, discuss the pros and cons of each solution. Have students choose the top three of each.

C Set a time limit (five minutes) and have students complete the task individually then compare their notes with a partner.

Evaluation
20–25 minutes

To test students' understanding of the unit language and content, have them take the Unit 11 Test, available on the Teacher Resource Center.

Unit Overview

This unit explores recreational activities and entertainment, and using superlatives and comparatives to express opinions.

KEY OBJECTIVES

Lesson 1	Identify recreational facilities, activities, and entertainment genres
Lesson 2	Describe weekend plans
Lesson 3	Use the superlative to describe popular entertainment
Lesson 4	Ask for and give opinions; agree and disagree with others' opinions
Lesson 5	Identify U.S points of interest; use maps for travel needs
Teamwork & Language Review	Review unit language

UNIT FEATURES

Academic Vocabulary	*relaxing*
Employability Skills	• Speculate about weekend activities • Negotiate times and dates of recreational activities • Interpret facts about U.S. sights • Design a journey using a map of the U.S. • Find solutions to reduce time spent watching TV • Understand teamwork • Communicate information • Listen actively • Work with others • Communicate verbally

Resources	**Class Audio** CD3, Tracks 49–63
	Workbook Unit 12, pages 79–85
	Teacher Resource Center
	    Multilevel Activities 2 Unit 12
	    Multilevel Grammar Exercises 2 Unit 12
	    Unit 12 Test
	Oxford Picture Dictionary Geography and Habitats, Places to Go, Outdoor Recreation, Winter and Water Sports, Individual Sports, Team Sports, Entertainment

Lesson Overview	Lesson Notes

MULTILEVEL OBJECTIVES

On-level: Identify words for recreation and entertainment

Pre-level: Recognize words for recreation and entertainment

Higher-level: Talk and write about recreation and entertainment

LANGUAGE FOCUS

Grammar: Simple present (*They play softball in May.*)

Vocabulary: Recreation and entertainment words, names of the months

For vocabulary support, see these **Oxford Picture Dictionary** topics: Outdoor Recreation, page 232; Winter and Water Sports, page 233; Individual Sports, page 234; Team Sports, page 235; Entertainment, pages 242–243

READINESS CONNECTION

In this lesson, students communicate information and speculate about recreational activities and entertainment.

PACING

To compress this lesson: Assign 1D and 2C for homework.

To extend this lesson: Have students interview a partner. (See end of lesson.)

And/or have students complete **Workbook 2 page 79** and **Multilevel Activities 2 Unit 12 page 128**.

CORRELATIONS

CCRS: L.6.A Use words and phrases acquired through conversations, reading and being read to, and responding to texts, including using frequently occurring conjunctions to signal simple relationships (e.g., *because*).

SL.1.A Participate in collaborative conversations with diverse partners in small and larger groups.

SL.2.A Confirm understanding of a text read aloud or information presented orally or through other media by asking and answering questions about key details and requesting clarification if something is not understood.

SL.3.A Ask and answer questions in order to seek help, get information, or clarify something that is not understood.

ELPS: 8. An ELL can determine the meaning of words and phrases in oral presentations and literary and informational text.

Warm-up and Review
10–15 minutes (books closed)

Draw a series of pictures on the board that illustrate things you like to do in your free time, such as use a camera, read a book, play volleyball, or hike a mountain. Have students guess the activities that go with the pictures. Ask: *What do you like to do in your free time?* Write students' answers on the board.

Introduction
5 minutes

1. Write *Recreational Activities* and *Entertainment* on the board. Categorize the words from the warm-up under these headings. For example: *Martin likes to play soccer. Playing soccer is a recreational activity. Soon likes to watch TV. TV is a form of entertainment.*

2. State the objective: *Today we will explore words for recreational activities and entertainment.*

1 Learn about recreational activities

Presentation
20–25 minutes

 A 1. Direct students to look at the pictures and say the months listed in the captions. Ask: *Do you do different activities in different months?*

2. Have students identify and circle the words they know. Have students share the activities they do.

B ◄)) **3-49** 1. Tell students that they will hear someone talking about the pictures and that they should listen for who is talking. Play the audio.

2. Have students compare answers with a partner. Play the audio again and check answers as a class.

Answer
The mother of the family is speaking.

 C ◄)) **3-50** 1. Ask students to listen and repeat the words.

2. While students are repeating, circulate and listen for pronunciation difficulties. Provide choral practice as necessary.

Guided Practice I
10–20 minutes

 D 1. Have students work individually to complete the sentences using the new vocabulary. Set a time limit (two to three minutes).

2. Encourage students to take turns reading the completed sentences with a partner. Check answers as a class.

Answers	
1. go camping	4. go skating
2. go biking	5. go fishing
3. go hiking	6. play softball

 E 1. Read the instructions and questions aloud.

2. Set a time limit (three minutes). Have students take turns asking and answering questions with a partner. Circulate and listen for any pronunciation or vocabulary difficulties.

2 Talk about entertainment

Guided Practice II
25–30 minutes

A 1. Ask: *Do you have a lot of free time for entertainment? When do have time for entertainment?* Introduce the new topic: *Now we're going to talk about some types of entertainment.*

2. Group students and assign roles: manager, researcher, administrative assistant, and reporter. Explain that students work with their groups to match the words and pictures.

3. Check comprehension of the exercise. Ask: *Who looks up the words in the picture dictionary?* [researcher] *Who writes the numbers in the book?* [administrative assistant] *Who tells the class your answers?* [reporter] *Who helps everyone and manages the group?* [manager]

4. Set a time limit (two minutes) and have students work together to complete the task. While students are working, copy the wordlist onto the board.

5. Call "time" and have the reporters from each group take turns calling out the numbers for the wordlist. Record students' answers on the board. If groups disagree, write each group's choice next to the word.

6. Draw students' attention to the illustrations. Prompt students to use vocabulary not labeled in the art. Ask: *What other items can you name?* [librarian, bookshelves, computer, signs etc.] *Wht kind of nonfiction is* The Life of Martin Luther King, Jr.*? [biography] Does this library look similar to your library? What is different?*

Answers	
2–action	6–mystery
9–history	5–romance
8–biography	7–science fiction
1–animation	4–documentary
3–horror	

MULTILEVEL STRATEGIES

For 2A, use mixed-level groups.

• **Pre-level** Assign these students the role of administrative assistant.

• **Higher-level** Assign these students the role of manager.

B 🔊 3-51 1. Play the audio. Ask students to listen and check their answers.

2. Have students correct the wordlist on the board and then write the correct numbers in their books as needed.

3. Have the groups from 2A work in pairs to practice the words. Set a time limit (two minutes).

Communicative Practice and Application
15–20 minutes

C 1. Ask: *What part of the library/bookstore do you spend the most time in? Are there kinds of entertainment you don't like/never do?*

2. Set a time limit (five minutes). Ask students to discuss the questions and answers with a partner.

Answers	
1. It's a romance.	4. It's a mystery.
2. *Night of Nightmares*	5. *Aliens from Mars*
3. *The Life of Martin Luther King, Jr.*	6. It's a history book.

D Read the instructions aloud. Have students take turns asking and answering the questions with a partner. Set a time limit (three minutes). Circulate and listen for any pronunciation or vocabulary difficulties. Have volunteers share their responses with the class.

TIP

After completing 2D, find out what kind of movies or TV shows your students like best. Put up cards around the room with the words *action*, *mystery*, *romantic*, *horror*, and *educational*. Tell students to stand next to the one they like the best. Assign a time limit (30 seconds), so they have to make a quick decision. Guide a class discussion about the results.

Evaluation
10–15 minutes

TEST YOURSELF

1. Make a two-column, three-row chart on the board with the headings *Recreational Activities* and *Entertainment*. Have students give examples for each column.

2. Have students copy the blank chart into their notebooks.

3. Set a time limit (five to ten minutes). Have students test themselves by writing the words they recall from the lesson in the chart.

4. Call "time" and have students check their spelling in *The Oxford Picture Dictionary* or another dictionary.

MULTILEVEL STRATEGIES

Target the *Test Yourself* to the level of your students.

• **Pre-level** Have these students work with their books open.

• **Higher-level** Have these students complete the chart and then write at least one sentence for each column in the chart.

EXTENSION ACTIVITY

Interview a Partner

Have students look at pictures of team sports and outdoor recreation that you bring to class or the ones in *The Oxford Picture Dictionary*. Have them ask their partners: *Do you like _____?*

Lesson Overview	Lesson Notes
MULTILEVEL OBJECTIVES	
On-, Pre-, and Higher-level: Read and write about entertainment activities	
LANGUAGE FOCUS	
Grammar: Future with *going to* (*I'm going to stay home this weekend.*) **Vocabulary:** Recreation and entertainment words For vocabulary support, see these **Oxford Picture Dictionary** topics: Places to Go, pages 228–229; Outdoor Recreation, page 232; Winter and Water Sports, page 233; Individual Sports, page 234; Team Sports, page 235; Entertainment, pages 242–243	
STRATEGY FOCUS	
After introducing the main idea of a paragraph, include some supporting details.	
READINESS CONNECTION	
In this lesson, students listen actively, read, and write about activities people do on weekends or in their free time.	
PACING	
To compress this lesson: Assign 2D for homework and/or skip 1F. **To extend this lesson:** Have students talk about going to the movies. (See end of lesson.) And/or have students complete **Workbook 2 page 80** and **Multilevel Activities 2 Unit 12 page 129**.	

CORRELATIONS	
CCRS: SL.1.A Participate in collaborative conversations with diverse partners in small and larger groups. SL.2.A Confirm understanding of a text read aloud or information presented orally or through other media by asking and answering questions about key details and requesting clarification if something is not understood. SL.3.A Ask and answer questions in order to seek help, get information, or clarify something that is not understood. R.1.A Ask and answer questions about key details in the text. R.7.A Use the illustrations and details in a text to describe its key ideas (e.g., maps, charts, photographs, political cartoons, etc.). W.2.A Write informative/explanatory texts in which they name a topic, supply some facts about the topic, and provide some sense of closure.	**ELPS:** 6. An ELL can analyze and critique the arguments of others orally and in writing. 9. An ELL can create clear and coherent level-appropriate speech and text.

Warm-up and Review
10–15 minutes (books closed)

Ask students to tell you the words for different kinds of movies and write them on the board:

romantic, action, drama, horror, mystery, science fiction. Ask students to tell you titles of well-known movies that fit into these categories.

Introduction
5 minutes

1. Tell students about your plans for the weekend. Ask volunteers to say what they plan to do.

2. State the objective: *Today we're going to read and write about weekend activities.*

1 Prepare to write

Presentation
20–25 minutes

A 1. Direct students' attention to the pictures and read the activities in 1B aloud. Build students' schema by asking questions about the pictures and the email. Ask: *What activities do you see in the pictures? Who are these people?*

2. Have students work with a partner. Give them one minute to discuss their answers to the questions. Elicit responses from the class.

B **3-52** 1. Introduce the model email and its purpose: *You're going to listen to and read an email about a family's weekend activities. Listen for the kinds of details in the different paragraphs.*

2. Read the instructions aloud and play the audio. Have students listen silently and check what Dina and her family will do.

Answers
go to the movies
go to a soccer game
go to a museum

C **3-52** 1. Play the audio again. Have students silently read along again.

2. Check comprehension. Ask: *Who is Gabriela?* [Lucinda's daughter] *Who is Pedro?* [Lucinda's husband] *Is the email formal or informal?* [formal] *What is the cheapest day at the Science Museum?* [Sunday] *Who wants to see a horror movie?* [Pedro and her children] *Is Gabriela going to play soccer on Saturday?* [yes] *What do Lucinda and Pedro like to do at the soccer game?* [talk to other parents]

3. Read the *Writer's Note* aloud. Ask: *How many paragraphs are there in the email?* [four] *What is the main idea of each paragraph?* [1. what she will do over the whole weekend, 2. visiting the science museum, 3. going to the movies, 4. request to write back]

Guided Practice I
5–10 minutes

D Have students work individually to mark the sentences *T* (true) or *F* (false). As a class, discuss answers and correct the false sentences on the board.

Answers
1. F
2. T
3. F
4. F

Guided Practice II
10–15 minutes

E **3-53** Tell students that they will listen to people talking about weekend activities. Direct students' attention to the ads and read them aloud.

2. Play the audio and have students complete the task individually. Don't check answers yet.

F **3-53** Play the audio again in segments. After the answer for each item comes up, stop the audio and give students a few seconds to edit or add to their answers. Check answers as a class.

Answers
1. Maria is going to try yoga on Saturday,
2. Jason is going to go biking with his kids.
3. Maria and Jason are going to go to the country music concert on Sunday. They are going to have a picnic.

2 Plan

Communicative Practice I
20–25 minutes

A 1. Read the instructions aloud and have students copy the chart into their notebooks.

2. To confirm that students have appropriate vocabulary to write their email in 3A, brainstorm activities not covered so far and write them on the board.

3. Have students fill in their charts. Set a time limit (five minutes).

B Set a time limit (five minutes). Have students take turns asking and answering questions with a partner and help each other add to their charts as needed. Circulate and listen for any pronunciation or vocabulary difficulties.

3 Write

Communicative Practice II and Application
10–15 minutes

A 1. Read the instructions aloud. Have students look at the email template as you read it aloud. For each blank, have a volunteer give a sample answer.

2. Set a time limit for writing (five to ten minutes). Remind students to use their lists from 2A to write their emails. Have students complete the template with their own information.

> **MULTILEVEL STRATEGIES**
>
> Adapt 3A to the level of your students.
>
> • **Pre-level** Provide these students with a paragraph template to fill out. *On Saturday, I'm going to go to _____ with my _____. We're going to _____. On Sunday, I'm going to go to _____ with my _____. We're going to _____.*
>
> • **Higher-level** Ask these students to add one extra sentence for each day and answer this question: *Why do you like this activity?*

B 1. Ask students to share their emails with a partner. Call on volunteers to share one thing they liked about their partner's email, and also what was the same or different between their own and their partner's email.

> **TIP**
>
> After completing 3B, have groups of three to four plan "the perfect weekend" based on things that they can do within an hour of their town/city. Have students present their plans to the class.

Evaluation
10 minutes

TEST YOURSELF

1. Read the instructions aloud. Assign a time limit (five minutes) and have students work individually.

2. Before collecting student work, invite two or three volunteers to share their sentences with the class. Ask students to raise their hands if they wrote similar answers.

> **EXTENSION ACTIVITY**
>
> **Talk about Movies**
>
> Have students practice movie words.
>
> 1. Have students work in pairs or groups of three.
>
> 2. Pass out recent entertainment sections from local newspapers to each group.
>
> 3. Ask groups to look up a movie location, time, and rating and share the information with the class. If you have access to the Internet in class, students can do this online by typing their zip code into a movie-ticket site.

Lesson Overview	Lesson Notes
MULTILEVEL OBJECTIVES	
On- and Higher-level: Use the superlative to ask questions and state opinions about movies and activities **Pre-level:** Use the superlative to ask questions about movies and activities	
LANGUAGE FOCUS	
Grammar: Superlative adjectives (*What was the best movie this year?*) **Vocabulary:** Superlative adjective forms For vocabulary support, see these **Oxford Picture Dictionary** topics: Places to Go, pages 228–229; Outdoor Recreation, page 232; Entertainment, pages 242–243	
STRATEGY FOCUS	
Use the comparative to talk about two things. Use the superlative to talk about three or more things.	
READINESS CONNECTION	
In this lesson, students practice using superlatives and comparatives to communicate opinions.	
PACING	
To compress this lesson: Assign 2A for homework and/or skip 3D. **To extend this lesson:** Have students make sentences with the superlative. (See end of lesson.) And/or have students complete **Workbook 2 pages 81–82, Multilevel Activities 2 Unit 12 page 130**, and **Multilevel Grammar Exercises 2 Unit 12.**	

CORRELATIONS	
CCRS: L.1.A Demonstrate command of the conventions of standard English grammar and usage when writing or speaking. f. Use frequently occurring adjectives. SL.1.A Participate in collaborative conversations with diverse partners in small and larger groups. SL.2.A Confirm understanding of a text read aloud or information presented orally or through other media by asking and answering questions about key details and requesting clarification if something is not understood. R.1.A Ask and answer questions about key details in the text.	**ELPS:** 7. An ELL can adapt language choices to purpose, task, and audience when speaking and writing. 10. An ELL can demonstrate command of the conventions of standard English to communicate in level-appropriate speech and writing.

Warm-up and Review
10–15 minutes (books closed)

Ask students to tell you the names of three department stores or supermarkets. Write the names on the board and ask which is the most expensive. Next, write *speaking, listening, reading,* and *writing* on the board and ask which is the most difficult to do in English. Leave this on the board also.

Introduction
5–10 minutes

1. Use your students' opinions from the warm-up to write two sentences on the board: _____ *is the most expensive store.* _____ *is the most difficult part of learning English.* Tell students that sentences using *most* with an adjective contain the superlative.

2. State the objective: *Today we're going to explore using the superlative.*

1 Explore the superlative

Presentation I
20–25 minutes

 1. Direct students to look at the pictures. Read the descriptions and questions aloud. Answer the questions in a short class discussion.

Answers
1. science fiction
2. romance
3. horror
4. action

B Read the instructions aloud and have students complete the task individually. Have a volunteer say the answer to the question.

Answer
The most exciting

C 1. Read through the chart word by word. Read the notes aloud. Then read the words again and have students repeat after you.

2. Use the sentences about the movies in 1A to illustrate points in the grammar chart: *How many syllables in* long? *What's the rule to make this word a superlative?*

3. Have a volunteer answer the question in the direction line.

Answer
adjectives with two or more syllables

TIP

Assess students' understanding of the charts. Refer to the sentences you wrote in the warm-up: *We said _____ was the most expensive store. What if we want to use the word* cheap? *What is the superlative of* cheap? *Which store is the cheapest? We said _____ was the most difficult part of learning English. What if we want to use the word* easy? *What is the superlative of* easy? *Which part of learning English is the easiest?*

Guided Practice I
10–15 minutes

D Have students work individually to complete the sentences. Have volunteers write the answers on the board.

Answers
1. the saddest
2. the worst
3. the scariest
4. the most famous
5. the best

MULTILEVEL STRATEGIES

Adapt 1C and 1D to the level of your students.

• **Pre-level** While other students are completing 1D, ask pre-level students to copy the superlative forms from 1C into their notebooks. Give them time to copy the answers to 1D after they are written on the board.

• **Higher-level** Ask these students to write three to five sentences using the superlative to express their opinions about movies or TV shows they have seen.

E Have students work in pairs to complete the task. Check answers as a class.

Answers
1. double consonant
2. irregular
3. change *y* to *i*
4. add *the most*
5. irregular

2 Practice questions with the superlative

Presentation II and Guided Practice II
15–20 minutes

 1. Read the advertisement aloud and draw students' attention to the picture of the person zip-lining. Ask students if they want to try zip-lining, bungee jumping, sky diving, or other "extreme" activities. Ask: *Which is the most exciting activity?*

2. Have students complete the sentences individually. Ask volunteers to write the answers on the board.

Answers
1. the most popular
2. the most expensive
3. the scariest
4. the cheapest

B 1. Read the instructions aloud. Have students work individually to write answers to the questions in 2A.

2. Have students compare their answers with a partner. Check answers as a class.

Answers
1. the most popular tourist destination in the U.S. is the Grand Canyon.
2. the most expensive hotel in the U.S. is in Las Vegas.
3. the scariest sport in the U.S. is zip-lining.
4. the cheapest type of vacation in the U.S. is camping.

3 Practice using the comparative and the superlative

Guided Practice III
20–30 minutes

A 1. Read the instructions and the *Grammar Note* aloud. Give students time to scan the brochure and ask any questions about vocabulary.

2. Play the audio and have students complete the task individually. Check answers as a class.

Answers
1. the most convenient
2. friendlier, more exciting
3. more relaxing
4. healthier

MULTILEVEL STRATEGIES

Adapt 3A to the level of your students.

• **Pre-level** Work with these students to establish if the sentence should be filled in with a superlative or a comparative.

• **Higher-level** Have these students take turns asking and answering questions about the brochure using superlatives or comparatives.

B Have students work in pairs. Set a time limit (five minutes) for pairs to discuss their opinions about the brochure in A. Suggest that students take brief notes to use in C. Circulate and monitor.

C 1. Read the instructions aloud and model the conversation with a volunteer. Have students copy the chart into their notebooks.

2. Have students work in groups of four to discuss the questions and fill in the chart. Circulate and monitor.

Answers
the most dangerous
the most relaxing
the most boring
the cheapest
the most expensive

D Write the chart from C on the board. Have students take turns sharing their group's responses with the class. Write their answers in the chart on the board and, as a class, briefly discuss which groups agree or disagree.

2. Extend the class discussion by asking follow-up questions: *Why is X the most boring? Why is X the most expensive? What do you need to buy for it? Why is X the most dangerous? What can happen?*

4 Answer a questionnaire about free-time activities

Communicative Practice and Application
20–25 minutes

A Read through the questions aloud and have students circle their answers individually. Ask students to think about their reasons and suggest they take notes to use in B.

B Read the instructions and sample sentence aloud. Have students work in groups of three to compare their answers and explain their reasons to each other.

C Have volunteers tell the class about one of their group member's answers. Lead a short class discussion about the most common responses.

Evaluation

10 minutes

TEST YOURSELF

Write *My opinion* and *My classmate's opinion* on the board and tell students to copy the phrases into their notebooks. Direct students to work individually to choose the answers of one of their classmates from 4B and write sentences under each heading. Collect and correct their writing.

Lesson Overview	Lesson Notes

MULTILEVEL OBJECTIVES

On- and Higher-level: Ask for and give opinions about recreational activities

Pre-level: Identify opinions about recreational activities

LANGUAGE FOCUS

Grammar: Comparative (*Basketball is more exciting than baseball.*); Superlative (*Basketball is the most exciting sport.*)

Vocabulary: Entertainment words, adjectives, *conference, presentation*

For vocabulary support, see this **Oxford Picture Dictionary** topic: Entertainment, pages 242–243

STRATEGY FOCUS

Ask for opinions.

READINESS CONNECTION

In this lesson, students verbally communicate about and practice how to use superlatives and comparatives to express opinions.

PACING

To compress this lesson: Skip 4B.

To extend this lesson: Have students make posters. (See end of lesson.)

And/or have students complete **Workbook 2 page 83** and **Multilevel Activities 2 Unit 12 page 131**.

CORRELATIONS

CCRS: SL.1.A Participate in collaborative conversations with diverse partners in small and larger groups.

SL.2.A Confirm understanding of a text read aloud or information presented orally or through other media by asking and answering questions about key details and requesting clarification if something is not understood.

SL.3.A Ask and answer questions in order to seek help, get information, or clarify something that is not understood.

RF.2.A Demonstrate understanding of spoken words, syllables, and sounds (phonemes).

ELPS: 2. An ELL can participate in level-appropriate oral and written exchanges of information, ideas, and analyses, in various social and academic contexts, responding to peer, audience, or reader comments and questions. 9. An ELL can create clear and coherent level-appropriate speech and text.

Warm-up and Review
10–15 minutes (books closed)

Ask students for their opinions about free-time activities: *Is basketball or baseball more exciting? Is listening to music or reading a book more relaxing? Are TV shows or movies more interesting?* Write comparative sentences about their responses. *Angel thinks basketball is more exciting than baseball.*

Introduction
5 minutes

1. Remind students that the sentences on the board are comparative because they talk about two things. Add a superlative sentence by asking for further information. *Angel, what do you think is the most exciting sport of all?* Write the sentence on the board. *Angel thinks soccer is the most exciting sport.*

2. State the objective: *Today we'll explore using the comparative and superlative to talk about opinions.*

1 Listen to learn: expressing opinions

Presentation I
20–30 minutes

A 1. Direct students to look at the pictures. Read the captions aloud. Ask students to number the pictures and then tell a partner their choices.

2. Ask for a show of hands to find out which activity is the most popular: *How many people chose* watch sports *as number one?*

B 🔊 **3-55** 1. Tell students they will hear three conversations of people giving their opinions. Explain that they should listen for the main topic of each conversation.

2. Ask students to listen silently and jot down their answers. Play the audio. Don't check answers yet.

C 🔊 **3-55** 1. Have students copy the chart into their notebooks. Play the audio and have students fill out their chart individually.

2. Have students compare answers with a partner. Play the audio again and check answers as a class.

Answers			
Questions	**Conversation 1**	**Conversation 2**	**Conversation 3**
Main topic of conversation	a TV show	a concert	a football game
Did the man like it?	yes	no	yes
Did the woman like it?	yes	no	no

2 Practice your pronunciation

Pronunciation Extension
10–15 minutes

A 🔊 **3-56** 1. Remind students: *If you put stress on the wrong syllable, it might be difficult for the listener to understand what you are saying. This is especially true for longer words.*

2. Don't read the words aloud. Tell students to read each word silently to themselves. Play the audio. Have students circle the stressed syllable for each word.

3. Play the audio again and have students repeat.

Answers
amazing (2nd syllable)
fantastic (2nd syllable)
horrible (1st syllable)
incredible (2nd syllable)
awesome (1st syllable)
terrible (1st syllable)

B 🔊 **3-57** Read the instructions aloud and play the audio. Ask students to write a sentence about the difference between the two replies.

C 🔊 **3-58** 1. Read the instructions aloud and have students read the sentences silently to themselves. Play the audio and have them check the correct box.

2. Check answers as a class. Play the audio again and have students repeat.

Answers
1. strong
2. normal
3. normal
4. strong

3 Practice asking for and giving opinions

Presentation II and Guided Practice II
15–25 minutes

A 🔊 **3-59** 1. Read the instructions aloud. Play the audio and have students read along silently.

2. Have volunteers answer the question. [They agree on the baseball game and disagree about the TV show.]

B Read the instructions and questions aloud. Have students work individually to answer the questions about the conversation in 3A. Discuss answers as a class. [*How was the ...? What did you think of it? I think so, too! I don't think it's very good.*]

C 🔊 **3-60** Give students time (one to two minutes) to read through the chart. Play the audio and have students repeat.

D 1. Read the instructions and the opinions aloud. Then read the adjectives in the *Need help?* box. Brainstorm other adjectives students may use to give their opinion (e.g., *fun, beautiful, scary, OK, wonderful, silly*).

2. Set a time limit (five minutes) and have students work in pairs to complete the task. Circulate and monitor. If time allows, have students share some of their partner's answers with the class.

4 Make conversation: agreeing and disagreeing with opinions

Communicative Practice I
15–20 minutes

A 1. Ask students if they like to give their opinion, or if doing so makes them uncomfortable. Explain that if they are worried about offending someone because they disagree about something, using a polite tone of voice makes a big difference in how their opinion sounds.

2. Read the template conversation aloud. Then ask the class for examples to fill each blank. Model the sample conversation with a volunteer.

3. Direct students' attention to the *Need help?* box. Read the sentences aloud and have them say which ones are used in the conversation.

4. Have students work in pairs to create their own conversation and take turns performing the parts.

B 1. Set a time limit (five to ten minutes). Ask pairs to share their conversation with another pair. Circulate and monitor.

2. Have pairs present their conversation to the class.

> ### TIP
> As mentioned in 4A, some students may be uncomfortable giving an opinion or disagreeing with an opinion. Practice intonation to make the opinion seem "softer." Also, provide students with other words and phrases that can be used to sound polite: *I think you're right about ____, but I also think that ____. That's a good point, but I ____. That's very true, but ____.*

AT WORK

Asking for opinions

Presentation III and Communicative Practice II
20–25 minutes

A **3-61** 1. Direct students to look at the pictures. Ask them to describe what they see and what they think the different situations are. Confirm that students understand the meaning of *conference* and *presentation*.

2. Play the audio and have students read along silently.

B **3-61** 1. Read the instructions and the example answer aloud. Play the audio and have students complete the task individually. Play the audio again and check answers as a class.

> **Answers**
> 1. It was fantastic. (strong opinion)
> 2. Oh, it was so-so. (normal)
> 3. I thought they were interesting. (normal)

C 1. Read the instructions aloud. Have students practice the conversations with a partner. Then have them give their own opinion about something in the classroom or school. Circulate and help as needed.

2. Have pairs share one of their conversations with the class.

> **MULTILEVEL STRATEGIES**
> For C, have same-level students sit and work together in pairs.
> • **Pre-level** Write the conversation from 4A on the board for students to use as a guide for their new conversations.
> • **Higher-level** Have these students think of one more situation and have a conversation.

Evaluation
10–15 minutes

TEST YOURSELF

Read the instructions aloud. Model the conversation with a student. Set a time limit (5 minutes). Have students act out the situation with a partner. Circulate and assess students' progress.

EXTENSION ACTIVITY

Make a Poster

Have students make posters to practice the comparative and the superlative.

1. Have students work in groups of three to four, and give each group a magazine.

2. Ask students to find and cut out three pictures from the magazine and then write about the three objects, using at least two sentences with the comparative and one with the superlative. Students will produce a wider variety of adjectives if different groups have different kinds of magazines, such as a clothing catalog, a furniture catalog, a magazine with people in it, and a nature magazine.

3. Have students make a small poster with the pictures and sentences.

4. Post the posters around the room and have everyone move around and look at other groups' work.

Lesson Overview	Lesson Notes

MULTILEVEL OBJECTIVES

On- and Higher-level: Read about and discuss tourist destinations in the United States

Pre-level: Read about tourist destinations in the United States

LANGUAGE FOCUS

Grammar: Simple present (*Washington D.C. is the capital of the United States.*)

Vocabulary: *Border, canyon, compass rose, sight, view*

For vocabulary support, see these **Oxford Picture Dictionary** topics: Geography and Habitats, page 214; Places to Go, pages 228–229

STRATEGY FOCUS

Identify the words that can help you find the location of places on a map. Try to visualize locations on a map as you read an article.

READINESS CONNECTION

In this lesson, students verbally communicate information about travel destinations in the United States.

PACING

To compress this lesson: Assign 2F for homework and/or for 2C, have students research their places for homework the day before class.

To extend this lesson: Have students make travel brochures. (See end of lesson.)

And/or have students complete **Workbook 2 page 84** and **Multilevel Activities 2 Unit 12 page 132**.

CORRELATIONS

CCRS: R.1.A Ask and answer questions about key details in the text.

R.4.A Ask and answer questions to help determine or clarify the meaning of words and phrases in a text.

R.7.A Use the illustrations and details in a text to describe its key ideas (e.g., maps, charts, photographs, political cartoons, etc.).

SL.1.A Participate in collaborative conversations with diverse partners in small and larger groups.

SL.6.A Speak audibly and express thoughts, feelings, and ideas clearly. Produce complete sentences when appropriate to task and situation.

ELPS: 1. An ELL can construct meaning from oral presentations and literary and informational text through level-appropriate listening, reading, and viewing. 3. An ELL can speak and write about level-appropriate complex literary and informational texts and topics.

Warm-up and Review
10–15 minutes (books closed)

Tell students about one or two of your favorite travel destinations in the U.S. Ask students what places in the U.S. they have visited and write the names on the board. Ask for words to describe the places and put those on the board too.

Introduction
5 minutes

1. Hold up a U.S. map and briefly describe the places that students mentioned or places you have been yourself. *Key West is in the south of Florida. It's a long chain of islands. It's very popular in the winter because it's warm.*

2. State the objective: *Today we're going to read about famous places to visit in the U.S.*

> **TIP**
>
> Bring pictures of famous U.S. tourist destinations. After the introduction, discuss where each place or landmark is and why it is important or famous. Encourage students to make comparative and superlative statements about the places: *Yellowstone is the most beautiful. Mt. McKinley is the farthest. The Statue of Liberty is the most famous.* It is also very useful to bring in or have Internet access to a map of the U.S. and the world.

1 Build reading strategies

Presentation I
10–20 minutes

 Direct students' attention to the definitions and photos. Have students read along silently as you read the sentences aloud. Help students with the definitions of *border*, *canyon*, *sight*, and *view* as needed. As a class, discuss which word goes with which photo.

Guided Practice Pre-reading
5–10 minutes

B Read the instructions aloud. Ask: *What will you do to preview the article?* [look at the title, skim the first sentence of a paragraph] Have students answer the question with a partner. Then check answers as a class. If any students answer incorrectly, ask them to support their answer using the pictures and title. Establish consensus about the correct answer as a class.

Guided Practice: While Reading
20–30 minutes

C 1. Read the instructions and the *Readers Note* aloud. Ask students to read the article silently and think about their answer to the question. Answer any questions about unfamiliar vocabulary.

2. Have students work in pairs to compare and discuss their answers, and then check answers as a class.

3. Check comprehension. Ask: *Where is the White House?* [Washington, D.C.] *Can you visit the White House?* [yes] *What is the Maid of the Mist?* [a boat at Niagara Falls] *Can you walk on the Golden Gate Bridge?* [yes] *Which sight has camping nearby?* [Grand Canyon]

> **MULTILEVEL STRATEGIES**
>
> Adapt 1C to the level of your students.
> - **Pre-level** Read the text aloud to these students as they follow along.
> - **On- and Higher-level** Pair students and have them read the article aloud to each other, taking turns to read each paragraph.

Guided Practice: Rereading
10–15 minutes

D **3-62** 1. Play the audio and have students listen as they silently read along again.

2. Provide an opportunity for students to extract evidence from the article. On the board, write all the numbers that are in the article. Give students one minute to read the article again and then close their books. Point to each number on the board and have students say what it refers to in the article. Check answers as a class.

3. Have students discuss their answers to the question with a partner. Circulate and monitor. Have volunteers report their partner's responses to the class.

Guided Practice: Post-reading
15 minutes

E Have students work individually to mark each sentences *T* (*true*) or *F* (*false*) then identify in the reading where they found the answer. Have volunteers come to the board and correct the false sentences.

Answers
1. F
2. T
3. T
4. T
5. F

F 1. Have students work individually to complete the sentences.

2. Have students read their sentences to a partner before checking answers as a class.

Answers
1. capital
2. view
3. border
4. sight

MULTILEVEL STRATEGIES

After the group comprehension check in 2F, call on volunteers and tailor your questions to the level of your students.

• **Pre-level** Ask *yes/no* questions. *Do people go camping at the Grand Canyon?* [yes]

• **On-level** Ask information questions. *What can you see from the Golden Gate Bridge?* [the Pacific Ocean and San Francisco]

• **Higher-level** Ask these students to compare the four places: *Which of these places would be easiest for a family with young children to visit? Why?*

2 Read a map

Communicative Practice
30–35 minutes

A 1. Direct students to find the compass rose on the map and ask them what it shows. [directions] Read the *Need help?* box aloud. Draw a compass rose of the board similar to the one on the map. Point to each point on the compass rose and have volunteers say which direction it indicates.

2. Ask students to work individually to fill in the blanks. Discuss the answers as a class.

B 1. Read the instructions aloud. Allow students time to write their own questions. Suggest that they write one question for each of the locations.

2. Set a time limit (ten minutes). Have students take turns asking and answering their questions with a partner. Circulate and help as needed.

TIP

If you have souvenirs or postcards from any of these places, bring them in and display them in the classroom. Tell students about your visit. Encourage students who have been to any famous places in the U.S. to bring in pictures or souvenirs.

C Read the instructions aloud. Allow students to use the Internet, if available, to find information about different sights in the U.S. Set a time limit (15 minutes) for students to choose their places and plan their route. Have students share their trips with the class. Alternatively, have students work at home and make a poster of their maps, places, and route and present it to the class.

Application
5–10 minutes

BRING IT TO LIFE

As a class, brainstorm a list of places for the students to research. Write them on the board and ask students to choose two places they are interested in. Have students discuss their answers with a partner.

EXTENSION ACTIVITY

Make a Travel Brochure

Have students make a travel brochure for a place they have visited.

1. Tell students they can use their hometown or a famous place in their native country.

2. Tell them to write a few sentences about the place and draw or bring in a picture of it. They could also print a picture from the Internet.

3. Post their work around the classroom.

Lesson Overview	Lesson Notes
MULTILEVEL OBJECTIVES	
On-, Pre-, and Higher-level: Expand upon and review unit grammar and life skills	
LANGUAGE FOCUS	
Grammar: Superlative adjectives (*What is the most exciting place to visit?*) **Vocabulary:** Adjectives For vocabulary support, see these **Oxford Picture Dictionary** topics: Geography and Habitats, page 214; Places to Go, pages 228–229; Outdoor Recreation, page 232	
READINESS CONNECTION	
In this review, students work in a team to review using the superlative and comparative to describe and complete a survey on recreational activities.	
PACING	
To extend this review: Have students complete **Workbook 2 page 85**, **Multilevel Activities 2 Unit 12 pages 133–136**, and **Multilevel Grammar Exercises 2 Unit 12**	

CORRELATIONS	
CCRS: R.1.A Ask and answer questions about key details in the text. R.7.A Use the illustrations and details in a text to describe its key ideas (e.g., maps, charts, photographs, political cartoons, etc.). SL.1.A Participate in collaborative conversations with diverse partners in small and larger groups. SL.3.A Ask and answer questions in order to seek help, get information, or clarify something that is not understood. SL.6.A Speak audibly and express thoughts, feelings, and ideas clearly. Produce complete sentences when appropriate to task and situation. W.2.A Write informative/explanatory texts in which they name a topic, supply some facts about the topic, and provide some sense of closure.	**ELPS:** 5. An ELL can conduct research and evaluate and communicate findings to answer questions or solve problems. 6. An ELL can analyze and critique the arguments of others orally and in writing.

Warm-up and Review
10–15 minutes (books closed)

1. Review the *Bring It to Life* assignment from Lesson 5.

2. Have students who did the exercise present the information about the place they researched.

3. Ask the class: *Do you want to go there? Is it far? Do you think it's expensive?*

4. Conduct a classroom poll to find out which place students think is the most beautiful, the most interesting, and the most expensive.

Introduction and Presentation
5 minutes

1. Write sentences using the superlative on the board to reflect the outcome of your classroom poll: *We think Yosemite is the most beautiful place. We think New York is the most expensive.*

2. State the objective: *Today we're going to review using superlatives to talk about recreational activities.*

3. Review the rules for the superlative. Ask: *What if we change* beautiful *to* ugly? *What's the superlative form? What if we change* expensive *to* cheap? Write the superlatives on the board. Ask: *Can we use* most *with one-syllable adjectives?*

4. Ask questions to elicit comparative forms: *Is _____ or _____ more expensive?* Write the sentence on the board: *_____ is more expensive than _____.*

5. Invite students to contrast the comparative with the superlative: *Which form uses* the? *Which form uses* than?

Guided Practice
15–20 minutes

 1. Direct students to work in groups of three to four and look at the picture. Ask: *Who are these people? How old are they? What are they doing?*

2. Set a time limit (five minutes) for teams to complete the task. Circulate and answer any questions.

3. Have students from each group share the group's responses with the class. If you have a large class, you may not want all of the groups to report their responses. Instead, have groups share their responses with each other. Call "time" and tell all groups to work with a new group and to repeat their responses. Repeat this process as desired, making sure each group gets to share their responses at least once.

Communicative Practice
30–45 minutes

 1. Have students work in their same groups from A. If necessary, have them review the information they discussed for that exercise.

2. Read the instructions aloud and model the sample conversation with a volunteer.

3. Tell groups that each student should have a turn to write a line for the conversation. Set a time limit (ten minutes).

C Have students complete the sentences individually and then check their answers with a partner.

Answers
1. more interesting
2. more relaxing
3. easier
4. the most popular
5. the healthiest

D 1. Read the instructions. Have students complete the exercise with their group from A and B.

2. Set a time limit (ten minutes) to complete the task. Circulate and assist groups as needed.

E 1. Put students in new groups of three to four. Read the instructions aloud. You can assign the topics to teams to make sure each topic is covered by at least one team.

2. Model the sample conversation with a volunteer. Write a sample survey chart on the board for students to copy into their notebooks that they will fill out as they interview their classmates.

3. Set a time limit depending on class size (10–15 minutes) for teams to complete the task.

F Have students work with their teams from E to discuss their findings. Explain that they should combine their data into one chart. Set a time limit (five minutes) to complete the task.

G Draw students' attention to the paragraph template. Have them copy the template into their notebooks and fill it in with the information in their combined chart from F.

H Have a volunteer from each team share their team's summary with the class.

PROBLEM SOLVING AT HOME

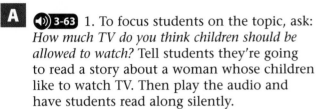

10–15 minutes

A ◀))**3-63** 1. To focus students on the topic, ask: *How much TV do you think children should be allowed to watch?* Tell students they're going to read a story about a woman whose children like to watch TV. Then play the audio and have students read along silently.

2. Check comprehension. Ask: *What do Tara's children like to do?* [watch TV] *How does Tara feel about it?* [She doesn't like it.]

B 1. Elicit several answers to question 1. Come to a class consensus on an answer.

2. Elicit solutions. Have volunteers write each one on the board until all of the class ideas have been put up.

3. Discuss the pros and cons of each solution.

> **TIP**
>
> To help students identify other things Tara's children can do, show the illustrations on the Hobbies and Games pages in *The Oxford Picture Dictionary* or use chalkboard drawings of alternative activities.

C Have students work in pairs to role-play the conversation between Tara and a friend. Circulate and monitor. Have pairs share their conversation with the class.

Evaluation

20–25 minutes

To test students' understanding of the unit language and content, have them take the Unit 12 Test, available on the Teacher Resource Center.